National Institute of
Standards and Technology
Technology Administration
U.S. Department of Commerce

NIST Special Publication 500-265

Proceedings of Workshop on Software Security Assurance Tools, Techniques, and Metrics

Paul E. Black (workshop Chair)
Michael Kass (Co-chair)
Elizabeth Fong (editor)

Information Technology Laboratory
National Institute of Standards & Technology
Gaithersburg MD 20899

February 2006

U.S. Department of Commerce
Carlos M. Gutierrez. Secretary

National Institute of Standards and Technology
William Jeffrey, Director

Proceedings of Workshop on Software Security Assurance Tools, Techniques, and Metrics

Paul E. Black (workshop chair)
Michael Kass (co-chair)
Elizabeth Fong (editor)
Information Technology Laboratory
National Institute of Standards and Technology
Gaithersburg, MD 20899

ABSTRACT

This is the proceedings of a workshop held on November 7 and 8, 2005 in Long Beach, California, USA, hosted by the Software Diagnostics and Conformance Testing Division, Information Technology Laboratory, of the National Institute of Standards and Technology. The workshop, "Software Security Assurance Tools, Techniques, and Metrics," is one of a series in the NIST Software Assurance Measurement and Tool Evaluation (SAMATE) project, which is partially funded by DHS to help identify and enhance software security assurance (SSA) tools. The goal of this workshop is to discuss and refine the taxonomy of flaws and the taxonomy of functions, come to a consensus on which SSA functions should first have specifications and standards tests developed, gather SSA tools suppliers for "target practice" on reference datasets of code, and identify gaps or research needs in SSA functions.

Keywords: Software assessment tools; software assurance; software metrics; software security; target practice, reference dataset; vulnerability

Foreword

The workshop on "Software Assurance Tools, Techniques, and Metrics" was held 7-8 November 2005 at the Long Beach, California, USA, co-located with the Automated Software Engineering Conference 2005.

This workshop consisted of eleven paper presentations for the first day. The second day morning consisted of "target practice" and the review of the nature of the reference dataset.

The Program Committee consisted of the following:

Freeland Abbott	Georgia Tech	Paul Ammann	George Mason U.
Elizabeth Fong	NIST	Michael Hicks	U. of Maryland
Michael Koo	NIST	Richard Lippmann	MIT
Robert A. Martin	MITRE Corp.	W. Bradley Martin	NSA
Nachiappan Nagappan	Microsoft Research	Samuel Redwine	James Madison U.
Ravi Sandhu	George Mason U.	Larry D. Wagoner	NSA

These proceedings have five main parts:
- Summary
- Workshop Announcement
- Workshop Agenda
- Reference Dataset Target Practice, and
- Papers

We thank those who worked to organize this workshop, particularly Elizabeth Fong, who handled much of the correspondence and Debra A. Brodbeck, who provided conference support. We appreciate the program committee for their efforts in reviewing the papers. We are grateful to NIST, especially the Software Diagnostics and Conformance Testing Division, for providing the organizers' time. On behalf of the program committee and the whole SAMATE team, thanks to everyone for taking their time and resources to join us.

Sincerely,

Dr. Paul E. Black

Table of Contents

Summary

This is the proceeding of the workshop on Software Security Assurance Tools, Techniques, and Metrics, held on November 7 and 8, 2005 at Long Beach, California, USA, co-located with the Automated Software Engineering Conference 2005. It was organized by the Software Diagnostics and Conformance Testing Division, Information Technology Laboratory, National Institute of Standards and Technology (NIST). Forty-two people attended, including people from government, universities, tool vendors and service providers, and research companies.

The workshop is one of a series in the NIST Software Assurance Measurement and Tool Evaluation (SAMATE) project, http://samate.nist.gov/ A previous workshop was on Defining the State of the Art in Software Security Tools, held on August 10 and 11, 2005 at the NIST in Gaithersburg, MD, USA.

The call for papers resulted in eleven accepted papers, which were presented on the first day of the workshop. The second day was devoted to the discussion of reference dataset and target practice with three SSA tool vendors, and included an invited presentation "Correctness by construction: The case for constructive static verification" by Rob Chapman.

The material and papers for the workshop were distributed on USB drives to the participants. The content of the USB drives was:

- Introduction,
- Workshop call of papers,
- Workshop agenda,
- Reference dataset target practice,
- Flaw taxonomies, and
- Accepted papers.

Here are summaries of the workshop conclusions:

- Today's SSA tool does not add much value to real, large software products.
- How do we score (rate) the risk of a piece of code is still a challenging question.
- There is a need to harmonize the different taxonomy of vulnerabilities.
- Very substantive feedbacks were gathered on the shared reference dataset. See write-up on SAMATE Reference Dataset "Target Practice" in this document.
- There were consensuses that the first SSA specification and standard tests will be the source code scanner tools.

Workshop CALL FOR PAPERS (SSATTM'05)

National Institute of Standards and Technology (NIST) workshop on
Software Security Assurance Tools, Techniques, and Metrics
7-8 November 2005
Co-located with ASE 2005, Long Beach, California, USA

Funded in part by the Department of Homeland Security (DHS), the National Institute of Standards and Technology (NIST) started a long-term, ambitious project to improve software security assurance tools. Security is the ability of a system to maintain the confidentiality, integrity, and availability of information processed and stored by a computer. Software security assurance tools are those that help software be more secure by building security into software or determining how secure software is. Among the project's goals are:

(1) develop a taxonomy of software security flaws and vulnerabilities,
(2) develop a taxonomy of software security assurance (SSA) tool functions and techniques which detect or prevent flaws, and
(3) develop testable specifications of SSA functions and explicit tests to evaluate how closely tools implement the functions. The test materials include reference sets of buggy code.

These goals extend into all phases of the software life cycle from requirements capture through design and implementation to operation and auditing.

The goal of the workshop is to convene researchers, developers, and government and industrial users of SSA tools to

- discuss and refine the taxonomy of flaws and the taxonomy of functions, which are under development,
- come to a consensus on which SSA functions should first have specifications and standard tests developed,
- gather SSA tools suppliers for "target practice" on reference datasets of code, and
- identify gaps or research needs in SSA functions.

REFERENCE DATASET "TARGET PRACTICE"

Sets of code with known flaws and vulnerabilities, with corresponding correct versions, can be references for tool testing to make research easier and to be a standard of evaluation. Working with others, we will bring reference datasets of many types of code, like Java, C, binaries, and bytecode. We welcome contributions of code you've used.

To help validate the reference datasets, we solicit proposals not exceeding 2 pages to participate in SSA tool "target practice" on the datasets. Tools can range from university projects to commercial products. Participation is intended to demonstrate the state of the art in finding flaws, consequently the proposals should not be marketing write-ups, but should highlight technical contributions: techniques used, precision achieved, classes of vulnerabilities detected,

7

suggestions for extensions to and improvements of the reference datasets, etc. Participants are expected to provide their own equipment.

TOPICS OF PAPERS:

SSATTM encourages contributions describing basic research, novel applications, and experience relevant to SSA tools and their evaluation. Topics of particular interest are:

- Benchmarks or reference datasets for SSA tools
- Comparisons of tools
- ROI effectiveness of SSA functions
- Flaw catching effectiveness of SSA functions
- Evaluating SSA tools
- Gaps or research needs in SSA functions
- SSA tool metrics
- Software security assurance metrics
- Surveys of SSA tools
- Relation between flaws and the techniques that catch them
- Taxonomy of software security flaws and vulnerabilities
- Taxonomy of SSA functions or techniques

PAPER SUBMISSION:

Papers should not exceed 8 pages in the conference format http://www.acm.org/sigs/pubs/proceed/template.html. Papers exceeding the length restriction will not be reviewed. Papers will be reviewed by at least two program committee members. All papers should clearly identify their novel contributions. All papers should be submitted electronically in PDF format by 26 August 2005 to Elizabeth Fong efong@nist.gov.

PUBLICATION:

Accepted papers will be published in the workshop proceedings. The workshop proceedings, along with a summary of discussions and the output of the reference dataset "target practice", will be published as a NIST Special Publication.

CURRENT PROGRAM COMMITTEE:

Freeland Abbott	Georgia Tech	Paul Ammann	George Mason U.
Paul E. Black	NIST	Elizabeth Fong	NIST
Michael Kass	NIST	Michael Koo	NIST
Richard Lippmann	MIT	Robert A. Martin	M ITRE Corp.
W. Bradley Martin	NSA	Samuel Redwine	James Madison U.
Larry D. Wagoner	NSA		

IMPORTANT DATES:

19 Aug: Paper and tool proposal submission deadline
19 Sep: Paper and proposal notification
15 Oct: Final camera-ready copy due
7-8 Nov: Workshop

Workshop Program

November 7, 2005
8:30 – 9:00   Welcome – Paul Black

9:00 – 10:30   Tools and Metrics – Session Chair: Elizabeth Fong
- Where do Software Security Assurance Tools Add Value – David Jackson, David Cooper
- Metrics that Matter – Brian Chess
- The Case for Common Flaw Enumeration – Robert Martin, Steven Christey, Joe Jarzombek

10:30 – 11:00 Break

11:00 – 12:30 Flaw Taxonomy and Benchmarks – Session Chair: Robert Martin
- Seven Pernicious Kingdoms: A Taxonomy of Software Security Errors – Katrina Tsipenyuk, Brian Chess, Gary McGraw
- A Taxonomy of Buffer Overflows for Evaluating Static and Dynamic Software Testing Tools – Kendra Kratkiewicz, Richard Lippmann
- ABM – A Prototype for Benchmarking Source Code Analyzers – Tim Newsham, Brian Chess

12:30 – 1:30   Lunch

1:30 – 4:00   New Techniques – Session Chair: Larry Wagoner
- A Benchmark Suite for Behavior-Based Security Mechanisms – Dong Ye, Micha Moffie, David Kaeli
- Testing and Evaluation of Virus Detectors for Handheld Devices – Jose A. Morales, Peter Clarke, Yi Deng
- Eliminating Buffer Overflows, Using the Compiler or a Standalone Tool – Thomas Plum, David Keaton
- A Secure Software Architecture Description Language – Jie Ren, Richard Taylor
- Prioritization of Threats Using the K/M Algebra – Supreeth Vendataraman, Warren Harrison

November 8, 2005
9:00 – 11:30   Reference Dataset Target Practice – Michael Kass

11:30 – 1:00 lunch

1:00 – 2:30 Invited Presentation -   Session Chair: Vadim Okun
- Correctness by Construction: The Case for Constructive Static Verification – Rod Chapman

SAMATE Reference Dataset "Target Practice"

Michael Kass[*]
National Institute of Standards and Technology

Introduction

The SAMATE Reference Dataset (SRD) is a rapidly growing set of contributed test cases for measuring software security assurance (SSA) tool capability against a functional specification for that tool. This initial distribution is a compilation of C source code test cases that will be used for evaluating the functional capability of C source code scanning tools. Contributions from MIT Lincoln Lab and Fortify Software Inc. make up this initial set. Additional contributions from Klocwork Inc. and Ounce Labs Inc. will be added soon.   We expect to expand the SRD to include other languages (e.g. C++, Java) as well as to include test suites for other SSA tools (such as requirements and software design documents).

MIT Contribution

Documentation for each test case is contained in the source files themselves. In the case of the MIT contribution, the first line of each test case contains a classification code describing the test case "signature" (in terms of code complexity). All MIT discrete test cases are "buffer overflow" examples, with permutations of some of the 22 coding variation factors to challenge a tool's ability to discover a buffer overflow or recognize a patched version of the overflow. Also, MIT contributed 14 models (scaled-down versions) of 3 real world applications (bind, sendmail, and wu-ftpd).

Fortify Software Test Case Contribution

 Fortify Software has contributed C code test cases, the majority of which are also buffer overflow vulnerabilities. Additionally a number of race condition, command injection and other vulnerabilities are also included in the test suite. Like the MIT test cases, the Fortify test cases are "self documenting", with keyword describing the type of software flaw present in the code. Additionally, to provide a uniform way of classifying the complexity of the test cases, the MIT classification code is placed at the top of each test file.

[*] This paper is authored by an employee of the U.S. Government and is in the public domain.
SSATTM'05, 11/7-11/8/05, Long Beach, CA, USA ISBN 1-59593-307-7/05/11

Klocwork Test Case Contribution

Klocwork Inc. has donated an initial contribution of C++ test cases, the majority of which are memory management related (e.g. memory leak, bad frees, use after frees) They intend to follow up with an additional donation of Java test cases.

Target Practice Test Suite

A subset of both the MIT (152 discrete test cases and 3 models) and Fortify (12) test cases make up the "target practice" test suite. A representative group of well-understood and documented tests are presented as a "starting point" to get initial feedback from tool developers and users as to how useful the test suite is. Both a "bad" (flawed) and "good" (patched) version exists for each test case.

Target Practice Test Suite Details

- 12 Fortify Test Cases – (stack overflow tests)
    - 6 "BAD"
    - 6 "OK"
- 152 MIT Discreet Test Cases – (inter-procedural, liaising, pointers, function-calls)
    - 76 "BAD"
    - 76 "OK"
- 6 MIT "Model" Test Cases – (global variable underflow, buffer overflow)
    - 3 "BAD"
    - 3 "OK"

Test Suite Execution

It is expected that each participant will run their tool against the target practice test suite before attending the workshop on Tuesday, so as to provide maximum time for discussion of the merits/deficiencies in the test suite. Tests are provided in two separate directories (MIT and Fortify). How a tool scans the test suite is at the discretion of the tool implementer/user.

Test Suite Evaluation

After running their tool on the Target Practice test suite, participants will be asked to fill out a questionnaire regarding usefulness of the test suite in the following areas:

- Validity of the tests
- Do test cases reflect real world examples?
- Test case coverage (What software flaws should we focus on initially?)
- Complexity (Were the tests challenging/enlightening for discovering a tool's capability?)
- Sufficient metadata for describing test case flaws and code complexity (e.g. MIT's metadata scheme - do we need more? If so what?)

Confidentiality of Test Results

At no time was a participant required to report anything about their tool's performance against the Target Practice test suite.

Discussion topics included:

Test Case *Validity*

- Do target practice test cases reflect real world examples?
- What should be the ratio of "manufactured" vs. "real world" test cases
- Should we initially "set a bar" with the SRD to which all tool developers agree is realistic?

FEEDBACK: Participants felt that discrete test cases provide a useful purpose in "establishing a minimal bar" of capability for source code scanners tools. One participant stated that some of the discreet test cases were "beyond the capability of tools today". Tools generally did well, with no "false positives" reported.

Test Case *Coverage*

- Where (what flaws) should we focus on initially?
- 95% of initial tests are "buffer overflow" examples for C code (where else should be put our resources?
- Coverage based upon: commonality, danger, and capability of tools?
- Should coverage be the primary goal of the SRD?

FEEDBACK: Participants pointed out that virtually all test cases were of the "buffer overflow variety, and that much more coverage of existing software flaws is necessary to make the SRD useful. Some suggested focusing on "race conditions" as the next are of developing tests. Others suggested creating test cases for "fringe areas" of research, since this could have a great impact in moving tool technology forward.

Test Case *Variation*

- Expressed in Taxonomy of Flaws vs. Test Case attributes? (e.g. buffer overflow/buffer underflow)
- Should variation be a primary goal for the SRD?

is truly effective. It was generally viewed that a large variety of examples of a particular type of source code flaw will be necessary in order to truly measure a tool's effectiveness of discovering such a flaw.

Test Case *Complexity*

- What is the minimal metadata necessary to describe test case complexity ?
- In order to search/retrieve test cases with particular complexity and variation, a common set of attributes is needed

FEEDBACK: It was generally agreed upon that some descriptors are necessary to permit a SRD user to "find" the test cases that are relevant to them. Simply providing a "flaw classification" will not provide the granularity necessary for someone to "cull" the tests they need from potentially thousands of test cases. The MIT metadata used to classify its buffer overflow test cases was used as an example. No consensus was reached on exactly what general list of descriptors is necessary to tag any source code test case.

Where Do Software Security Assurance Tools Add Value?

David Jackson
QinetiQ
WWA109 Malvern Technology Centre
Malvern, WR14 3PS, UK
[+44] (0)1684 896689
DMJackson@QinetiQ.com

David Cooper
CESG
Room A2h, Hubble Road,
Cheltenham, GL51 0EX, UK
[+44] (0)1242 221491 ext 39049
David.Cooper@cesg.gsi.gov.uk

ABSTRACT

In developing security information technology products, we are presented with a wide choice of development and assurance processes, and of tools and techniques to support those processes. By considering a structured break-down of the goals of a development, and building on the results of a survey of the applicability of tools to certification, this paper proposes a framework for assessing the value of tools – both security specific and more general – to security assurance.

Categories and Subject Descriptors

D.2.9 [**Software Engineering**]: Management–software quality assurance (SQA); Software/Program Verification–Validation

General Terms

Management, Measurement, Security.

Keywords

Software Assurance; Common Criteria for Information Security Evaluation

1. INTRODUCTION

Security is important in all aspects of life, and the increasing pervasiveness and capability of information technology makes IT infrastructure security increasingly so [1]. The continual and increasing publicity given to failures of IT security demonstrate the importance of developing and assuring systems to appropriate levels of security.

In spite of this attention, security remains a difficult attribute to assess and value [2]. Although the benefits of improved security can be difficult to quantify, as technologists and managers we are required to define and implement security measures which are appropriate to the threat and to the application. In the area of software security, these choices are further complicated by the wide range of techniques and tools have been used or proposed. Efforts are being made to categorize these tools and techniques,

and to measure the effectiveness with which they perform their functions, but the variety of different approaches makes direct comparisons difficult.

This paper is a preliminary attempt to identify the role of various assurance activities and tools in the development of a software product, and the potential benefits of employing them. We believe that virtually all developments aimed at a non-trivial distribution will require some degree of security assurance.

This paper is based on the authors' experience in a number of recent projects relating to software security assurance. Its principle inputs are:

- A study carried out on behalf of the UK Government CESG into the use of tools in support of Common Criteria (CC) evaluation [4];

- The SafSec project, which is investigating cost-effective safety and security certification approaches for Integrated Modular Avionics (IMA) [5]; and

- Discussions around the NIST workshop on "Defining the State of the Art in Software Assurance Tools" [6].

The work described here is the first attempt to combine the goal-based approach proposed by SafSec with the survey results of the other projects, and also takes into account the recent revision of the Common Criteria [17]. As a result, it poses questions for future research which are more wide-ranging than earlier studies.

2. BACKGROUND – THE ASSURANCE PROBLEM

Various approaches are used by those responsible for developing, deploying and maintaining IT equipment and systems. Historically, most of the emphasis on information security came from government and military applications. Information security techniques developed which were appropriate for these highly-regulated environments. These are typified by formal product approval schemes such as that established by the Common Criteria for Information Technology Security Evaluation [3] (hereafter Common Criteria or CC). In purely commercial applications, less rigorous division will typically exist between development and security assessment, but effective security processes will still generally contain elements of both [7]. In order to examine where the benefits of particular technologies in supporting security assurance lie, we will consider a general model of product development, taken from [5].

SSATTM'05, 11/7-11/8/05, Long Beach, CA, USA

2.1 Lifecycle of a Secure Product

Figure 1 High-level Goals of a Product Development

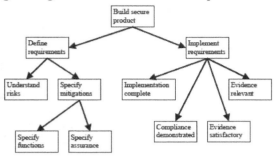

The security aspects of a development address a number of goals; these goals do not necessarily represent particular activities, but rather aspects of development which must be made, and maintained, valid through the course of development and deployment. A high-level view of a typical project is shown in Figure 1, which is based on that adopted by the SafSec project [5]. The notation is based on Kelly's Goal Structuring Notation (GSN) [8]. The key goals are grouped into those which derive security specifications (understanding the risks, specifying mitigations) and those which ensure the specifications are implemented (completion and control of implementation, generation and adequacy of assurance evidence).

Although the emphasis given to these goals will differ widely between products according to the priorities of particular industries and applications, at some level each of these areas must be addressed by an adequately assured development.

Given a breakdown of the goals which a product development is seeking to achieve, we can assess the value of project activities by considering their contribution to meeting particular goals. Ultimately, we might assess the relative merits of different strategies by considering the relative economy (in terms of the necessary supporting solutions) with which each supports the goal. Obviously if the goals have been characterized purely in terms of security, only security aspects of the development will be illuminated by such an analysis.

2.2 Common Criteria Evaluation & Practical Security

In regulated applications, these development goals are often satisfied by adopting a formal certification scheme, of which the Common Criteria are the most widely accepted. Certification schemes generally involve additional time and expense in meeting their requirements, and thus the value of such schemes has been questioned. Areas in which the results of a certification program may differ from expectations include:

- Measurement of results: Is the objective to minimize vulnerabilities discovered or published, or to achieve a level of confidence that no significant risks remain?

- The scope of assessment: some evaluations are carried out under constraints which are too stringent to be widely practicable.

- Development processes: development technologies are continually evolving, and future developments may not match the expectations of the certification scheme.

Our previous work [4] includes a study aimed at addressing some of these issues and reviewing both assurance technologies and the CC assurance criteria to identify potential improvements to development and evaluation processes. The baseline for the work described here is the current formal release of the common criteria, version 2.2. The implications of the new draft of the CC, version 3, are discussed in Section 4.4 below.

2.2.1 Current evaluation practice

Current evaluation practice is driven by the evaluation method [9]. Many requirements are focused on a product's documentation, rather than any formal artifact. This documentation – models of the design, or representations of the implementation, for example – is typically largely manually generated and intended for manual review. The CC evaluation process also makes assumptions about the development process. The information available is assumed to be consistent with a waterfall-style development: security functions are identified at the requirements level, and their presence and correct implementation verified through successive levels of design representation, culminating in their demonstration (by testing) in the final product. In consequence, only a small proportion of the evaluation effort is typically spent examining the product (code). Focus on implementation of identified security functions also poses pragmatic problems for evaluators: to make a sensible judgment on security issues, a thorough understanding of the product is necessary, but the targeted documentation provided to trace the security functions will not necessarily help build this understanding. Emphasis on the presence of specific security measures is also seen as encouraging the de-scoping of valuable, but difficult-to-assure, measures from the security targets which are claimed. This could result in the accreditation of products with increasingly unrealistic constraints on their operation, as opposed to real improvements in security. These factors do not encourage the types of assurance (e.g. scanning for potential vulnerabilities, or automated checks for compliance with implementation rules) that are amenable to automation (apart from standard document automation functions such as searching and indexing.). The product development process is, of course, likely to make some use of tools, for example to manage and organize source code, to generate and monitor tests, or to carry out customized consistency or style checks. Typically, however, such tools are used purely to benefit the development, not to contribute to the formal security assurance process. Evaluation may be facilitated by tools which contribute to the management of development (such as tools for configuration management, impact analysis, change control, or automated build and testing) but to no greater extent than any other process is facilitated by having good control of its inputs.

2.2.2 Desirable changes

The perceived weaknesses of current assurance regimes lead us to try and identify desirable features of future assurance approaches. Key attributes identified by a range of stakeholders in the CC scheme included:

- Assurance should not introduce significant delay or additional cost into product development.

- Emphasis should be placed on identifying vulnerabilities in the product, rather than exploring attributes of the documentation.

- Assurance requirements should not list specific documents and checks, but allow flexibility to choose development environments and life-cycles which reflect current practices, and the goals to be addressed.

- Encouragement of broader good practice and approaches that facilitate understanding and assurance of the whole product, not simply a set of security functions. Also promotion of security targets which are broad enough to be practically applicable, rather than restricted to facilitate accreditation.

- Provision of concrete advice on the application of specific techniques, the use of tools in specific areas, and the identification and elimination of particular high-risk structures.

- Maintenance of the existing high standards for the quality of assurance, eg by maintaining mutual recognition and repeatability, and demanding appropriate validation of tools.

However, it was emphasized that any changes should not jeopardize the assurance of systems which are not covered by available tools, or introduce unrealistic expectations of the developers (e.g. by demanding manual resolution of many false positive reports from tools).

3. CLASSIFICATION OF ASSURANCE TOOLS AND TECHNOLOGIES

The tool survey carried out as part of the CC investigation examined a broad range of technologies, on the grounds that many tools might contribute to developing a secure system even if they are not specifically security-related. The classification used there is summarized here.

- Tools which aid human comprehension of software, including

    o Reverse-engineering to graphical representations

    o Enhanced code navigation

    o Automatic documentation

    o Presentation of multiple views

    o Configuration management

    o Integrated development environments

    There are also tools targeted specifically at audit and assessment, which typically include a number of the above functions.

- Configuration management tools. Some form of configuration management is essential, but in this category we include related tools for controlling and supporting development. Additional facilities offered include:

    o Comprehensive documentation management (not just source code)

    o Change management

    o Version / variant management

    o Traceability

    o Build management

    o Access control

    o Integration with the development environment

- Test support and dynamic analysis tools, covering not only conventional testing, but also other assurance activities based on execution of (a variant of) the product. Examples include:

    o Test execution frameworks

    o Test case generation, both white-box (based on the implementation) and black-box (based on a separate specification of intended behavior)

    o Test coverage analysis

    o Memory and execution profiling

- Subset conformance tools. Some forms of security risk can be avoided by eliminating certain classes of structure from allowable implementations, essentially defining a subset of the implementation language. These subsets can be standardized (as, for example, the MISRA subset of C [10]) or company- or project-specific.

- Detection of general implementation weaknesses. Many means of exploiting vulnerabilities make use of errors in software implementation, even if the errors themselves do not constitute a direct vulnerability. Detection and elimination of general programming errors will improve the overall quality of a software product and reduce the potential for security functions to be bypassed or subverted.

- Run-time error detection. One specific class of software weakness which can be difficult to identify by testing is the occurrence of run-time exceptions such as overflow and arithmetic errors. Several approaches have been developed to identify where such errors may occur.

- Vulnerability detection. Of all the classes of flaws which we may search for in a product, those which present known vulnerabilities offers the most direct benefit. A range of tools is available according to the implementation technology and vulnerability classes of concern. This area is the main focus of many other surveys, including [11].

- Executable code analysis. Many of the attributes noted above can be determined either at source code level or by direct examination of object code or byte-code. Source code tools have potential access to richer information about the design intent that object-code tools, but the latter have the advantage of applying directly to the delivered product, and could, for example, be applied to third-party or legacy components.

- Program correctness tools. Although typically applicable only to higher levels of assurance requirement, and thus of limited general applicability, some tools do exist which address the question of program correctness in a broader sense. As many security vulnerabilities are likely to lie outside the intended behaviour of a program, these are able to provide high levels of confidence in the security of a product. Typically, however, they require additional design and implementation effort, such as the preparation of formal specifications or program annotations.

Another recent proposal for a taxonomy of security assurance tools [11] identified the following classes:

- External
  - Network Scanners
  - Web Application Scanners
  - Web Services Network Scanners
  - Dynamic Analysis Tools
- Internal
  - Software Requirements Verification Tools
  - Software Design/Modeling Verification Tools
  - Source Code Scanning Tools, further divided into identification of range and type errors, calls to vulnerable library functions, environmental problems synchronization and timing errors, locking problems, protocol errors, general logic errors and other flaws (file cycling issues, access control implementation, configuration violations)
  - Byte Code Scanning Tools
  - Binary Code Scanning Tools
  - Database Scanning Tools

This breakdown provides more detail on security-specific tools, and includes, in its external category, tools that, being most useful after deployment, were not judged relevant to a product assurance process for the purposes of our earlier study. It provides less detail on tools which are not security specific. Ongoing work to develop a more general taxonomy is taking place as part of the NIST SAMATE project [6].

If tools are to be used in creating or assessing assurance evidence, it is necessary for the tools themselves to be fit for the purpose, in order to establish the requisite confidence in the results they produce. The problem of tool qualification is not unique to security, and has been addressed, for example, by the aerospace safety community [12]. The benchmark for any tool which replaces a life-cycle process is that its output should be at least equivalent to the processes replaced; this means that if the output of a tool is cross-checked independently by some other activity, the requirements place on the tool itself may be relaxed.

Attributes which may be expected of a qualified tool include:

- Clear definition of the function performed and requirements satisfied
- Accuracy
- Repeatability
- Completeness and lack of ambiguity of output
- Characterization of operating environment and behavior under abnormal conditions
- Demonstration of requirements coverage, and analysis of the degree of coverage achieved
- Evidence of previous evaluations, of previous successful deployments, and of the pedigree of other tools developed by the same process
- A traceable defect recording and corrective action system

Ultimately, if the requirements on a class of tool can be characterized with sufficient accuracy, we could expect to develop certification criteria and independent testing schemes.

4. POTENTIAL BENEFITS

The CC classify security requirements into security functional requirements (specifying particular security-related functions which a system must provide) and assurance requirements (specifying the measures to be taken to ensure correct implementation of the functional requirements). Assurance requirements are further subdivided into families:

- Configuration management (ACM)
- Delivery and operation (ADO)
- Development (ADV)
- Guidance documentation (AGD)
- Life cycle support (ALC)
- Tests (ATE)
- Vulnerability assessment (AVA)

Seven pre-defined packages of assurance requirements are defined, representing increasing levels of assurance – the Evaluation Assurance Levels (EAL) 1–7 where EAL 1 is the least stringent, and EAL 7 the most.

Analysis of the capabilities of the various classes of software development and assurance tools against the CC requirements led us to consider three areas in which tools can facilitate the development of an assured product, as follows.

- Tools employed in the development, but which support or facilitate assurance,
- Tools of direct use in evaluating security, and
- Tools which support the implementation of security functional requirements rather than providing evidence that security assurance requirements have been met.

These areas are discussed in the following sub-sections.

One additional aspect of tool use became clear in the course of the analysis: there are many areas in which tools which may not necessarily assist in one-off assurance of a particular development but contribute substantially to the effective maintenance and re-use of assurance evidence. Such re-use is important in many situations:

o   In re-assurance of a modified or updated product,

o   In assurance of a product in distinct, but related, environments (eg across different platforms), and

o   In developing composite systems that make use of previous assurance evidence about their components.

Of particular importance in these cases is the need to be able to identify where modifications have been made, and where dependencies arise which may need to be re-considered in the light of those changes. Our experience indicates that even given such facilities, re-assuring a complex system can still be difficult if an attempt is made to re-use parts of previous work in the production of complete new assurance arguments; re-use is more likely to be effective if complete assurance arguments are used as a whole, forming a baseline against which later assurance is documented as an assured set of changes.

4.1   Tools employed in development

Many tools used in development are useful in supporting assurance, because many of the factors which facilitate assurance also directly facilitate the development itself. Nevertheless, some development tool functions are of greater relevance than others. Areas of particular relevance are described below

4.1.1   Configuration Management (CC Assurance Class ACM).

Tool support for change and build management provides both developers and assessors with confidence that the product delivered – and its supporting configuration information, documentation, training material, etc – are derived from valid sources and controlled appropriately. All serious product developments will use some forms of configuration management policy and tools; nevertheless, choice of appropriate tools can greatly simplify assuring an appropriate level of configuration management. Features of particular relevance include: comprehensive coverage of all documents (not simply code); access control; change control; traceability; and version comparison/impact analysis to support re-use of assurance evidence.

4.1.2   Life cycle support (CC Assurance Class ALC)

Confidence in the control of the development life-cycle is an important component of assurance. While few tools control the life-cycle directly, and lifecycle definition and control are general project-management issues beyond the scope of this paper, a number of aspects of assurance benefit from an appropriate development tool environment. Configuration management tools which provide formal release control, for example, may be used to enforce compliance to particular life-cycle features. Development security (Class ALC_DVS) may also be enhanced by use of a CM system which enforces appropriate access controls and audit mechanisms. The level of assurance required

of all tools used is also a life-cycle issue: maintenance of satisfactory assurance may require keeping all tools under configuration management, for example, and the use of additional tools (such as subset-conformance checkers) to ensure that other tools (such as compilers) are only employed within the limits of their own assurance. Direct assurance of one tool, a compiler for example, may also be established through the use of another (a de-compiler or compiler validation suite). See Section 3.

4.1.3   Development (CC Assurance Class ADV)

The CC approach to development concentrates on establishing consistency between increasingly detailed levels of design representation. Assurance of this consistency can be facilitated by tools which maintain traceability between representations. Integrated development environments using semi-formal notations such as UML [13] can be used to support such a lifecycle, the rigorous separation of functional specification, high-level design, low-level design and implementation representation which (the current version of) the CC requires is not necessarily natural in such frameworks. See Section 4.4 for further discussion. The task of demonstrating correspondence between implementation and low-level design is facilitated by many of the software quality tools identified in Section 3: subset conformance, detection of run-time errors and software weaknesses all support this goal, as do some forms of object code verification.

4.1.4   Testing (CC Assurance Class ATE)

Some degree of test automation is likely to be used in any substantial product development, and any mechanisms which encourage the repeatable and controlled execution of tests will provide a degree of assurance in the design process. Some assurance benefits maybe expected from coverage analysis tools, although measurement of the proportion of a design which is exercised may not be a good prediction of the actual performance of the tests in detecting security-related errors. Management tools, such as configuration management and traceability tools, will also be applicable to tests and the test process.

4.2   For evaluators

The areas in which tools are directly applicable to assurance are perhaps more restricted than the general benefits of development tools, but the specific value which could potentially be obtained in some cases is nevertheless substantial. In the analysis, it proved useful to consider areas in which evaluators seek confidence, such as:

•   Correct functionality is crucial, but in the majority of cases restricted to an informal review

•   Identification of specific risky constructs, including error conditions, common vulnerabilities such as buffer overflows, and issues regarding concurrency.

•   Consistency between design representations, and across interfaces between different elements.

•   Sensitivities to platform and compiler attributes, which may become weaknesses if external dependencies change.

- General structure and behaviour of the program, as a prerequisite for assessing other issues, and also to illuminate information flow, for example.

Note that although these issues were examined from the perspective of an evaluator or assessor, developers are likely to use the same tools and techniques in order to reduce the risk that issues may be discovered later in the product life cycle.

4.2.1 Assurance of correct development (CC Assurance Class ADV)

The bulk of the information available to an assessor arises from the development process – any evaluation will therefore expect to make use of the tools discussed in the previous section. The applicability of other tools will depend largely on the nature of the information available: for medium and low-level assessment (the vast majority of cases) much of this information will be informal. In these cases, the key documentation (functional specifications, high- and low-level designs) may be natural language texts – there may be scope for the use of documentation tools such as readability metrics and indexing tools, but little true automation may be expected (NASA's Automated Requirement Measurement tool (ARM) is an interesting extension to an important class of documents [14].) Where semi-formal notations are used, mechanical consistency checks may be implemented (often as part of an IDE) ,but acceptance of such checks a assurance evidence is hampered by lack of commonly agreed representations and semantics for such checks.

In contrast, source code is by its nature formal and suited to the provision of mechanical support for the key assurance challenge of accessing and comprehending large quantities of technical information. Navigation and documentation aids (such as cross referencing and indexing tools) are important supports to assessment activities. Tools which provide some degree of abstraction (such as generating a call-tree or dependence graph) can be used to support comparison of the implementation with a low-level design, and can assist in identifying security-enforcing functions and their dependencies.

4.2.2 Assurance testing (CC Assurance Class ATE)

Assurance activities will typically include both an assessment of testing carried out during development and an element of independent testing. Both classes of activities will be facilitated by tools as discussed in the previous section (Section 4.1). The identification of specific vulnerabilities is also likely to involve testing in addition to the activities discussed in the next section.

4.2.3 Vulnerability identification (CC Assurance Class AVA)

The search for specific vulnerabilities is an essential element of security assurance. This is an area in which a number of specific vulnerability detection tools have been proposed (See Section 3) and their use is obviously a potentially valuable source of evidence, but the value of their results will be crucially dependent on parameters which are not necessarily easy to characterize, such as the proportion of identified problems which are not, in fact vulnerabilities (false positives) and the proportion of vulnerabilities which are present but not detected (false negatives). Similar concerns also apply to tools which look for general weaknesses which may be associated with breaches, such as run-time errors. The characterization and qualification of these tools is an important area of research (see also Section 3).

4.2.4 Manual assurance is essential

Although we have identified a number of areas in which tool support may support the assurance activities, there are a number of areas where no substitute to manual review and assessment is practical. This is the case, for example, in areas where the key attributes are the clarity and completeness of documentation, such as prevention of accidental misuse and installation and operational guidance generally. General purpose tools will also have limited use in some technical analysis, such as determination if the strength of security functions is appropriate.

4.3 Functional requirements

The discussion above has concentrated on assurance requirements – constraints on how a product is constructed – rather than the function it actually performs. In general, tools will not be able to confirm functional correctness of a product, although customised tool-supported analysis may be justifiable for some specific projects. There are some specific areas, however, where tool support can be valuable in assuring functional correctness, including:

- Control and data flow analyses. The more sophisticated program analysis tools can derive the flow of data and control through a program. This can be valuable in demonstrating the adequacy of various controls and policies, such as ensuring that security functions are invoked prior to any action which might compromise security (mediation).

- Failure mode analysis. Tools which detect vulnerabilities or general weaknesses in implementation provide information about the possible ways in which an implementation or function may fail. This is necessary to establish the appropriateness of measures which manage failures such as fault-tolerance or fail-secure functionality.

- Protocol and algorithm correctness. Although full proof of correctness of an implementation is not likely to be practical for the vast majority of security products, there are elements which, because of their extreme criticality or wide deployment, may be subject to more stringent constraints. In these cases, formal verification with specialist tool support may be appropriate. Typical applications might be security protocols or algorithms used by fundamental network infrastructure. ([15], [16], for example).

4.4 Evolution of the CC Evaluation Scheme

Our review identified a number of recommendations which we felt should be considered for changes to the CC and the evaluation methodology which advises how the criteria should be applied. The key recommendations regarding the methodology were:

- To require a search for known failure modes in the chosen implementation language, and mechanical enforcement of rules necessary to conform to well-defined language subsets.

- To link the sizes chosen for sampling activities to general software quality measures (allowing sample size reduction to be argued for developments showing demonstrably good quality).

- To encourage security targets to be defined according to practical application rather than to simplify evaluation.

Recommendations regarding the Common Criteria themselves were addressed more cautiously, because of the need to maintain consensus among all participants. The key suggestions were in the following areas:

- Fault elimination: Strengthening the functional specification of security functions to place greater emphasis on interfaces, and on the assumptions which the security functions make for correct behavior (e.g. integrity of memory, restrictions on flow of control). (Class ADV_FSP); inclusion in the development of evidence for the robustness of separation between security functions and other functions; and allowing tool support for maintenance of design representations, and relaxing requirements for strict refinement between design representations (while maintaining the necessary consistency).

- Fault discovery and removal: the requirement identified above, to search for known failure modes and insecurities, should ultimately be reflected in the CC.

- Failure tolerance. Designing systems to be tolerant of faults and failures is a crucial element in other product integrity domains, but is not emphasized in the CC. A requirement should be added to require analysis of possible failures and demonstrating that the design is appropriately robust.

- General changes: In other communities, standards-setting is moving towards a less prescriptive goal-oriented approach. The CC could be made less prescriptive, stating objectives of a successful evaluation and criteria which the recorded evidence must meet, but leaving open the means of meeting these objectives. This would facilitate competitive improvement of the evaluation process. To maintain mutual recognition in the light of this change, recognition should be based on establishing that different approaches are consistent in their effectiveness and findings, rather than that they produce identical results.

Since the completion of the work reported in [4], a new draft issue of the Common Criteria and the evaluation methodology has been published [17]. The new draft addresses many of the recommendations made here:

- Greater emphasis is placed on architectural integrity, and on demonstrating that other functions do not interfere with the security functions, although explicit failure mode analysis is not required.

- More explicit requirements are placed on specification of the interfaces of security functions.

- The development assurance family (ADV) has been revised to simplify the constraints placed on design documentation.

- The vulnerability analysis requirements include requirements to search for known classes of vulnerabilities.

The evaluation methodology remains too abstract to provide concrete advice on the use of tools, although clearly tool support will be advantageous for those activities which are required to be methodical.

Although the new version does significantly introduce noticeable simplification and significant re-structuring in many requirements, the majority of key assurance activities remain the same; the value and applicability of tool support will, therefore, remain unchanged.

5. CONCLUSIONS & FUTURE WORK
This paper takes results from number of existing studies:

- a goal-based view of the objectives of a secure product development [5],

- a review of the applicability of tools to security assurance [4] and

- Emerging work on taxonomies of software security tools [11],

and presents a summary which highlights where software tools may be expected to add value to development programs.

5.1 Applicability of Tools
Our review identified a number of areas where existing security evaluations could be supported by existing tools:

- Control of changes and configurations of products, product variants and assurance evidence
- Identification of general weaknesses, violations of coding standards and subsets, and potential run-time errors
- Identification of known vulnerabilities
- Assisting in an assessors understanding of a potentially large volume of potentially complex information

In the short term, use of tools in these areas appears most likely to improve the value of assurance (in terms of reduction of vulnerabilities discovered in service) rather than to decrease cost. We believe that it may be possible to achieve savings, primarily in the cost of developing the information required to support assurance, if increased use of automated document management and change control tools, and increased use of tools to enforce coding standards and subsets, were combined with a shift in the focus of development and evaluation processes.

Any successful deployment of tools will require that the tools themselves are adequately assured.

5.2 Varieties of assurance

The security of a product depends on many factors, and consequently can be improved and demonstrated by a range of different measures. The benefits of different assurance measures can be comprehended, and trade-off decisions facilitated, by considering their contribution to a structured assurance argument. Such an argument can provide a framework for planning assurance activities and identifying the support which tools can provide.

Some of the more important measures are specific to security assurance, such as searching implementations for known vulnerabilities, but we believe that systematic examination of the goals of a secure development demonstrates that more general assurance tools provide significant value in areas including general software quality, robustness of architectures, configuration management and change control. Our studies further indicate that for benefits in cost as well as quality, security assurance must be an integral element of the development process, taken into consideration as key design decisions are being made.

5.3 Future Work

Although the opportunity for tool-supported security assurance is attractive, there are several questions which must be resolved if security assurance tools are to be widely adopted:

- Classification of tools and techniques, and development of common understandings of the value and function of each class, is necessary both to justify the adoption of tools, and to provide a basis for tool assurance. To support cost-benefit analysis, the classification must reflect benefits (eg risks reduced) rather than functional behaviour.

- Practical tools must be usable: issues such as consistent and informative output, reduction of false positive and false negative results, and scalability to large code bases are paramount.

- The qualitative discussion of assurance presented here must be refined to give quantitative cost-benefit arguments for tool adoption. A systematic approach to assurance will be required to allow tradeoffs to be made not only between the cost of assurance and the cost of failure, but between mechanisms which may each improve security in very different ways.

6. ACKNOWLEDGMENTS

The authors would like to acknowledge the support of CESG, Praxis High Integrity Systems Ltd, and all the stakeholders involved in the Common Criteria study [4]. Particular thanks are due to Keith Banks for his contributions to [4], and to Phil Core for his comments on drafts of this paper. The referees also provided useful comments.

7. REFERENCES

[1] U.S. Department of Homeland Security, The National Strategy to Secure Cyberspace, February 2003

[2] Anderson, R.J., Why Information Security is Hard – An Economic Perspective, *Proc. Annual Computer Security Applications Conference*, 2001

[3] Common Criteria for Information Technology Security Evaluation, Version 2.2, January 2004 Available from www.commoncriteriaportal.org

[4] Praxis Critical Systems Ltd, EAL4 Common Criteria Evaluations Study, September 2004, available from http://www.cesg.gov.uk/site/iacs/itsec/media/techniques_tools/eval4_study.pdf

[5] U.K Defence Procurement Agency and Praxis High Integrity Systems Limited, SafSec Project, www.safsec.com

[6] U.S. National Institute of Standards and Technology, SAMATE Project, http://samate.nist.gov

[7] Secure Software Inc., The CLASP Application Security Process, 2005.

[8] Kelly, T.P., Arguing Safety – A Systematic Approach to Safety Case Management, DPhil Thesis YCST99-05, Department of Computer Science, University of York, UK, 1998

[9] Common Methodology for Information Technology Security Evaluation, Version 2.2, January 2004

[10] Motor Industry Software Reliability Association, MISRA-C:2004 - Guidelines for the use of the C language in critical systems, ISBN 0 9524156 2 3, 2004

[11] U.S. National Institute of Standards and Technology, SAMATE Project Tools Survey, http://samate.nist.gov/index.php/Tools

[12] RTCA Inc, DO-178B, Software Considerations in Airborne Systems and Equipment Certification, 1992

[13] Booch, G., Rumbaugh, J. and Jacobson, I., The Unified Modeling Language User Guide Addison-Wesley 1998

[14] NASA, Automated Requirement Measurement (ARM), http://satc.gsfc.nasa.gov/tools/arm/

[15] Lowe, G., An Attack on the Needham-Schroeder Public-Key Authentication Protocol. *Information Processing Letters 56*, 3, 1995, 131-133.

[16] Reed, J.N., Jackson, D.M., Deinov, B., and Reed, G.M., Automated Formal Analysis of Networks: FDR models for arbitrary topologies and flow-control mechanisms, *Proc. Joint European Conferences on Theory and Practice of Software* LNCS 1382, Springer 1998.

[17] Common Criteria for Information Technology Security Evaluation, Draft Version 3.0, July 2005

Metrics That Matter:

Quantifying Software Security Risk

Brian Chess
Fortify Software
2300 Geng Road, Suite 102
Palo Alto, CA 94303
1-650-213-5600

brian@fortifysoftware.com

Abstract

Any endeavor worth pursuing is worth measuring, but software security presents new measurement challenges: there are no established formulas or procedures for quantifying the security risk present in a program. This document details the importance of measuring software security and discusses the less-than-satisfying approaches that are prevalent today. A new set of metrics is then proposed for ensuring an accurate and comprehensive view of software projects ranging from legacy systems to newly deployed web applications. Many of the new metrics make use of source code analysis results.

1. Introduction: Why measure?

What would happen if your company cut its security budget in half? What if the budget was doubled instead? In most companies today, no one knows the answers to these questions. Security remains more art than science, and nothing is more indicative of this fact than the inability of security practitioners to quantify the effects of their work.

Software security is no exception: nearly every major business-critical application deployed today contains vulnerabilities—buffer overflow and cross-site scripting are commonplace, and so are many other, less well-known, types of vulnerabilities. These problems can be exploited to cause considerable harm by external hackers or malicious insiders. Security teams know that these errors exist, but are, for the most part, ill equipped to quantify the problem. Any proposed investment in improving this situation is bound to bring up questions such as:
- Are the applications more secure today than yesterday—or less secure?
- Does security training really make a difference?
- How will we know when our systems are secure?

This paper examines the current state of practice for measuring software security. It then suggests two new approaches to the problem: quantifying the secure development lifecycle, and focusing on the root cause of many vulnerabilities using metrics built with source code analysis results.

2. The State of Practice: Three Flawed Approaches to Measuring Security

1. Build then Break: Penetration Testing as a Metric
The de facto method that most organizations use for measuring software security today can be summarized as "build then break." Developers create applications with only a minimum of attention paid to security, and the applications are deployed. The operations team then attempts to compensate for the problematic software with perimeter security. When the team takes inventory of all of the ways that data moves through and around the perimeter defenses, it becomes clear that the perimeter security is insufficient. At this point, the operations team may bring in penetration testers to find the problems before hackers or malicious insiders do. The penetration testers generally have a fixed schedule for performing their work, and their goal is to find a small number of serious problems to justify their consulting fee. Once these problems are resolved, everyone is happy. But there's no reason to believe that the penetration test revealed all of the problems with the application. In fact, subsequent audits usually prove that it did not. There's also very little feedback to the developers, so penetration tests often find the same types of problems over and over again.

2. Measure Software Security as Part of Software Quality
A naive approach to software security calls for treating security as just another aspect of software quality. The problem is that traditional quality assurance is aimed at verifying a set of features against a specification. Software security, however, requires much more than well-implemented security features. The reality is that a typical process for achieving good results with respect to traditional quality issues does not guarantee good results with respect to security issues. In other words, you have to focus specifically on security in order to improve it. Good security is not a byproduct of good quality.

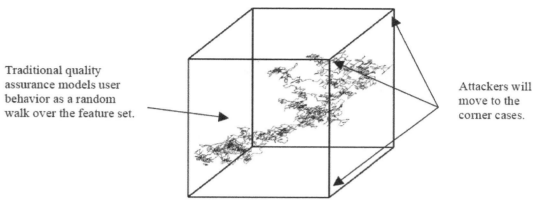

Traditional quality assurance models user behavior as a random walk over the feature set.

Attackers will move to the corner cases.

Figure 1: A quality-oriented approach to security leaves many opportunities for attackers.

Further complicating this approach, the majority of Quality Assurance (QA) departments lack the requisite security expertise to carry out adequate security tests. Finally, as Figure 1 illustrates, any approach to quality that is based on the behavior of regular users will leave many untested opportunities for attackers.

3. *The Feel-Good Metric: If It Hasn't been Hacked Yet, It's Probably Okay*

Because security so often goes unquantified, the bottom-line measure for security is often gut-feel. Human nature and the nature of security are in conflict on this point: people and organizations tend to gain comfort with the status quo over time, but security may actually degrade as time passes. New types of attacks and new applications for old types of attacks can harm a program's security—even as an organization becomes more and more complacent because security "hasn't been a problem yet!"

A similar fallacy holds that the security of a program can be correlated to the breadth of its adoption. Interestingly, this line of reasoning always seems to work in favor of the status quo. For applications with a small user base, people assume that attackers will not take an interest. For applications with a large user base, people assume that any security issues will be flushed out of the system shortly after release. In truth, security is no more related to breadth of adoption than it is to longevity. The BugTraq mailing list (where news of many new vulnerabilities debuts) is filled with entries about small and obscure applications. Furthermore, the long history of buffer overflows in widely adopted programs as varied as SendMail and Internet Explorer shows that neither age nor a large install base prevents attackers from finding new exploits.

3. A Positive Trailing Indicator

There are encouraging signs that the longstanding neglect, ignorance, or apathy shown to software security is beginning to change. Microsoft has adopted the Trustworthy Computing Security Development Lifecycle (SDL) process for the creating software that needs to withstand malicious attack [4]. The process adds a series of security-focused activities and deliverables to each of the phases of Microsoft's software development process. These activities and deliverables include risk analysis during software design, the application of source

code analysis tools during implementation, and code reviews and security testing during a focused "security push." Before software subject to the SDL can be released, it must undergo a final security review by a team independent from its development group. When compared to software that has *not* been subject to the SDL, software that *has* undergone the SDL has experienced a significantly reduced rate of external discovery of security vulnerabilities. Figure 2 shows the number of security bulletins for Windows 2000 in its first 12 months after release versus the number of security bulletins for Windows Server 2003 in its first 12 months after release. The number of issues has been reduced by more than 50%, even as the size and complexity of the operating system has increased.

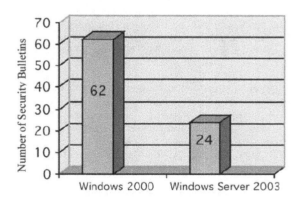

Figure 2. A measurable improvement in Microsoft OS security: the number of security bulletins issued in the first 12 months following two major OS releases.

However, Figure 2 is an example of a *trailing indicator*. It only demonstrates that security has been improved after the OS has been released. It provides strong evidence that the SDL has a beneficial effect on the security of the resulting operating system, but if Microsoft only releases an operating system every five or six years, it requires five or six years to know whether there is a measurable improvement in software security from the previous release. That is far too slow. Security must be measured on an ongoing basis throughout the software development lifecycle, and for that we need *leading indicators* for software security.

4. Software security metrics you can use now

Having explained the measurement problem and how *not* to solve it, we now turn to two practical methods for measuring software security.

1. *Quantify the Secure Development Lifecycle*

Software security must be addressed as part of the software development lifecycle [*1,2*]. There are practical steps that development groups can take during each phase of the lifecycle in order to improve the security of the resulting system. These steps include:

- **Evaluate** the current state of software security and create a **plan** for dealing with it throughout the development life cycle.
- **Specify** the threats, identify both business and technical risks, and plan countermeasures.
- **Review** the code for security vulnerabilities introduced during development.
- **Test** code for vulnerabilities based on the threats and risks identified earlier.
- **Build a gate** to prevent applications with vulnerabilities from going into production. Require signoff from key development and security personnel.
- **Measure** the success of the security plan so that the process can be continually improved. Yes, your measurement efforts should be measured!
- **Educate** stakeholders about security so they can implement the security plan effectively.

Each of these steps can be measured. For example, if your security plan includes educating developers, you can measure what percentage of developers have received software security training. [1]

Of course, not all organizations will adopt all steps to the same degree. By tracking and measuring the adoption of secure development practices, you will have the data to draw correlations within your organization. For example, you will likely find that the up-front specification of threats and risks correlates strongly to a faster and easier security signoff prior to release.

2. *Use Source Code Analysis to Measure Security*

All software organizations, regardless of programming language, development methodology, or product category, have one thing in common: they all have source code. The source code is a very direct embodiment of the system, and many vulnerabilities manifest themselves in the source [3]. It follows that the source code is the one key artifact to measure as part of assessing software security. Of course, source code review is useful for more than just metrics. The following sections discuss some source code analysis fundamentals and then look at how source code analysis results can provide the raw material for powerful software security metrics.

---

[1] It seems reasonable to assume that Microsoft also produces metrics related to their SDL, but they have published very little on the topic.

5. Source Code Analysis

Source code analyzers process code looking for known types of security defects. In an abstract sense, a source code analyzer searches the code for patterns that represent potential vulnerabilities and presents the code that matches these patterns to a human auditor for review. The three key attributes for good source code analysis are accuracy, precision, and robustness.

A source code analyzer should accurately identify vulnerabilities that are of concern to the type of program being analyzed. For example, web applications are typically at risk for SQL injection, cross-site scripting, and access control problems, among others. Further, the analysis results should indicate the likely importance of each result.

The source code analyzer must also be precise, pointing to a manageable number of issues without generating a large number of false positives. Furthermore, if a program is analyzed today, and subsequently re-analyzed tomorrow, it is likely that only a small amount of code will have changed. The source code analyzer must be able to give the same name to the same issue today and tomorrow, allowing for the ability to track when issues appear and disappear. This capability is critical for extracting meaningful metrics from source code analysis results.

Finally, the source code analyzer must be robust: it must be able to deal with large, complex bodies of code. Of course, not every issue the source code analyzer identifies will be a true vulnerability. Therefore, part of being robust is allowing human auditors to evaluate and prioritize potential issues. A preferred scenario has a human auditor classify the output from the analyzer into 1) severe vulnerabilities that must be corrected immediately, 2) bad practices, and 3) issues that are not relevant to the organization. An even better application of source code analysis allows developers to analyze their own code as they write it, making source code analysis part of the daily process of program development.

6. Security Metrics Based on Source Code Analysis

The best metrics that can be derived from source code analysis results are, to a certain extent, dependent upon the way in which an organization applies source code analysis. We will consider the following scenarios:

1. Developers use the source code analyzer on a regular basis as part of their development work. They are proactively coding with security in mind.
2. A software security team uses the source code analyzer as part of a periodic code review process. A large body of code has been created with little regard for security. The organization plans to remediate this code over time.

Of course, the first scenario is preferable, but most organizations cannot achieve that overnight. For the near future, it is likely that both scenarios will co-exist in most organizations.

Metrics for Secure Coding

After a development team adopts a source code analysis tool and tunes it for the security policies that are important for their project, they can use source code analysis results in aggregate for trending and project comparison purposes. Figure 3 shows a comparison between two projects, one red and one blue, where the source code analysis results have been grouped by severity. The graph suggests a plan of action: eliminate the critical issues for the red project, then move on to the high-importance issues for the blue project.

It can also be useful to look at the types of issues found broken down by category. Figure 4 shows the results for the same two projects in this fashion. Here, the differences between the red and the blue project become pronounced: the blue project has a significant number of buffer overflow issues. A strategy for preventing buffer overflow is in order.

Vulnerability Severities by Project

Figure 3: Source code analysis results broken down by severity for two projects.

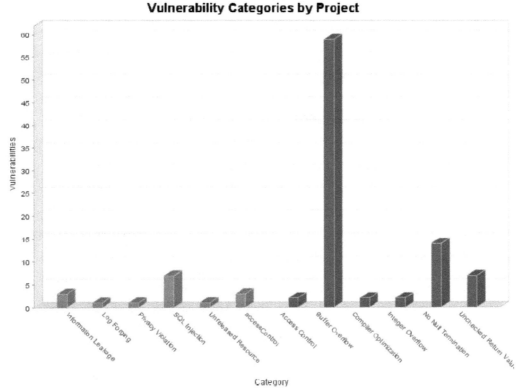

Vulnerability Categories by Project

Figure 4: Source code analysis issues organized by vulnerability type.

25

Source code analysis results can also be used to examine vulnerability trends. Teams that are focused on security will decrease the number of source code analysis findings over time as they increasingly use the automation to mitigate security problems. A sharp increase in the number of issues found is likely to indicate a new security concern. Figure 5 shows the number of issues found during each nightly build. Trend indicators show how the project is evolving. In this case, the spike in the number of issues found is a result of the development group taking over a module from a group that has not been focused on security. This code represents a risk that will need mitigation throughout the remaining portion of the development life cycle.

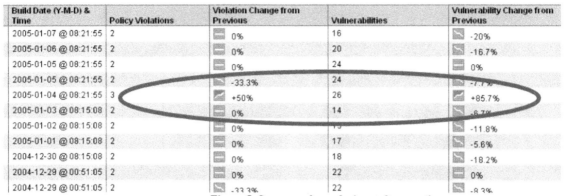

Build Date (Y-M-D) & Time	Policy Violations	Violation Change from Previous	Vulnerabilities	Vulnerability Change from Previous
2005-01-07 @ 08:21:55	2	0%	16	-20%
2005-01-06 @ 08:21:55	2	0%	20	-16.7%
2005-01-05 @ 08:21:55	2	0%	24	0%
2005-01-05 @ 08:21:55	2	-33.3%	24	-7.7%
2005-01-04 @ 08:21:55	3	+50%	26	+85.7%
2005-01-03 @ 08:15:08	2	0%	14	-6.7%
2005-01-02 @ 08:15:08	2	0%	15	-11.8%
2005-01-01 @ 08:15:08	2	0%	17	-5.6%
2004-12-30 @ 08:15:08	2	0%	18	-18.2%
2004-12-29 @ 00:51:05	2	0%	22	0%
2004-12-29 @ 00:51:05	2	-33.3%	22	-8.3%

Figure 5: Source code analysis results over time.

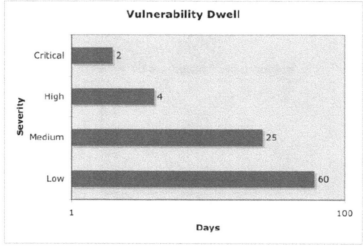

Figure 6: Vulnerability dwell as a function of priority.

Metrics for Legacy codebases

For large codebases where security has not historically been a priority, the security challenge has a different flavor. In most cases, it is not possible to instantaneously remodel the entire codebase for security purposes. Instead, an audit team needs to prioritize the problems and work to remove the worst ones. Of course, new development will continue even as the triage takes place.

Metrics for legacy codebases leverage the ability of the source code analyzer to give the same issue the same name across different builds. By following the same issue over time and associating it with the feedback provided by a human auditor, the source code analyzer can provide insight into the evolution of the project.

For example, the source code analysis results can reveal the way a development team responds to security vulnerabilities. After an auditor identifies a vulnerability, how long on average does it take for the developers to make a fix? This metric is named "Vulnerability Dwell." Figure 6 shows a project where the developers fix critical vulnerabilities within two days and take progressively longer to address less severe problems.

Because a legacy codebase often continues to evolve, auditors will need to return to the same projects again and again over time. But how often? Every month? Every six months? The rate of auditing should keep pace with the rate of development, or rather the rate at which potential security issues are introduced into the code. By tracking individual issues over time, the output from a source code analysis tool can show an audit team how many unaudited issues a project contains.

Figure 7 presents a typical graph. At the point the project is first audited, audit coverage goes to 100%. Then, as the code evolves over time, the audit coverage decays until the project is audited again.

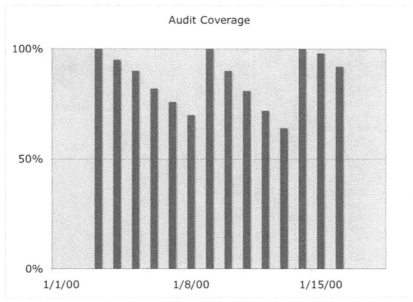

Figure 7: Audit coverage over time.

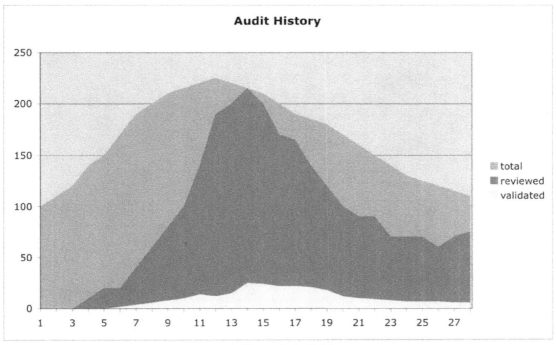

Figure 8: Audit history.

Another view of this same data gives a more comprehensive view of the project. An audit history shows the total number of issues, number of issues reviewed, and number of vulnerabilities identified as a function of time. This view takes into account not just the work of the auditors, but the effect the developers have on the project, too. Figure 8 shows an audit (shown in red) conducted over several product builds. At the same time the audit is taking place, the number of issues in the codebase (shown in blue) is growing. As the auditors work, they report vulnerabilities (shown in yellow). When the blue and red meet, the auditors have looked at all of the issues. Development work is not yet complete though, and soon the project once again contains unaudited issues. As the developers respond to some of the vulnerabilities identified by the audit team, the number of issues begins to decrease and some of the identified vulnerabilities are fixed. At the far right side of the graph, the uptick in the red indicates that another audit is beginning.

7. Conclusion

While software security has been a universally recognized risk, there has been an absence of established procedures for quantifying the security risk present software. Only by measuring can organizations conquer the software security problem.

The first step in this journey is the adoption of security-focused activities and deliverables throughout each phase of the software development process. These activities and deliverables include risk analysis during software design, code review during development, and security-oriented testing that targets the risks that are specific to the application at hand. By tracking and measuring the security activities adopted into the development process, an organization can begin to quantify their software security risk.

The data produced by source code analysis tools can be particularly useful for this purpose, giving insight into whether or not code review is taking place and whether or not the results of the review are being acted upon.

8. REFERENCES

[1] G. McGraw. *Software Security: Building Security In.* Addison-Wesley, to appear in 2006.

[2] G. McGraw et al. Building Security In. *IEEE Security and Privacy Magazine*, 2004-2005.

[3] C. E. Landwehr, A. R. Bull, J. P. McDermott, W. S. Choi. A Taxonomy of Computer Program Security Flaws, with Examples. *ACM Computing Surveys*, Vol. 26, No. 3, September 1994, pp. 211-254.

[4] S. Lipner and M. Howard. The Trustworthy Computing Security Development Lifecycle. In *Proceedings of the 20th Annual Computer Security Applications Conference* (ACSAC'04), 2004, pp. 2-13.

The Case for Common Flaw Enumeration

Robert A. Martin
MITRE Corporation
202 Burlington Road
Bedford, MA 01730
1-781-271-3001

ramartin@mitre.org

Steven M. Christey
MITRE Corporation
202 Burlington Road
Bedford, MA 01730
1-781-271-3961

coley@mitre.org

Joe Jarzombek
National Cyber Security Division
Department of Homeland Security
Arlington, VA 22201
1-703-235-5126

joe.jarzombek@dhs.gov

ABSTRACT
Software acquirers want assurance that the software products they are obtaining are reviewed for known types of security flaws. The acquisition groups in large government and private organizations are moving forward to use these types of reviews as part of future contracts. The tools and services that can be used for this type of review are fairly new at best. However, there are no nomenclature, taxonomies, or standards to define the capabilities and coverage of these tools and services. This makes it difficult to comparatively decide which tool/service is best suited for a particular job. A standard taxonomy of software security vulnerabilities can serve as a unifying language of discourse and measuring stick for tools and services. Leveraging the diverse thinking on this topic from academia, the commercial sector, and government, we can pull together the most valuable breadth and depth of content and structure to serve as a unified standard. As a starting point, we plan to leverage the wide acceptance and use of the Common Vulnerabilities and Exposures (CVE) list of publicly known software security flaws. In conjunction with industry and academia, we propose to extend the coverage of the CVE concept [1] into security-based code assessment tools and services. Our objective is to help shape and mature this new code security assessment industry and also dramatically accelerate the use and utility of these capabilities for organizations in reviewing the software systems they acquire or develop.

Categories and Subject Descriptors
D.2.4 [Software Engineering]: Software/Program Verification

General Terms
Software, Security, Testing, Verification, Flaws, Faults.

Keywords
taxonomies, static analysis, security flaws, weaknesses, idiosyncrasies, WIFF, Common Vulnerabilities and Exposures, CVE, vulnerabilities, secure software, software security assurance.

1. INTRODUCTION
More and more organizations want assurance that the software products they acquire and develop are free of known types of security flaws. High quality tools and services for finding security flaws in code are new. The question of which tool/service is appropriate/better for a particular job is hard to answer given the lack of structure and definition in the code assessment industry.

There are several efforts currently ongoing to begin to resolve some of these shortcomings including the Department of Homeland Security (DHS) National Cyber Security Division (NCSD) sponsored Software Assurance Metrics and Tool Evaluation (SAMATE) project [2] being led by the National Institute of Standards and Technology (NIST), and the Department of Defense (DOD) sponsored Code Assessment Methodology Project (CAMP) which is part of the Protection of Vital Data (POVD) effort [3] being conducted by Concurrent Technologies Corporation (CTC), among others. While these efforts are well placed, timely in their objectives and will surely yield high value in the end, they both would benefit from a common description of the underlying security vulnerabilities in software that they are targeted to resolve. Without such a common taxonometric description, many of these efforts cannot move forward in a meaningful fashion or be aligned and integrated with each other to provide strategic value.

Past efforts at developing this kind of taxonomy have been limited by a very narrow technical domain focus or have largely focused on high-level theories, taxonomies, or schemes that do not reach the level of detail or variety of security issues that are found in today's products. As an alternate approach, under sponsorship of DHS NCSD, MITRE investigated the possibility of leveraging the CVE initiative's experience in analyzing nearly 13,000 real-world vulnerabilities reported and discussed by industry and academia.

As part of the creation of the CVE List, over the last five years MITRE's CVE initiative, sponsored by DHS NCSD, has developed a preliminary classification and categorization of vulnerabilities, attacks, faults, and other concepts that can be used to help define this arena. However, the current groupings used in the development of CVE, while sufficient for that task, are too rough to be used to identify and categorize the functionality offered within the offerings of the code security assessment industry. Additional fidelity and succinctness is needed to support this type of usage and there needs to be additional details and description for each of the different nodes and groupings such as the effects, behaviors, and implementation details, etc.

As part of MITRE's participation in the DHS-sponsored NIST SAMATE project MITRE took a first cut at revising the internal CVE category work for usage in the code assessment industry. The resultant document, called the Preliminary List Of Vulnerability Examples for Researchers (PLOVER) [4], is a working document that lists over 1,400 diverse, real-world examples of vulnerabilities, identified by their CVE name. The vulnerabilities are organized within a detailed conceptual framework that currently enumerates 290 individual types of Weaknesses, Idiosyncrasies, Faults, Flaws (WIFFs), with a large number of real-world vulnerability examples for each type of WIFF. PLOVER represents the first cut of a truly bottom-up effort to take real-world observed faults and flaws that *do* exist in code, abstract them and group them into common classes representing more general potential vulnerabilities that *could* exist in code, and then finally to organize them in an appropriate relative structure so as to make them accessible and useful to a diverse set of audiences for a diverse set of purposes. The initial details of this enumeration can be found at the end of this paper.

Working with the community under the NIST SAMATE project, we are establishing acceptable definitions and descriptions of these CWEs. When completed, this will serve as a mechanism for describing code vulnerability assessment capabilities in terms of their coverage of the different CWEs. If necessary, this will also be scoped to specific languages, frameworks, platforms and machine architectures. More work is required to group PLOVER WIFFs into a taxonomy more useful for SAMATE.

2. OBJECTIVES

As discussed above, we are leveraging PLOVER as a starting point for the creation of a formal enumeration of the set of software security Weaknesses, Idiosyncrasies, Faults, Flaws (WIFFs) to serve as a common language for describing software security vulnerabilities, to serve as a standard measuring stick for software security tools targeting these vulnerabilities, and to provide a common glue for vulnerability identification, mitigation and prevention efforts. When complete, this Common WIFF Enumeration (CWE) will not only encompass a large portion of the CVE List's 12,000 plus CVE names but it will also include detail and breadth from a diverse set of other industry and academic sources and examples. Once a comprehensively broad set of CWEs has been identified and collected, we will again look to these other sources and examples for approaches to organizing this enumeration in order to provide more simplicity to various potential users through taxonometric layering.

Working with the community under the DHS-sponsored NIST SAMATE project we are proceeding to establish acceptable definitions and descriptions of these CWEs to support finding these types of software security flaws in code prior to fielding. When completed this will be a mechanism for describing each of the industry's software security flaw code assessment capabilities in terms of their coverage of the different CWEs. If necessary, this will also be scoped to specific languages, frameworks, platforms and machine architectures.

Additionally, we are working with researchers and software suppliers to determine what sort of metadata and resources (e.g. code exemplars, patterns, code snippets, etc.) will be needed to allow tools to be tailored or enhanced to identify CWEs in code. This work will also align with and leverage the SAMATE project's various sub-efforts including its development of a corpus of data to determine precision and recall statistics for verifying the effectiveness of these types of code assessment tools with respect to finding CWEs.

Beyond the creation of the vulnerability taxonomy for the stated reasons, a further end goal of this effort will be to take the findings and results of this work and roll them into the CVE initiative as the foundation of a new type of compatibility that can be directly used by organizations in their selection and evaluation of tools and/or services for assessing their acquired software for known types of flaws.

3. APPROACH

A main theme of this effort is to leverage the existing work on this topic area [5]-[14] in light of the large number of diverse real-world vulnerabilities in CVE. We will leverage as many sources and examples as we can gain access to as well as collaborate with key industry players who are currently tackling this subject. We will work in conjunction with researchers at the NIST, The Open Web Application Security Project (OWASP), Ounce Labs, Cigital, Fortify Software, Cenzic, Microsoft, Klocwork, and Secure Software, and other interested parties, to develop specific and succinct definitions of the CWE list elements that adequately describe and differentiate the various CWEs while capturing their specific effects, behaviors, exploit mechanisms, and implementation details. In addition, we will assign the appropriate CWE to the CVE names so that each CWE group will have a list of the CVE names that belong to that CWE category of software security flaws. In constructing the CWE list, we will strive for maximum comprehensive coverage across appropriate conceptual, business and technical domains.

In our efforts to define organizational structure to the CWE list elements, we will look not only to PLOVER, but also to leading thoughts in this area including the McGraw/Fortify "Kingdoms" taxonomy [15], Howard, LeBlanc & Viega's *19 Deadly Sins* [16], Secure Software's CLASP [17], among others. In defining the organizational structure, we will strive for simplicity and appropriateness of description for leveraging by various audiences and for various purposes through the use of taxonometric layering. We currently foresee using a three tiered approach, in which the lowest level consists of the full CWE list (likely hundreds of nodes) and that is applicable to tool vendors and detailed research efforts. The middle tier would consist of descriptive affinity groupings of CWEs (likely 25-50 nodes) that are useful to software security and software development practitioners. The top level would consist of high-level groupings of the middle tier nodes (likely 5-10 nodes) to define strategic classes of vulnerability and is useful for high level discourse among software practitioners, business people, tool vendors, researchers, etc.

Once an initial CWE list and organizational structure have been defined, we will collaborate with our colleagues in the industry to further refine the required attributes of CWE list elements into a more formal schema defining the metadata structure necessary to support the various uses of the taxonomy. This schema will also be driven by a desire to align with and support the other SAMATE and CAMP efforts such as software metrics, software security tool metrics, the software security tool survey, the methodology for validating software security tool claims, and the reference datasets.

With a schema defined, an initial comprehensive list of CWEs identified and defined and an organizational structure in place, this set of content will be submitted to a much broader audience of industry participants to discuss, review and revise. This cycle will iterate until a general consensus can be reached on what will become the first release of the specification (a defacto standard).

4. IMPACT AND TRANSITION OPPORTUNITIES

The completion of this effort will yield consequences of three types: direct impact and value, alignment with and support of other existing efforts, and enabling of new follow-on efforts to provide value that is not currently being pursued.

Following is a list of the direct impacts this effort will yield. Each impact could be the topic of much deeper ongoing discussion.

1. Provide a common language of discourse for discussing, finding and dealing with the causes of software security vulnerabilities as they are manifested in code.

2. Allow software security tool vendors and service providers to make clear and consistent claims of the security vulnerability causes that they cover to their potential user communities in terms of the CWEs that they look for in a particular code language. Additionally, a new type of CVE Compatibility will be developed to allow security tool and service providers to publicly declare their capability's coverage of CWEs

3. Allow purchasers to compare, evaluate and select software security tools and services that are most appropriate to their needs including having some level of assurance of the level of CWEs that a given tool would find. Software purchasers would be able to compare coverage of tool and service offerings against the list of CWEs and the programming languages that are used in the software they are acquiring.

4. Enable the verification of coverage claims made by software security tool vendors and service providers (this is supported through CWE metadata and alignment with the SAMATE reference dataset).

5. Enable government and industry to leverage this standardization in the contractual terms and conditions.

Following is a list of alignment opportunities with existing efforts that are provided by the results of this effort. Again, each of these items could be the topic of much deeper ongoing discussion.

1. Mapping of CWEs to CVEs. This mapping will help bridge the gap between the potential sources of vulnerabilities and examples of their observed instances providing concrete information for better understanding the CWEs and providing some validation of the CWEs themselves.

2. Bidirectional alignment between the vulnerability taxonomy and the SAMATE metrics effort.

3. The SAMATE software security tool/service capability framework effort that is tasked with designing a framework and schema to quantitatively and qualitatively describe the capabilities of tools and services would be able to leverage this vulnerability taxonomy as the core layer of the framework. This framework effort is not an explicitly called

out item in the SAMATE charter but is implied as necessary to meet the project's other objectives.

4. The SAMATE software security tool and services survey effort would be able to leverage this vulnerability taxonomy as part of the capability framework to effectively and unambiguously describe various tools and services in a consistent apples-to-apples fashion.

5. There should be bidirectional alignment between this source of vulnerability taxonomy and the SAMATE reference dataset effort such that CWEs could reference supporting reference dataset entries as code examples of that particular CWE for explanatory purposes and reference dataset entries could reference the associated CWEs that they are intended to demonstrate for validation purposes. Further, by working with industry, an appropriate method could be developed for collecting, abstracting, and sharing code samples from the code of the products that the CVE names are assigned to with the goal of gathering these code samples from industry researchers and academia so that they could be shared as part of the reference dataset and aligned with the vulnerability taxonomy. These samples would then be available as tailoring and enhancement aides to the developers of code assessment security tools. We could actively engage closed source and open source development organizations that work with the CVE initiative to assign CVE names to vulnerabilities to identify an approach that would protect the source of the samples while still allowing us to share them with others. By using the CVE-based relationships with these organizations, we should be able to create a high-quality collection of samples while also improving the accuracy of the security code assessment tools that are available to the software development groups to use in vetting their own product's code

6. The SAMATE software security tool/service assessment framework effort that is tasked with designing a test and validation framework to support the validation of tool/service vendor claims by either the purchaser directly or through a 3rd party, would rely heavily on this sources of vulnerability taxonomy as its basis of analysis. To support this, we would work with researchers to define the mechanisms used to exploit the various CWEs for the purposes of helping to clarify the CWE groupings and as a possible verification method for validating the effectiveness of the tools that identify the presence of CWEs in code by exploring the use of several testing approaches on the executable version of the reviewed code. The effectiveness of these test approaches could be explored with the goal of identifying a method or methods that are effective and economical to apply to the validation process

7. Bidirectional mapping between CWEs and Coding Rules, such as those deployed as part of the DHS NCSD "Build Security In" (BSI) website [18], used by tools and in manual code inspections to identify vulnerabilities in software.

8. There should be bidirectional alignment between the vulnerability taxonomy and the CAMP malware repository effort similar to the alignment with the SAMATE reference dataset described in #5 above.

Following is a list of new, unpursued follow-on opportunities for creating added value to the software security industry.

1. Expansion of the Coding Rules Catalog on the DHS BSI website to include full mapping against the CWEs for all relevant technical domains.

2. Identification and definition of specific domains (language, platform, functionality, etc.) and relevant protection profiles based on coverage of CWEs. These domains and profiles could provide a valuable tool to security testing strategy and planning efforts.

With this fairly quick research and refinement effort, this work should be able to help shape and mature this new code security assessment industry, and dramatically accelerate the use and utility of these capabilities for organizations and the software systems they acquire, develop, and use.

5. Initial Weaknesses, Idiosyncrasies, Faults, Flaws (WIFFs) Enumeration

The following section introduces the current content we have derived through studying a large portion of the CVE list. The listing below, which is comprised of 290 specific types of weakness, idiosyncrasies, faults and flaws (WIFFs) is not exhaustive and will certainly evolve.

Our purpose in coining the term "WIFFs" is avoid the use of the term "vulnerability" for these items. The term "vulnerability" is frequently used in the community to apply to other concepts including bugs, attacks, threats, risks, and impact. Also, there are widely varying opinions regarding what "risk level" must be associated with a problem in order to call it a vulnerability, e.g. in terms of denial-of-service attacks and minor information leaks. Finally, not every instance of the items listed below, or those collected in this overall effort, will need to be removed or addressed in the applications they reside in. While they most certainly need to be examined and evaluated for their potential impact to the application, there will certainly be a large number of these items that could be safely left as is, or dealt with by making some minimal adjustments or compensations to keep them from manifesting into exploitable vulnerabilities. If we went forward using the term "vulnerability" for these items, there would be a built-in bias and predisposition to remove and eliminate each and every one of them, which would be a massive and unnecessary waste of time and resources.

The items below have not been categorized except in the most obvious and expeditious manner. With the incorporation of the other contributions from academia and industry sources we will most certainly reorganize these groupings as more examples and specifics are added. With this caveat we provide the following summary of the 28 main categories which contain the 290 individual types of WIFFs we have enumerated to-date.

1. Buffer overflows, format strings, etc. [BUFF] (10 types)

    These categories cover the increasingly diverse set of WIFFs that are generally referred to as "buffer overflows." The specific types in this group are: Buffer Boundary Violations ("buffer overflow"), Unbounded Transfer ("classic overflow"), Boundary beginning violation ("buffer underflow"), Out-of-bounds Read, Buffer over-read, Buffer under-read, Array index overflow, Length Parameter

Inconsistency, Other length calculation error, Format string vulnerability

2. Structure and Validity Problems [SVM] (10 types)

    These categories cover certain ways in which "well-formed" data could be malformed. The specific types in this group are: Missing Value Error, Missing Parameter Error, Missing Element Error, Extra Value Error, Extra Parameter Error, Undefined Parameter Error, Undefined Value Error, Wrong Data Type, Incomplete Element, Inconsistent Elements

3. Special Elements (Characters or Reserved Words) [SPEC] (19 types)

    These categories cover the types of special elements (special characters or reserved words) that become security-relevant when transferring data between components. The specific types in this group are: General Special Element Problems, Parameter Delimiter, Value Delimiter, Record Delimiter, Line Delimiter, Section Delimiter, Input Terminator, Input Leader, Quoting Element, Escape, Meta, or Control Character / Sequence, Comment Element, Macro Symbol, Substitution Character, Variable Name Delimiter, Wildcard or Matching Element, Whitespace, Grouping Element / Paired Delimiter, Delimiter between Expressions or Commands, Null Character / Null Byte

4. Common Special Element Manipulations [SPECM] (11 types)

    These categories include different ways in which special elements could be introduced into input to software as it operates. The specific types in this group are: Special Element Injection, Equivalent Special Element Injection, Leading Special Element, Multiple Leading Special Elements, Trailing Special Element, Multiple Trailing Special Elements, Internal Special Element, Multiple Internal Special Element, Missing Special Element, Extra Special Element, Inconsistent Special Elements

5. Technology-Specific Special Elements [SPECTS] (17 types)

    These categories cover special elements in commonly used technologies and their associated formats. The specific types in this group are: Cross-site scripting (XSS), Basic XSS, XSS in error pages, Script in IMG tags, XSS using Script in Attributes, XSS using Script Via Encoded URI Schemes, Doubled character XSS manipulations, e.g. "<<script", Null Characters in Tags, Alternate XSS syntax, OS Command Injection, Argument Injection or Modification, SQL injection, LDAP injection, XML injection (aka Blind Xpath injection), Custom Special Character Injection, CRLF Injection, Improper Null Character Termination

6. Pathname Traversal and Equivalence Errors [PATH] (47 types)

    These categories cover the use of file and directory names to either "escape" out of an intended restricted directory, or access restricted resources by using equivalent names. The specific types in this group are: Path Traversal, Relative Path Traversal, "/directory/../filename", "../filedir",

"/./filedir", "directory/../../filename", "..\filename" ("dot dot backslash"), "\..\filename" ("leading dot dot backslash"), "\directory\..\filename", "directory\..\..\filename", "..." (triple dot), "...." (multiple dot), "....//" (doubled dot dot slash), Absolute Path Traversal, /absolute/pathname/here, "../../..//", \absolute\pathname\here ("backslash absolute path"), "C:dirname" or C: (Windows volume or "drive letter"), "\\UNC\share\name\" (Windows UNC share), Path Equivalence, Trailing Dot - "filedir.", Internal Dot - "file.ordir", Multiple Internal Dot - "file...dir", Multiple Trailing Dot - "filedir....", Trailing Space - "filedir ", Leading Space - " filedir", file[SPACE]name (internal space), filedir/ (trailing slash, trailing /), //multiple/leading/slash ("multiple leading slash"), /multiple//internal/slash ("multiple internal slash"), /multiple/trailing/slash// ("multiple trailing slash"), \multiple\\internal\backslash, filedir\ (trailing backslash), /./ (single dot directory), filedir* (asterisk / wildcard), dirname/fakechild/../realchild/filename, Windows 8.3 Filename, Link Following, UNIX symbolic link (symlink) following, UNIX hard link, Windows Shortcut Following (.LNK), Windows hard link, Virtual Files, Windows MS-DOS device names, Windows ::DATA alternate data stream, Apple ".DS_Store", Apple HFS+ alternate data stream

7. Channel and Path Errors [CP] (13 types)

These categories cover the ways in which the use of communication channels or execution paths could be security-relevant. The specific types in this group are: Channel Errors, Unprotected Primary Channel, Unprotected Alternate Channel, Alternate Channel Race Condition, Proxied Trusted Channel, Unprotected Windows Messaging Channel ("Shatter"), Alternate Path Errors, Direct Request aka "Forced Browsing", Miscellaneous alternate path errors, Untrusted Search Path, Mutable Search Path, Uncontrolled Search Path Element, Unquoted Search Path or Element

8. Cleansing, Canonicalization, and Comparison Errors [CCC] (16 types)

These categories cover various ways in which inputs are not properly cleansed or canonicalized, leading to improper actions on those inputs. The specific types in this group are: Encoding Error, Alternate Encoding, Double Encoding, Mixed Encoding, Unicode Encoding, URL Encoding (Hex Encoding), Case Sensitivity (lowercase, uppercase, mixed case), Early Validation Errors, Validate-Before-Canonicalize, Validate-Before-Filter, Collapse of Data into Unsafe Value, Permissive Whitelist, Incomplete Blacklist, Regular Expression Error, Overly Restrictive Regular Expression, Partial Comparison

9. Information Management Errors [INFO] (19 types)

These categories involve the inadvertent or intentional publication or omission of sensitive data, which is not resultant from other types of WIFFs. The specific types in this group are: Information Leak (information disclosure), Discrepancy Information Leaks, Response discrepancy infoleak, Behavioral Discrepancy Infoleak, Internal behavioral inconsistency infoleak, External behavioral inconsistency infoleak, Timing discrepancy infoleak, Product-Generated Error Message Infoleak, Product-External Error Message Infoleak, Cross-Boundary Cleansing Infoleak, Intended information leak, Process information infoleak to other processes, Infoleak Using Debug Information, Sensitive Information Uncleared Before Use, Sensitive memory uncleared by compiler optimization, Information loss or omission, Truncation of Security-relevant Information, Omission of Security-relevant Information, Obscured Security-relevant Information by Alternate Name

10. Race Conditions [RACE] (6 types)

These categories cover various types of race conditions. The specific types in this group are: Race condition enabling link following, Signal handler race condition, Time-of-check Time-of-use race condition, Context Switching Race Condition, Alternate Channel Race Condition, Other race conditions

11. Permissions, Privileges, and ACLs [PPA] (20 types)

These categories include the improper use, assignment, or management of permissions, privileges, and access control lists. The specific types in this group are: Privilege / sandbox errors, Incorrect Privilege Assignment, Unsafe Privilege, Privilege Chaining, Privilege Management Error, Privilege Context Switching Error, Privilege Dropping / Lowering Errors, Insufficient privileges, Misc. privilege issues, Permission errors, Insecure Default Permissions, Insecure inherited permissions, Insecure preserved inherited permissions, Insecure execution-assigned permissions, Fails poorly due to insufficient permissions, Permission preservation failure, Ownership errors, Unverified Ownership, Access Control List (ACL) errors, User management errors

12. Handler Errors [HAND] (4 types)

These categories, which are not very mature, cover various ways in which "handlers" are improperly applied to data. The specific types in this group are: Handler errors, Missing Handler, Dangerous handler not cleared/disabled during sensitive, Raw Web Content Delivery, File Upload of Dangerous Type

13. User Interface Errors [UI] (7 types)

These categories cover WIFFs in a product's user interface that lead to insecure conditions. The specific types in this group are: Product UI does not warn user of unsafe actions, Insufficient UI warning of dangerous operations, User interface inconsistency, Unimplemented or unsupported feature in UI, Obsolete feature in UI, The UI performs the wrong action, Multiple Interpretations of UI Input, UI Misrepresentation of Critical Information

14. Interaction Errors [INT] (7 types)

These categories cover WIFFs that only occur as the result of interactions or differences between multiple products that are used in conjunction with each other. The specific types in this group are: Multiple Interpretation Error (MIE), Extra Unhandled Features, Behavioral Change, Expected behavior violation, Unintended proxy/intermediary, HTTP response splitting, HTTP Request Smuggling

15. Initialization and Cleanup Errors [INIT] (6 types)

These categories cover incorrect initialization. The specific types in this group are: Insecure default variable initialization, External initialization of trusted variables or values, Non-exit on Failed Initialization, Missing Initialization, Incorrect initialization, Incomplete Cleanup.

16. Resource Management Errors [RES] (11 types)

These categories cover ways in which a product does not properly manage resources such as memory, CPU, network bandwidth, or product-specific objects. The specific types in this group are: Memory leak, Resource leaks, UNIX file descriptor leak, Improper resource shutdown, Asymmetric resource consumption (amplification), Network Amplification, Algorithmic Complexity, Data Amplification, Insufficient Resource Pool, Insufficient Locking, Missing Lock Check

17. Numeric Errors [NUM] (6 types)

These categories cover WIFFs that involve erroneous manipulation of numbers. The specific types in this group are: Off-by-one Error, Integer Signedness Error (aka "signed integer" error), Integer overflow (wrap or wraparound), Integer underflow (wrap or wraparound), Numeric truncation error, Numeric Byte Ordering Error

18. Authentication Error [AUTHENT] (12 types)

These categories cover WIFFs that cause authentication mechanisms to fail. The specific types in this group are: Authentication Bypass by Alternate Path/Channel, Authentication bypass by alternate name, Authentication bypass by spoofing, Authentication bypass by replay, Man-in-the-middle (MITM), Authentication Bypass via Assumed-Immutable Data, Authentication Logic Error, Missing Critical Step in Authentication, Authentication Bypass by Primary WIFF, No Authentication for Critical Function, Multiple Failed Authentication Attempts not Prevented, Miscellaneous Authentication Errors

19. Cryptographic errors [CRYPTO] (13 members)

These categories cover problems in the design or implementation of cryptographic algorithms and protocols, or their misuse within other products. The specific types in this group are: Plaintext Storage of Sensitive Information, Plaintext Storage in File or on Disk, Plaintext Storage in Registry, Plaintext Storage in Cookie, Plaintext Storage in Memory, Plaintext Storage in GUI, Plaintext Storage in Executable, Plaintext Transmission of Sensitive Information, Key Management Errors, Missing Required Cryptographic Step, Weak Encryption, Reversible One-Way Hash, Miscellaneous Crypto Problems

20. Randomness and Predictability [RAND] (9 types)

These categories cover WIFFs in security-relevant processing that depends on sufficient randomness to be effective. The specific types in this group are: Insufficient Entropy, Small Space of Random Values, PRNG Seed Error, Same Seed in PRNG, Predictable Seed in PRNG, Small Seed Space in PRNG, Predictable from Observable State, Predictable Exact Value from Previous Values, Predictable Value Range from Previous Values

21. Code Evaluation and Injection [CODE] (4 types)

These categories cover WIFFs in components that process and evaluate data as if it is code. The specific types in this group are: Direct Dynamic Code Evaluation, Direct Static Code Injection, Server-Side Includes (SSI) Injection, PHP File Inclusion

22. Error Conditions, Return Values, Status Codes [ERS] (4 types)

These categories cover WIFFs that occur when a product does not properly handle rare or erroneous operating conditions. The specific types in this group are: Unchecked Error Condition, Missing Error Status Code, Wrong Status Code, Unexpected Status Code or Return Value

23. Insufficient Verification of Data [VER] (7 types)

These categories cover WIFFs in which the source and integrity of incoming data are not properly verified. The specific types in this group are: Improperly Verified Signature, Use of Less Trusted Source, Untrusted Data Appended with Trusted Data, Improperly Trusted Reverse DNS, Insufficient Type Distinction, Cross-Site Request Forgery (CSRF), Other Insufficient Verification

24. Modification of Assumed-Immutable Data [MAID] (2 types)

These categories cover WIFFs in which data that is assumed to be immutable by a product, can be modified by an attacker. The specific types in this group are: Web Parameter Tampering, PHP External Variable Modification

25. Product-Embedded Malicious Code [MAL] (7 types)

These categories cover WIFFs for intentionally malicious code that has been introduced into a product sometime during the software development lifecycle. The specific types in this group are: Back Door, Back Door, Developer-Introduced Back Door, Outsider-Introduced Back Door, Hidden User-Triggered Functionality, Logic Bomb, Time Bomb

26. Common Attack Mitigation Failures [ATTMIT] (3 types)

These categories cover certain design problems that are more frequently known by the attacks against them. The specific types in this group are: Insufficient Replay Protection, Susceptibility to Brute Force Attack, Susceptibility to Spoofing

27. Containment errors (container errors) [CONT] (3 types)

These categories cover WIFFs that involve the storage or transfer of data outside of its logical boundaries. The specific types in this group are: Sensitive Entity in Accessible Container, Sensitive Data Under Web Root, Sensitive Data Under FTP Root

28. Miscellaneous WIFFs [MISC] (7 types)

These categories do not fit cleanly within any of the other main categories. The specific types in this group are: Double-Free Vulnerability, Incomplete Internal State Distinction, Other Types of Truncation Errors, Signal Errors, Improperly Implemented Security Check for Standard, Misinterpretation Error, Business Rule Violations or Logic Errors

6. ACKNOWLEDGMENTS

The work contained in this paper was funded by DHS NCSD.

7. REFERENCES

[1] "The Common Vulnerabilities and Exposures (CVE) Initiative," MITRE Corporation, (http://cve mitre.org).

[2] "The Software Assurance Metrics and Tool Evaluation (SAMATE) project," National Institute of Science and Technology (NIST), (http://samate nist.gov).

[3] Code Assessment Methodology Project (CAMP), part of the Protection of Vital Data (POVD) effort, Concurrent Technologies Corporation, (http://www.ctc.com).

[4] "The Preliminary List Of Vulnerability Examples for Researchers (PLOVER)," MITRE Corporation, (http://cve mitre.org/docs/plover/).

[5] Householder, A. D., Seacord, R. C., "A Structured Approach to Classifying Security Vulnerabilities," CMU/SEI-2005-TN-003, January 2005.

[6] Leek, T., Lippmann, R., Zitser, M., "Testing Static Analysis Tools Using Exploitable Buffer Overflows From Open Source Code," Foundations of Software Engineering December, 2005 Newport Beach, CA.

[7] Waters, J. K., "Don't Let Your Applications Get You Down," Application Development Trends, July 2005.

[8] Wang, C., Wang, H., "Taxonomy of Security Considerations and Software Quality," Communications of the ACM, June 2003, Vol. 46. No. 6.

[9] Plante, A., "Beefed up OWASP 2.0 introduced at BlackHat," SearchSecurity.com, 28 July, 2005.

[10] Viega, J., "Security, Problem Solved?," QUEUE, June 2005.

[11] Ball, T., Das, M., DeLine, R., Fahndrich, M., Larus, J. R., Pincus, J., Rajamani, S. K., Venkatapathy, R., "Righting Software," IEEE Software, May/June 2004.

[12] Ranum, M. J., "SECURITY, The root of the problem," QUEUE, June 2004.

[13] Messier, M., Viega, J., "It's not just about the buffer overflow," QUEUE, June 2004.

[14] Weber, S., Karger, P. A., Paradkar, A., "A Software Flaw Taxonomy: Aiming Tools at Security," ACM Software Engineering for Secure Systems – Building Trustworthy Applications (SESS'05) St. Louis, Missouri, USA., June 2004.

[15] McGraw, G., Chess, B., Tsipenyuk, K., "Seven Pernicious Kingdoms: A Taxonomy of Software Security Errors". "NIST Workshop on Software Security Assurance Tools, Techniques, and Metrics," November, 2005 Long Beach, CA.

[16] Howard, M., LeBlanc, D., and Viega, J., "19 Deadly Sins of Software Security". McGraw-Hill Osborne Media, July 2005.

[17] Viega, J., The CLASP Application Security Process, Secure Software, Inc., http://www.securesoftware.com, 2005.

[18] Department of Homeland Security National Cyber Security Division's "Build Security In" (BSI) web site, (http://buildsecurityin.us-cert.gov).

Seven Pernicious Kingdoms:
A Taxonomy of Software Security Errors

Katrina Tsipenyuk
Fortify Software
2300 Geng Road, Suite 102
Palo Alto, CA 94303
1-650-213-5600

katrina@fortifysoftware.com

Brian Chess
Fortify Software
2300 Geng Road, Suite 102
Palo Alto, CA 94303
1-650-213-5600

brian@fortifysoftware.com

Gary McGraw
Cigital
21351 Ridgetop Circle, Suite 400
Dulles, VA 20166
1-703-404-9293

gem@cigital.com

ABSTRACT
We want to help developers and security practitioners understand common types of coding errors that lead to vulnerabilities. By organizing these errors into a simple taxonomy, we can teach developers to recognize categories of problems that lead to vulnerabilities and identify existing errors as they build software.

The information contained in our taxonomy is most effectively enforced via a tool. In fact, all of the errors included in our taxonomy are amenable to automatic identification using static source code analysis techniques.

We demonstrate why our taxonomy is not only simpler, but also more comprehensive than other modern taxonomy proposals and vulnerability lists. We provide an in-depth explanation and one or more code-level examples for each of the errors on a companion web site: http://vulncat fortifysoftware.com.

Categories and Subject Descriptors
D.4.6 [**Operating Systems**]: Security and Protection – *access controls, authentication, cryptographic controls, information flow controls, invasive software*. K.6.5 [**Management of Computing and Information Systems**]: Security and Protection – *authentication, invasive software, unauthorized access*.

General Terms
Security, standardization.

Keywords
Software security, security defects, taxonomy, static analysis tools.

1. INTRODUCTION
We believe that software developers play a crucial role in building secure computer systems. Because roughly half of all security defects are introduced at the source code level [15], coding errors (a k.a. "bugs") are a critical problem in software security.

SSATTM'05, 11/7-11/8/05, Long Beach, CA, USA
(c) 2005 ACM 1-59593-307-7/05/11.

In defining this taxonomy of coding errors, our primary goal is to organize sets of security rules that can be used to help software developers understand the kinds of errors that have an impact on security. We believe that one of the most effective ways to deliver this information to developers is through the use of tools. Our hope is that, by better understanding how systems fail, developers will better analyze the systems they create, more readily identify and address security problems when they see them, and generally avoid repeating the same mistakes in the future.

When put to work in a tool, a set of security rules organized according to this taxonomy is a powerful teaching mechanism. Because developers today are by and large unaware of the myriad ways they can introduce security problems into their work, publication of a taxonomy like this should provide tangible benefits to the software security community.

Defining a better classification scheme can also lead to better tools: a better understanding of the problems will help researchers and practitioners create better methods for ferreting them out.

We propose a simple, intuitive taxonomy, which we believe is the best approach for our stated purpose of organizing sets of software security rules that will teach software developers about security. Our approach is an alternative to a highly specific list of attack types and vulnerabilities offered by CVE (Common Vulnerabilities and Exposures) [7], which lacks in the way of categorization and is operational in nature. Our classification scheme is amenable to automatic identification and can be used with static analysis tools for detecting real-world security vulnerabilities in software. Our approach is also an alternative to a number of broad classification schemes that focus exclusively on operating-system-related vulnerabilities [1,2,3,12,19]. We discuss these taxonomies in Section 2.

Section 3 motivates our work and discusses the relationship between coding errors and corresponding attacks. It also defines terminology used throughout the rest of this paper. Section 4 describes the scheme we propose. We refer to a type of coding error as a *phylum* and a related set of phyla as a *kingdom*. A complete description of each phylum is available on this paper's companion web site [8]. Section 5 draws parallels between two other vulnerability lists [11,17]. Section 6 concludes.

2. RELATED WORK

All scientific disciplines benefit from a method for organizing their topic of study, and software security is no different. The value of a classification scheme is indisputable: a taxonomy is necessary in order to create a common vocabulary and an understanding of the ways computer security fails. The problem of defining a taxonomy has been of great interest since the mid-1970s. Several classification schemes have been proposed since then [4].

One of the first studies of computer security and privacy was the RISOS (Research Into Secure Operating Systems) project [1]. RISOS proposed and described seven categories of operating system security defects. The purpose of the project was to understand security problems in existing operating systems, including MULTICS, TENEX, TOPS-10, GECOS, OS/MVT, SDS-940, and EXEC-8, and to determine ways to enhance the security of these systems. The categories proposed in the RISOS project include:

- Incomplete Parameter Validation
- Inconsistent Parameter Validation
- Implicit Sharing of Privileges / Confidential Data
- Asynchronous Validation / Inadequate Serialization
- Inadequate Identification / Authentication / Authorization
- Violable Prohibition / Limit
- Exploitable Logic Error

The study shows that there are a small number of fundamental defects that recur in different contexts.

The objective of the Protection Analysis (PA) project [3] was to enable anybody (with or without any knowledge about computer security) to discover security errors in the system by using a pattern-directed approach. The idea was to use formalized patterns to search for corresponding errors. The PA project was the first project to explore automation of security defects detection. However, the procedure for reducing defects to abstract patterns was not comprehensive, and the technique could not be properly automated. The database of vulnerabilities collected in the study was never published.

Landwehr, Bull, McDermott, and Choi [12] classify each vulnerability from three perspectives: genesis (how the problem entered the system), time (at which point in the production cycle the problem entered the system), and location (where in the system the problem is manifest). Defects by genesis were broken down into intentional and inadvertent, where the intentional class was further broken down into malicious and non-malicious. Defects by time of introduction were broken down into development, maintenance, and operation, where the development class was further broken down into design, source code, and object code. Defects by location were broken down into software and hardware, where the software class was further broken down into operating system, support, and application. A very similar scheme was proposed by Weber, Karger, and Paradkar [21]. However, their scheme classifies vulnerabilities only according to genesis.

The advantage of this type of hierarchical classification is the convenience of identifying strategies to remedy security problems. For example, if most security issues are introduced inadvertently, increasing resources devoted to code reviews becomes an effective way of increasing security of the system. The biggest disadvantage of this scheme is inability to classify some existing vulnerabilities. For example, if it is not known how the vulnerability entered the system, it cannot be classified by genesis at all.

Another scheme relevant to our discussion is ODC (Orthogonal Defect Classification) [19] proposed and widely used at IBM. ODC categorizes defects according to error type (a low-level programming mistake) and trigger event (environment characteristics that caused a defect). Additionally, each defect is characterized by severity and symptom. However, ODC focuses on operating system quality issues rather than security issues.

The schemes discussed above have several limitations in common. One of them is the breadth of the categories making classification ambiguous. In some cases, one issue can be classified in more than one category. The category names, while useful to some groups of researchers, are too generic to be quickly intuitive to a developer in the context of day-to-day work. Additionally, these schemes focus mostly on operating system security problems and do not classify the ones associated with user-level software security. Furthermore, these taxonomies mix implementation-level and design-level defects and are not consistent about defining the categories with respect to the cause or effect of the problem.

The work done by Landwehr, Bull, McDermott, and Choi was later extended by Viega [20]. In addition to classifying vulnerabilities according to genesis, time, and location, he also classifies them by consequence (effects of the compromise resulting from the error) and other miscellaneous information, including platform, required resources, severity, likelihood of exploit, avoidance and mitigation techniques, and related problems. Each category is discussed in detail and provides specific examples, including, in some cases code excerpts. This "root-cause" database, as Viega calls it, strives to provide a lexicon for the underlying problems that form the basis for the many known security defects. As a result, not all of the issues in this taxonomy are security problems. Furthermore, the "root-cause" database allows the same problem to be classified differently depending upon the interests of the person doing the classification.

A good list of attack classes is provided by Cheswick, Bellovin, and Rubin [5]. The list includes:

- Stealing Passwords
- Social Engineering
- Bugs and Back Doors
- Authentication Failures
- Protocol Failures
- Information Leakage
- Exponential Attacks—Viruses and Worms
- Denial-of-Service Attacks
- Botnets
- Active Attacks

A thorough description with examples is provided for each class. These attack classes are applicable to a wide range of software, including user-level enterprise software. This fact distinguishes the list from other classification schemes. The classes are simple and intuitive. However, this list defines attack classes rather than categories of common coding errors that cause these attacks. A similar, but a more thorough list of attack patterns is given by Hoglund and McGraw [10]. Attack-based approaches are based on knowing your enemy and assessing the possibility of similar attack. They represent the black-hat side of the software security equation. A taxonomy of coding errors is more positive in nature. This kind of thing is most useful to the white-hat side of the software security world. In the end, both kinds of approaches are valid and necessary.

The classification scheme proposed by Aslam [2] is the only precise scheme discussed here. In this scheme, each vulnerability belongs to exactly one category. The decision procedure for classifying an error consists of a set of questions for each vulnerability category. Aslam's system is well-defined and offers a simple way for identifying defects by similarity. Another contribution of Aslam's taxonomy is that it draws on software fault studies to develop its categories. However, it focuses exclusively on implementation issues in the UNIX operating system and offers categories that are still too broad for our purpose.

The most recent classification scheme we are aware of is PLOVER (Preliminary List of Vulnerability Examples for Researchers) [6], which is a starting point for the creation of a formal enumeration of WIFFs (Weaknesses, Idiosyncrasies, Faults, Flaws) called CWE (Common WIFF Enumeration) [13]. Twenty-eight main categories that comprise almost three hundred WIFFs put Christey's and Martin's classification scheme at the other end of the ambiguity spectrum—the vulnerability categories are much more specific than in any of the taxonomies discussed above. Their bottom-up approach is complimentary to our efforts. PLOVER and CWE are extensions of Christey's earlier work in assigning CVE (Common Vulnerabilities and Exposures) [7] names to publicly known vulnerabilities. An attempt to draw parallels between theoretical attacks and vulnerabilities known in practice is an important contribution and a big step forward from most of the earlier schemes.

3. MOTIVATION

Most existing classification schemes, as is evident, begin with a theoretical and comprehensive approach to classifying security defects. Most research to date has been focusing on making the scheme deterministic and precise, striving for a one-to-one mapping between a vulnerability and the category the vulnerability belongs to. Another facet of the same goal has been to make classification consistent for different levels of abstraction: the same vulnerability should be classified into the same category regardless of whether it is considered from a design or implementation perspective.

Most of the proposed schemes focus on classifying operating-systems-related security defects rather than the errors in software security. Furthermore, categories that comprise many of the existing taxonomies were meant to be both broad and rigorously defined instead of intuitive and specific. Overall, most of the schemes cannot easily be applied to organizing security rules used by a software developer who wants to learn how to build secure software.

To further our goal of educating software developers about common errors, we forgo the breadth and complexity essential to theoretical completeness in favor of practical language centered on programming concepts that are approachable and meaningful to developers.

Before we proceed, we need to define the terminology borrowed from Biology which we use to talk about our classification scheme throughout the rest of the paper.

Definition 1. By *phylum* we mean a specific type of coding error. For example, Illegal Pointer Value is a phylum.

Definition 2. A *kingdom* is a collection of phyla that share a common theme. For example, Input Validation and Representation is a kingdom.

In defining our taxonomy, we value concrete and specific problems that are a real concern to software security over abstract and theoretical ones that either have not been seen in practice or are a result of high-level unsafe specification decisions. We did not make it a goal to create a theoretically complete classification scheme. Instead, we offer a scheme that is open-ended and amenable to future expansion. We expect the list of important phyla to change over time. We expect the important kingdoms to change too, though at a lesser rate. Any evolution will be influenced by trends in languages, frameworks, and libraries; discovery of new types of attacks; new problems and verticals toward which software is being applied; the regulatory landscape, and social norms.

We value simplicity over parallelism in order to create kingdoms that are intuitive to software developers who are not security experts. As opposed to most of the classification schemes discussed in Section 2, our taxonomy focuses on code-level security problems that occur in a range of software applications rather than errors that are most applicable to specific kinds of software, such as operating systems. For example, Buffer Overflow and Command Injection [8] are a part of our taxonomy, while analysis of keystrokes and timing attacks on SSH [18], as well as other kinds of covert-channel-type attacks, are not included. There is no reason to believe that the kingdoms we have chosen would not work for operating systems or other types of specialized software, however there are many more developers working on business applications and desktop programs than on operating systems.

To better understand the relationship between the phyla our taxonomy offers, consider a recently found vulnerability in Adobe Reader 5.0 x for Unix [9]. The vulnerability is present in a function `UnixAppOpenFilePerform()` that copies user-supplied data into a fixed-size stack buffer using a call to `sprintf()`. If the size of the user-supplied data is greater than the size of the buffer it is being copied into, important information, including the stack pointer, is overwritten. By supplying a malicious PDF document, an attacker can execute arbitrary commands on the target system. The attack is possible because of a simple coding error—the absence of a check that makes sure that the size of the user-supplied data is no greater than the size of the destination buffer. In our experience, developers will associate this check with a failure to code defensively around the call to `sprintf()`. We classify this coding error according to the attack it enables—Buffer Overflow. We choose Input Validation and Representation as the name of the kingdom Buffer Overflow phylum belongs to because the lack of proper input validation is the reason the attack is possible.

The coding errors represented by our phyla can all be detected by static source code analysis tools. Source code analysis offers developers an opportunity to get quick feedback about the code that they write. We see great potential for educating developers about coding errors by having them use a source code analysis tool.

4. THE TAXONOMY

We now provide a summary of our taxonomy, which will also appear in McGraw's new book [14]. We split the phyla into "seven-plus-one" high-level kingdoms that should make sense to a majority of developers. Seven of these kingdoms are dedicated to errors in source code, and one is related to configuration and environment issues. We present them in order of importance to software security:

1. **Input Validation and Representation**
2. **API Abuse**
3. **Security Features**
4. **Time and State**
5. **Errors**
6. **Code Quality**
7. **Encapsulation**
*. **Environment**

Brief descriptions of the kingdoms and phyla are provided below. Complete descriptions with source code examples are available on the internet at http://vulncat.fortifysoftware.com.

Our taxonomy includes coding errors that occur in a variety of programming languages. The most important among them are C and C++, Java, and the .NET family including C# and ASP. Some of our phyla are language-specific because the types of errors they represent are applicable only to specific languages. One example is the Double Free phylum. It identifies incorrect usage of low-level memory routines. This phylum is specific to C and C++ because neither Java nor the managed portions of the .NET languages expose low-level memory APIs.

In addition to being language-specific, some of our phyla are framework-specific. For example, the Struts phyla apply only to the Struts framework and the J2EE phyla are only applicable in the context of the J2EE applications. Log Forging, on the other hand, is a more general phylum.

Our phylum list is certainly incomplete, but it is adaptable to changes in trends and discoveries of new defects that will happen over time. We focus on finding and classifying security-related defects rather than more general quality or reliability issues. The Code Quality kingdom could potentially contain many more phyla, but we feel that the ones that we currently include are the ones most likely to affect software security. Finally, we concentrate on classifying errors that are most important to real-world enterprise developers—we derive this information from the literature, our colleagues, and our customers.

1. **Input Validation and Representation**

Input validation and representation problems are caused by metacharacters, alternate encodings and numeric representations. Security problems result from trusting input. The issues include: Buffer Overflows, Cross-Site Scripting attacks, SQL Injection, and many others.

- **Buffer Overflow.** Writing outside the bounds of allocated memory can corrupt data, crash the program, or cause the execution of an attack payload.
- **Command Injection.** Executing commands from an untrusted source or in an untrusted environment can cause an application to execute malicious commands on behalf of an attacker.
- **Cross-Site Scripting.** Sending unvalidated data to a Web browser can result in the browser executing malicious code (usually scripts).
- **Format String.** Allowing an attacker to control a function's format string may result in a buffer overflow.
- **HTTP Response Splitting.** Writing unvalidated data into an HTTP header allows an attacker to specify the entirety of the HTTP response rendered by the browser.
- **Illegal Pointer Value.** This function can return a pointer to memory outside of the buffer to be searched. Subsequent operations on the pointer may have unintended consequences.
- **Integer Overflow.** Not accounting for integer overflow can result in logic errors or buffer overflows.
- **Log Forging.** Writing unvalidated user input into log files can allow an attacker to forge log entries or inject malicious content into logs.
- **Path Manipulation.** Allowing user input to control paths used by the application may enable an attacker to access otherwise protected files.
- **Process Control.** Executing commands or loading libraries from an untrusted source or in an untrusted environment can cause an application to execute malicious commands (and payloads) on behalf of an attacker.
- **Resource Injection.** Allowing user input to control resource identifiers may enable an attacker to access or modify otherwise protected system resources.
- **Setting Manipulation.** Allowing external control of system settings can disrupt service or cause an application to behave in unexpected ways.
- **SQL Injection.** Constructing a dynamic SQL statement with user input may allow an attacker to modify the statement's meaning or to execute arbitrary SQL commands.
- **String Termination Error.** Relying on proper string termination may result in a buffer overflow.
- **Struts: Duplicate Validation Forms.** Multiple validation forms with the same name indicate that validation logic is not up-to-date.
- **Struts: Erroneous validate() Method.** The validator form defines a `validate()` method but fails to call `super.validate()`.
- **Struts: Form Bean Does Not Extend Validation Class.** All Struts forms should extend a Validator class.
- **Struts: Form Field Without Validator.** Every field in a form should be validated in the corresponding validation form.

- **Struts: Plug-in Framework Not In Use.** Use the Struts Validator to prevent vulnerabilities that result from unchecked input.
- **Struts: Unused Validation Form.** An unused validation form indicates that validation logic is not up-to-date.
- **Struts: Unvalidated Action Form.** Every Action Form must have a corresponding validation form.
- **Struts: Validator Turned Off.** This Action Form mapping disables the form's `validate()` method.
- **Struts: Validator Without Form Field.** Validation fields that do not appear in forms they are associated with indicate that the validation logic is out of date.
- **Unsafe JNI.** Improper use of the Java Native Interface (JNI) can render Java applications vulnerable to security bugs in other languages.
- **Unsafe Reflection.** An attacker may be able to create unexpected control flow paths through the application, potentially bypassing security checks.
- **XML Validation.** Failure to enable validation when parsing XML gives an attacker the opportunity to supply malicious input.

2. API Abuse

An API is a contract between a caller and a callee. The most common forms of API abuse are caused by the caller failing to honor its end of this contract. For example, if a program fails to call `chdir()` after calling `chroot()`, it violates the contract that specifies how to change the active root directory in a secure fashion. Another good example of library abuse is expecting the callee to return trustworthy DNS information to the caller. In this case, the caller abuses the callee API by making certain assumptions about its behavior (that the return value can be used for authentication purposes). One can also violate the caller-callee contract from the other side. For example, if a coder subclasses `SecureRandom` and returns a non-random value, the contract is violated.

- **Dangerous Function.** Functions that cannot be used safely should never be used.
- **Directory Restriction.** Improper use of the `chroot()` system call may allow attackers to escape a chroot jail.
- **Heap Inspection.** Do not use `realloc()` to resize buffers that store sensitive information.
- **J2EE Bad Practices: `getConnection()`.** The J2EE standard forbids the direct management of connections.
- **J2EE Bad Practices: Sockets.** Socket-based communication in web applications is prone to error.
- **Often Misused: Authentication.** Do not rely on the name the `getlogin()` family of functions returns because it is easy to spoof.
- **Often Misused: Exception Handling.** A dangerous function can throw an exception, potentially causing the program to crash.
- **Often Misused: File System.** Passing an inadequately-sized output buffer to a path manipulation function can result in a buffer overflow.
- **Often Misused: Privilege Management.** Failure to adhere to the principle of least privilege amplifies the risk posed by other vulnerabilities.
- **Often Misused: Strings.** Functions that manipulate strings encourage buffer overflows.

- **Unchecked Return Value.** Ignoring a method's return value can cause the program to overlook unexpected states and conditions.

3. Security Features

Software security is not security software. Here we're concerned with topics like authentication, access control, confidentiality, cryptography, and privilege management.

- **Insecure Randomness.** Standard pseudo-random number generators cannot withstand cryptographic attacks.
- **Least Privilege Violation.** The elevated privilege level required to perform operations such as `chroot()` should be dropped immediately after the operation is performed.
- **Missing Access Control.** The program does not perform access control checks in a consistent manner across all potential execution paths.
- **Password Management.** Storing a password in plaintext may result in a system compromise.
- **Password Management: Empty Password in Config File.** Using an empty string as a password is insecure.
- **Password Management: Hard-Coded Password.** Hard coded passwords may compromise system security in a way that cannot be easily remedied.
- **Password Management: Password in Config File.** Storing a password in a configuration file may result in system compromise.
- **Password Management: Weak Cryptography.** Obscuring a password with a trivial encoding does not protect the password.
- **Privacy Violation.** Mishandling private information, such as customer passwords or social security numbers, can compromise user privacy and is often illegal.

4. Time and State

Distributed computation is about time and state. That is, in order for more than one component to communicate, state must be shared, and all that takes time.

Most programmers anthropomorphize their work. They think about one thread of control carrying out the entire program in the same way they would if they had to do the job themselves. Modern computers, however, switch between tasks very quickly, and in multi-core, multi-CPU, or distributed systems, two events may take place at exactly the same time. Defects rush to fill the gap between the programmer's model of how a program executes and what happens in reality. These defects are related to unexpected interactions between threads, processes, time, and information. These interactions happen through shared state: semaphores, variables, the file system, and, basically, anything that can store information.

- **Deadlock.** Inconsistent locking discipline can lead to deadlock.
- **Failure to Begin a New Session upon Authentication.** Using the same session identifier across an authentication boundary allows an attacker to hijack authenticated sessions.
- **File Access Race Condition: TOCTOU.** The window of time between when a file property is checked and when the file is used can be exploited to launch a privilege escalation attack.

- **Insecure Temporary File.** Creating and using insecure temporary files can leave application and system data vulnerable to attack.
- **J2EE Bad Practices: System.exit().** A Web application should not attempt to shut down its container.
- **J2EE Bad Practices: Threads.** Thread management in a Web application is forbidden in some circumstances and is always highly error prone.
- **Signal Handling Race Conditions.** Signal handlers may change shared state relied upon by other signal handlers or application code causing unexpected behavior.

5. Errors

Errors and error handling represent a class of API. Errors related to error handling are so common that they deserve a special kingdom of their own. As with API Abuse, there are two ways to introduce an error-related security vulnerability: the most common one is handling errors poorly (or not at all). The second is producing errors that either give out too much information (to possible attackers) or are difficult to handle.

- **Catch NullPointerException.** Catching NullPointerException should not be used as an alternative to programmatic checks to prevent dereferencing a null pointer.
- **Empty Catch Block.** Ignoring exceptions and other error conditions may allow an attacker to induce unexpected behavior unnoticed.
- **Overly-Broad Catch Block.** Catching overly broad exceptions promotes complex error handling code that is more likely to contain security vulnerabilities.
- **Overly-Broad Throws Declaration.** Throwing overly broad exceptions promotes complex error handling code that is more likely to contain security vulnerabilities.

6. Code Quality

Poor code quality leads to unpredictable behavior. From a user's perspective that often manifests itself as poor usability. For an attacker it provides an opportunity to stress the system in unexpected ways.

- **Double Free.** Calling free() twice on the same memory address can lead to a buffer overflow.
- **Inconsistent Implementations.** Functions with inconsistent implementations across operating systems and operating system versions cause portability problems.
- **Memory Leak.** Memory is allocated but never freed leading to resource exhaustion.
- **Null Dereference.** The program can potentially dereference a null pointer, thereby raising a NullPointerException.
- **Obsolete.** The use of deprecated or obsolete functions may indicate neglected code.
- **Undefined Behavior.** The behavior of this function is undefined unless its control parameter is set to a specific value.
- **Uninitialized Variable.** The program can potentially use a variable before it has been initialized.
- **Unreleased Resource.** The program can potentially fail to release a system resource.
- **Use After Free.** Referencing memory after it has been freed can cause a program to crash.

7. Encapsulation

Encapsulation is about drawing strong boundaries. In a web browser that might mean ensuring that your mobile code cannot be abused by other mobile code. On the server it might mean differentiation between validated data and unvalidated data, between one user's data and another's, or between data users are allowed to see and data that they are not.

- **Comparing Classes by Name.** Comparing classes by name can lead a program to treat two classes as the same when they actually differ.
- **Data Leaking Between Users.** Data can "bleed" from one session to another through member variables of singleton objects, such as Servlets, and objects from a shared pool.
- **Leftover Debug Code.** Debug code can create unintended entry points in an application.
- **Mobile Code: Object Hijack.** Attackers can use Cloneable objects to create new instances of an object without calling its constructor.
- **Mobile Code: Use of Inner Class.** Inner classes are translated into classes that are accessible at package scope and may expose code that the programmer intended to keep private to attackers.
- **Mobile Code: Non-Final Public Field.** Non-final public variables can be manipulated by an attacker to inject malicious values.
- **Private Array-Typed Field Returned From a Public Method.** The contents of a private array may be altered unexpectedly through a reference returned from a public method.
- **Public Data Assigned to Private Array-Typed Field.** Assigning public data to a private array is equivalent giving public access to the array.
- **System Information Leak.** Revealing system data or debugging information helps an adversary learn about the system and form an attack plan.
- **Trust Boundary Violation.** Commingling trusted and untrusted data in the same data structure encourages programmers to mistakenly trust unvalidated data.

*. Environment

This section includes everything that is outside of the source code but is still critical to the security of the product that is being created. Because the issues covered by this kingdom are not directly related to source code, we separated it from the rest of the kingdoms.

- **ASP .NET Misconfiguration: Creating Debug Binary.** Debugging messages help attackers learn about the system and plan a form of attack.
- **ASP .NET Misconfiguration: Missing Custom Error Handling.** An ASP .NET application must enable custom error pages in order to prevent attackers from mining information from the framework's built-in responses.
- **ASP .NET Misconfiguration: Password in Configuration File.** Do not hardwire passwords into your software.
- **Insecure Compiler Optimization.** Improperly scrubbing sensitive data from memory can compromise security.
- **J2EE Misconfiguration: Insecure Transport.** The application configuration should ensure that SSL is used for all access-controlled pages.

41

- **J2EE Misconfiguration: Insufficient Session-ID Length.** Session identifiers should be at least 128 bits long to prevent brute-force session guessing.
- **J2EE Misconfiguration: Missing Error Handling.** A Web application must define a default error page for 404 errors, 500 errors and to catch `java.lang.Throwable` exceptions to prevent attackers from mining information from the application container's built-in error response.
- **J2EE Misconfiguration: Unsafe Bean Declaration.** Entity beans should not be declared remote.
- **J2EE Misconfiguration: Weak Access Permissions.** Permission to invoke EJB methods should not be granted to the `ANYONE` role.

5. SEVEN PLUS OR MINUS TWO

There are several other software security problem lists that have been recently developed and made available. The first at one month old, is called the 19 Deadly Sins of Software Security [11]. The second is the OWASP Top Ten Most Critical Web Application Security Vulnerabilities available on the web [17]. Both share one unfortunate property—an overabundance of complexity. People are good at keeping track of seven things (plus or minus two) [16]. We used this as a hard constraint and attempted to keep the number of kingdoms in our taxonomy down to seven (plus one).

By discussing these lists with respect to the scheme we propose, we illustrate and emphasize the superiority of our taxonomy. The main limitation of both lists is that they mix specific types of errors and vulnerability classes, and talk about them at the same level of abstraction. The nineteen deadly sins include the Buffer Overflows and Failing to Protect Network Traffic categories at the same level, even though the first is a very specific coding error, while the second could be a class comprised of various kinds of errors. OWASP's Top Ten includes Cross Site Scripting (XSS) Flaws and Insecure Configuration Management at the same level as well.

Our classification scheme consists of two hierarchical levels: kingdoms and phyla. The kingdoms represent the classes of errors, while the phyla that comprise the kingdoms represent specific errors. We would like to point out that even though the structure of our classification scheme is different from the structure of the lists described above, the categories that comprise these lists can be easily mapped to our kingdoms. Here is the mapping for the nineteen sins:

1. **Input Validation and Representation**
   Buffer Overflows
   Command Injection
   Cross-Site Scripting
   Format String Problems
   Integer Range Errors
   SQL Injection
2. **API Abuse**
   Trusting Network Address Information
3. **Security Features**
   Failing to Protect Network Traffic
   Failing to Store and Protect Data
   Failing to Use Cryptographically Strong Random Numbers

   Improper File Access
   Improper Use of SSL
   Use of Weak Password-Based Systems
   Unauthenticated Key Exchange
4. **Time and State**
   Signal Race Conditions
   Use of "Magic" URLs and Hidden Forms
5. **Errors**
   Failure to Handle Errors
6. **Code Quality**
   Poor Usability
7. **Encapsulation**
   Information Leakage
*. **Environment**

Here is the mapping for the OWASP Top Ten:

1. **Input Validation and Representation**
   Buffer Overflows
   Cross-Site Scripting (XSS) Flaws
   Injection Flaws
   Unvalidated Input
2. **API Abuse**
3. **Security Features**
   Broken Access Control
   Insecure Storage
4. **Time and State**
   Broken Authentication and Session Management
5. **Errors**
   Improper Error Handling
6. **Code Quality**
   Denial of Service
7. **Encapsulation**
*. **Environment**
   Insecure Configuration Management

6. CONCLUSION

We present a simple, intuitive taxonomy of common coding errors that affect security. We discuss the relationship between vulnerability phyla we define and corresponding attacks, and provide descriptions of each kingdom in the proposed taxonomy.

We point out the important differences between the scheme we propose and those discussed in related work. The classification scheme we present is designed to organize security rules, and thus be of help to software developers who are concerned with writing secure code and being able to automate detection of security defects. These goals make our scheme simple, intuitive to a developer, practical rather than theoretical and comprehensive, amenable to automatic identification of errors with static analysis tools, as well as adaptable with respect to changes in trends that can happen over time.

7. ACKNOWLEDGEMENTS

We would like to acknowledge the workshop reviewers for providing valuable feedback on our approach. We are grateful to Jacob West and Bob Martin for useful discussions of our work, and we thank Andy Vaughan for last-minute proof-reading of the paper.

8. REFERENCES

[1] R.P. Abbott, J. S. Chin, J.E. Donnelley, W.L. Konigsford, S. Tokubo, and D.A. Webb. Security Analysis and Enhancements of Computer Operating Systems. NBSIR 76-1041, National Bureau of Standards, ICST, Washington, D.C., 1976.

[2] T. Aslam. *A Taxonomy of Security Faults in the Unix Operating System*. Master's Thesis, Purdue University, 1995.

[3] R. Bisbey and D. Hollingworth. Protection Analysis Project Final Report. ISI/RR-78-13, DTIC AD A056816, USC/Information Sciences Institute, 1978.

[4] M. Bishop. *Computer Security: Art and Science*. Addison-Wesley, December 2002.

[5] W. Cheswick, S. Bellovin, and A. Rubin. *Firewalls and Internet Security: Repelling the Wily Hacker*, Second Edition. Addison-Wesley, 2003.

[6] S. Christey. PLOVER—Preliminary List of Vulnerability Examples for Researchers. Draft, August 2005. http://cve mitre.org/docs/plover/.

[7] CVE – Common Vulnerabilities and Exposures. http://www.cve mitre.org/.

[8] Fortify Descriptions. http://vulncat.fortifysoftware.com.

[9] Fortify Extra. Adobe Reader for Unix Remote Buffer Overflow. http://extra.fortifysoftware.com/archives/2005/07/adobe_reader_fo_1 html.

[10] G. Hoglund and G. McGraw. *Exploiting Software: How to Break Code*. Addison-Wesley, February 2004.

[11] M. Howard, D. LeBlanc, and J. Viega. *19 Deadly Sins of Software Security*. McGraw-Hill Osborne Media, July 2005.

[12] C. E. Landwehr, A. R. Bull, J. P. McDermott, W. S. Choi. A Taxonomy of Computer Program Security Flaws, with Examples. *ACM Computing Surveys*, Vol. 26, No. 3, September 1994, pp. 211-254.

[13] R. Martin, S. Christey, and J. Jarzombek. The Case for Common Flaw Enumeration. *NIST Workshop on Software Security Assurance Tools, Techniques, and Metrics (SSATTM) Proceedings*, November 2005, Long Beach, CA.

[14] G. McGraw. *Software Security: Building Security In*. Addison-Wesley, to appear in 2006.

[15] G. McGraw. From the Ground Up: The DIMACS Software Security Workshop. *IEEE Security & Privacy*, Vol. 1, No. 2, March-April 2003, pp. 59-66.

[16] G. Miller. The Magic Number Seven, Plus or Minus Two: Some Limits on our Capacity for Processing Information. *Psychological Review*, Vol. 63, No. 2, 1956.

[17] OWASP Top Ten Most Critical Web Application Security Vulnerabilities. http://www.owasp.org/documentation/topten html.

[18] D. Song, D. Wagner, and X. Tian. Timing Analysis of Keystrokes and Timing Attacks on SSH. *10th USENIX Security Symposium Proceedings*, August 2001, pp. 337-352.

[19] M. Sullivan and R. Chillarege. Software Defects and Their Impact on System Availability – A Study of Field Failures in Operating Systems. *IEEE International Symposium on Fault Tolerant Computing (FTCS) Proceedings*, 1991, Montreal, Canada.

[20] J. Viega.. The CLASP Application Security Process. Volume 1.1 Training Manual.

[21] S. Weber, P. Karger, and A. Paradkar. A Software Flaw Taxonomy: Aiming Tools at Security. *Software Engineering for Secure Systems – Building Trustworthy Applications (SESS) Proceedings*, 2005, St. Louis, MO.

A Taxonomy of Buffer Overflows for Evaluating Static and Dynamic Software Testing Tools*

Kendra Kratkiewicz
MIT Lincoln Laboratory
244 Wood Street
Lexington, MA 02420-9108
Phone: 781-981-2931
Email: KENDRA@LL.MIT.EDU

Richard Lippmann
MIT Lincoln Laboratory
244 Wood Street
Lexington, MA 02420-9108
Phone: 781-981-2711
Email: LIPPMANN@LL.MIT.EDU

ABSTRACT

A taxonomy that uses twenty-two attributes to characterize C-program overflows was used to construct 291 small C-program test cases that can be used to diagnostically determine the basic capabilities of static and dynamic analysis buffer overflow detection tools. Attributes in the taxonomy include the buffer location (e.g. stack, heap, data region, BSS, shared memory); scope difference between buffer allocation and access; index, pointer, and alias complexity when addressing buffer elements; complexity of the control flow and loop structure surrounding the overflow; type of container the buffer is within (e.g. structure, union, array); whether the overflow is caused by a signed/unsigned type error; the overflow magnitude and direction; and whether the overflow is discrete or continuous. As an example, the 291 test cases were used to measure the detection, false alarm, and confusion rates of five static analysis tools. They reveal specific strengths and limitations of tools and suggest directions for improvements.

Categories and Subject Descriptors

D.2.4 [Software Engineering] Software/Program Verification, D.2.5 [Software Engineering] Testing and Debugging, K.4.4 [Computers and Society] Electronic Commerce Security.

General Terms

Measurement, Performance, Security, Verification.

Keywords

Security, taxonomy, buffer overflow, static analysis, evaluation, exploit, test, detection, false alarm, source code.

1. INTRODUCTION

Buffer overflows are among the most important types of errors that occur in C code. They are of particular interest as they are potentially exploitable by malicious users, and have historically accounted for a significant percentage of the software vulnerabilities published each year [18, 20], such as in NIST's ICAT Metabase [9], CERT advisories [1], Bugtraq [17], and other security forums. Buffer overflows have also been the basis for many damaging exploits, such as the Sapphire/Slammer [13]

SSATTM'05, 11/7-11/8/05, Long Beach, CA, USA.
© 2005 ACM 1-59593-307-7/05/11

and Blaster [15] worms.

A buffer overflow vulnerability occurs when data can be written outside the memory allocated for a buffer, either past the end or before the beginning. Buffer overflows may occur on the stack, on the heap, in the data segment, or the BSS segment (the memory area a program uses for uninitialized global data), and may overwrite from one to many bytes of memory outside the buffer. Even a one-byte overflow can be enough to allow an exploit [10]. Buffer overflows have been described at length in many papers, including [20], and many descriptions of exploiting buffer overflows can be found online.

This paper focuses on developing a taxonomy of buffer overflows and using the taxonomy to create test cases that can be used to diagnostically evaluate the capabilities of static and dynamic buffer overflow detection tools. The first part of this paper describes the taxonomy and test cases that are available at http://www.ll.mit.edu/IST/corpora.html. The second part demonstrates how to use the test cases to evaluate five static analysis tools formerly evaluated by Zitser [20, 21]. While Zitser's study evaluated the ability of ARCHER [19], BOON [18], Splint [6, 12], UNO [8], and PolySpace C Verifier [14] to detect fourteen known buffer overflows in open-source software, the current evaluation focuses on determining those type of overflows that each tool can detect and those that cause false alarms.

2. BUFFER OVERFLOW TAXONOMY

Using a comprehensive taxonomy makes it possible to develop test cases that cover a wide range of buffer overflows and make diagnostic tool assessments. The most comprehensive previous taxonomy contained thirteen attributes and was developed by Zitser [20]. This taxonomy was modified and expanded to address problems encountered with its application, while still attempting to keep it small and simple enough for practical application. The new taxonomy consists of the twenty-two attributes listed in Table 1.

Table 1. Buffer Overflow Taxonomy Attributes

Attribute Number	Attribute Name
1	Write/Read
2	Upper/Lower Bound
3	Data Type
4	Memory Location
5	Scope
6	Container
7	Pointer

*This work was sponsored by the Advanced Research and Development Activity under Force Contract F19628-00-C-0002. Opinions, interpretations, conclusions, and recommendations are those of the authors and are not necessarily endorsed by the United States Government.

8	Index Complexity
9	Address Complexity
10	Length/Limit Complexity
11	Alias of Buffer Address
12	Alias of Buffer Index
13	Local Control Flow
14	Secondary Control Flow
15	Loop Structure
16	Loop Complexity
17	Asynchrony
18	Taint
19	Runtime Environment Dependence
20	Magnitude
21	Continuous/Discrete
22	Signed/Unsigned Mismatch

Details on the possible values for each attribute are available in [11], and are summarized below. For each attribute, the possible values are listed in ascending order (i.e. the 0 value first).

Write/Read: describes the type of memory access (write, read). While detecting illegal writes is of more interest in preventing buffer overflow exploits, illegal reads could allow unauthorized access to information or could constitute one operation in a multi-step exploit.

Upper/Lower Bound: describes which buffer bound is violated (upper, lower). While the term "buffer overflow" suggests an access beyond the upper bound of a buffer, one of the vulnerabilities analyzed by Zitser [21] allowed access below a buffer's lower bound (e.g. buf[-1]).

Data Type: indicates the type of data stored in the buffer (character, integer, floating point, wide character, pointer, unsigned character, unsigned integer). Although character buffers are often manipulated with unsafe string functions in C and some tools focus on detecting overflows of those buffers, buffers of all types may be overflowed and should be analyzed.

Memory Location: indicates where the buffer resides (stack, heap, data region, BSS, shared memory). Non-static variables defined locally to a function are on the stack, while dynamically allocated buffers (e.g., those allocated by calling a malloc function) are on the heap. The data region holds initialized global or static variables, while the BSS region contains uninitialized global or static variables. Shared memory is typically allocated, mapped into and out of a program's address space, and released via operating system specific functions. While a typical buffer overflow exploit may strive to overwrite a function return value on the stack, buffers in other locations have been exploited and should be considered as well.

Scope: describes the difference between where the buffer is allocated and where it is overrun (same, inter-procedural, global, inter-file/inter-procedural, inter-file/global). This is important because many tools perform local and not inter-procedural analyses, and many actual overflows are inter-procedural (e.g. [21]). The scope is local if the buffer is allocated and overrun within the same function. It is inter-procedural if the buffer is allocated in one function and overrun in another function within the same file. Global scope indicates that the buffer is allocated as a global variable, and is overrun in a function within the same file. Scope is inter-file/inter-procedural if the buffer is allocated

in a function in one file, and overrun in a function in another file. Inter-file/global scope describes a buffer that is allocated as a global in one file, and overrun in a function in another file. Any scope other than "same" may involve passing the buffer address as an argument to another function; in this case, the *Alias of Buffer Address* attribute must also be set accordingly. Note that the test suite used in this evaluation does not contain an example for "inter-file/global."

Container: indicates whether the buffer resides in some type of container (no, array, struct, union, array of structs, array of unions). The ability of static analysis tools to detect overflows within containers (e.g., overrunning one array element into the next, or one structure field into the next) and beyond container boundaries (i.e., beyond the memory allocated for the container as a whole) may vary according to how the tools model these containers and their contents.

Pointer: indicates whether the buffer access uses a pointer dereference (no, yes). Note that it is possible to use a pointer dereference with or without an array index (e.g. *pBuf or (*pBuf)[10]); the *Index Complexity* attribute must be set accordingly. In order to know if the memory location referred to by a dereferenced pointer is within buffer bounds, a code analysis tool must keep track of what pointers point to; this points-to analysis is a significant challenge.

Index Complexity: indicates the complexity of the array index (constant, variable, linear expression, non-linear expression, function return value, array contents, N/A). This attribute applies only to the user program, and is not used to describe how buffer accesses are performed inside C library functions.

Address Complexity: describes the complexity of the address or pointer computation (constant, variable, linear expression, non-linear expression, function return value, array contents). Again, this attribute is used to describe the user program only, and is not applied to C library function internals.

Length/Limit Complexity: indicates the complexity of the length or limit passed to a C library function that overruns the buffer (N/A, none, constant, variable, linear expression, non-linear expression, function return value, array contents). "N/A" is used when the test case does not call a C library function to overflow the buffer, whereas "none" applies when a C library function overflows the buffer, but the function does not take a length or limit parameter (e.g. strcpy). The remaining attribute values apply to the use of C library functions that do take a length or limit parameter (e.g. strncpy). Note that if a C library function overflows the buffer, the overflow is by definition inter-file/inter-procedural in scope, and involves at least one alias of the buffer address. In this case, the *Scope* and *Alias of Buffer Address* attributes must be set accordingly. Code analysis tools may need to provide their own wrappers for or models of C library functions in order to perform a complete analysis. This and the previous two attributes assess the ability of tools to analyze complex address and index computations.

Alias of Buffer Address: indicates if the buffer is accessed directly or through one or two levels of aliasing (no, one, two). Assigning the original buffer address to a second variable and subsequently using the second variable to access the buffer constitutes one level of aliasing, as does passing the original buffer address to a second function. Similarly, assigning the second variable to a third and accessing the buffer through the third variable would be classified as two levels of aliasing, as would passing the buffer address to a third function from the second.

Alias of Buffer Index: indicates whether or not the index is aliased (no, one, two, N/A). If the index is a constant or the results of a computation or function call, or if the index is a variable to which is directly assigned a constant value or the results of a computation or function call, then there is no aliasing of the index. If, however, the index is a variable to which the value of a second variable is assigned, then there is one level of aliasing. Adding a third variable assignment increases the level of aliasing to two. If no index is used in the buffer access, then this attribute is not applicable. This and the previous attribute assess how well tools analyze the difficult problem of aliases.

Local Control Flow: describes what kind of program control flow most immediately surrounds or affects the overflow (none, if, switch, cond, goto/label, setjmp/longjmp, function pointer, recursion). For the values "if", "switch", and "cond", the buffer overflow is located within the conditional construct. "Goto/label" signifies that the overflow occurs at or after the target label of a goto statement. Similarly, "setjmp/longjmp" means that the overflow is at or after a longjmp address. Buffer overflows that occur within functions reached via function pointers are assigned the "function pointer" value, and those within recursive functions receive the value "recursion". The values "function pointer" and "recursion" necessarily imply a global or inter-procedural scope, and may involve an address alias. The *Scope* and *Alias of Buffer Address* attributes should be set accordingly.

Control flow involves either branching or jumping to another context within the program; hence, only path-sensitive code analysis can determine whether or not the overflow is actually reachable. A code analysis tool must be able to follow function pointers and have techniques for handling recursive functions in order to detect buffer overflows with the last two values for this attribute.

Secondary Control Flow: has the same values as *Local Control Flow,* the difference being the location of the control flow construct. *Secondary Control Flow* either precedes the overflow or contains nested, local control flow. Some types of secondary control flow may occur without any local control flow, but some may not. The *Local Control Flow* attribute should be set accordingly.

The following example illustrates an if statement that precedes the overflow and affects whether or not it occurs. Because it precedes the overflow, as opposed to directly containing the overflow, it is labeled as secondary, not local, control flow.

```
int main(int argc, char *argv[])
{
  char buf[10];
  int i = 10;

  if (i > 10)
  {
    return 0;
  }

  /*  BAD  */
  buf[i] = 'A';
```

```
  return 0;
}
```

Only control flow that affects whether or not the overflow occurs is classified. In other words, if a preceding control flow construct has no bearing on whether or not the subsequent overflow occurs, it is not considered to be secondary control flow, and this attribute would be assigned the value "none."

The following example illustrates nested control flow. The inner if statement directly contains the overflow, and we assign the value "if" to the *Local Control Flow* attribute. The outer if statement represents secondary control flow, and we assign the value "if" to the *Secondary Control Flow* attribute as well.

```
int main(int argc, char *argv[])
{
  char buf[10];
  int i = 10;

  if (sizeof buf <= 10)
  {
    if (i <= 10)
    {
      /*  BAD  */
      buf[i] = 'A';
    }
  }

  return 0;
}
```

Some code analysis tools perform path-sensitive analyses, and some do not. Even those that do often must make simplifying approximations in order to keep the problem tractable and the solution scalable. This may mean throwing away some information, and thereby sacrificing precision, at points in the program where previous branches rejoin. Test cases containing secondary control flow may highlight the capabilities or limitations of these varying techniques.

Loop Structure: describes the type of loop construct within which the overflow occurs (none, standard for, standard do-while, standard while, non-standard for, non-standard do-while, non-standard while). A "standard" loop is one that has an initialization, a loop exit test, and an increment or decrement of a loop variable, all in typical format and locations. A "non-standard" loop deviates from the standard loop in one or more of these areas. Examples of standard for, do-while, and while loops are shown below, along with one non-standard for loop example:

Standard for loop:
```
for (i=0; i<11; i++)
{
    buf[i] = 'A';
}
```

Standard do-while loop:
```
i=0;
do
{
    buf[i] = 'A';
    i++;
} while (i<11);
```

Standard while loop:
```
i=0;
```

```
        while (i<11)
        {
            buf[i] = 'A';
            i++;
        }
```
A non-standard `for` loop:
```
        for (i=0; i<11; )
        {
            buf[i++] = 'A';
        }
```

Non-standard loops may necessitate secondary control flow (such as additional if statements). In these cases, the *Secondary Control Flow* attribute should be set accordingly. Any value other than "none" for this attribute requires that the *Loop Complexity* attribute be set to something other than "not applicable."

Loops may execute for a large number or even an infinite number of iterations, or may have exit criteria that depend on runtime conditions; therefore, it may be impossible or impractical for static analysis tools to simulate or analyze loops to completion. Different tools have different methods for handling loops; for example, some may attempt to simulate a loop for a fixed number of iterations, while others may employ heuristics to recognize and handle common loop constructs. The approach taken will likely affect a tool's capabilities to detect overflows that occur within various loop structures.

Loop Complexity: indicates how many loop components (initialization, test, increment) are more complex than the standard baseline of initializing to a constant, testing against a constant, and incrementing or decrementing by one (N/A, none, one, two, three). Of interest here is whether or not the tools handle loops with varying complexity in general, rather than which particular loop components are handled or not.

Asynchrony: indicates if the buffer overflow is potentially obfuscated by an asynchronous program construct (no, threads, forked process, signal handler). The functions that may be used to realize these constructs are often operating system specific (e.g. on Linux, `pthread` functions; `fork`, `wait`, and `exit`; and `signal`). A code analysis tool may need detailed, embedded knowledge of these constructs and the O/S-specific functions in order to properly detect overflows that occur only under these special circumstances.

Taint: describes whether and how a buffer overflow may be influenced externally (no, argc/argv, environment variables, file read or stdin, socket, process environment). "Taintable" buffer overflows that can be influenced by users external to a program are the most crucial to detect because they make it possible for attackers to create exploits. The occurrence of a buffer overflow may depend on command line or stdin input from a user, the value of environment variables (e.g. `getenv`), file contents (e.g. `fgets`, `fread`, or `read`), data received through a socket or service (e.g. `recv`), or properties of the process environment, such as the current working directory (e.g. `getcwd`). As with asynchronous constructs, code analysis tools may require detailed modeling of O/S-specific functions to properly detect related overflows. Note that the test suite used in this evaluation does not contain an example for "socket."

Runtime Environment Dependence: indicates whether or not the occurrence of the overrun depends on something determined at runtime (no, yes). If the overrun is certain to occur on every execution of the program, it is not dependent on the runtime environment; otherwise, it is. Examples of overflows that depend on the runtime environment include tainted overflows just described and overflows that depend on the value of a random number generator.

Magnitude: indicates the size of the overflow (none, 1 byte, 8 bytes, 4096 bytes). "None" is used to classify the "OK" or patched versions of programs that contain overflows. One would expect static analysis tools to detect buffer overflows without regard to the size of the overflow, unless they contain an off-by-one error in their modeling of library functions. The same is not true of dynamic analysis tools that use runtime instrumentation to detect memory violations; different methods may be sensitive to different sizes of overflows, which may or may not breach page boundaries, etc. The various overflow sizes were chosen with dynamic tool evaluations in mind. Overflows of one byte test both the accuracy of static analysis modeling, and the sensitivity of dynamic instrumentation. Eight and 4096 byte overflows are aimed more exclusively at dynamic tool testing, and are designed to cross word-aligned and page boundaries. One byte overflows are of interest because such overflows have enabled past exploits [10].

Continuous/Discrete: indicates whether the buffer overflow accesses another arbitrary location outside the buffer directly (discrete) or accesses consecutive elements within the buffer before overflowing past the bounds (continuous). Loop constructs are likely candidates for containing continuous overflows. C library functions that overflow a buffer while copying memory or string contents into it demonstrate continuous overflows. An overflow labeled as continuous should have the loop-related attributes or the Length Complexity attribute (indicating the complexity of the length or limit passed to a C library function) set accordingly. Some dynamic tools rely on "canaries" at buffer boundaries to detect continuous overflows [5], and therefore may miss discrete overflows.

Signed/Unsigned Mismatch: indicates if the buffer overflow is caused by using a signed or unsigned value where the opposite is expected (no, yes). Typically, a signed value is used where an unsigned value is expected, and gets interpreted as a very large unsigned or positive value, causing an enormous buffer overflow. This error was responsible for two of the vulnerabilities analyzed by Zitser [21].

This taxonomy is specifically designed for developing simple diagnostic test cases. It may not fully characterize complex buffer overflows that occur in real code, and specifically omits complex details related to the overflow context.

For each attribute (except for Magnitude), the zero value is assigned to the simplest or "baseline" buffer overflow, shown below:

```
int main(int argc, char *argv[])
{
    char buf[10];
    /*  BAD  */
    buf[10] = 'A';
    return 0;
}
```

47

Each test case includes a comment line as shown with the word "BAD" or "OK." This comment is placed on the line before the line where an overflow might occur and it indicates whether an overflow does occur. The buffer access in the baseline program is a write operation beyond the upper bound of a stack-based character buffer that is defined and overflowed within the same function. The buffer does not lie within another container, is addressed directly, and is indexed with a constant. No C library function is used to access the buffer, the overflow is not within any conditional or complicated control flows or asynchronous program constructs, and does not depend on the runtime environment. The overflow writes to a discrete location one byte beyond the buffer boundary, and cannot be manipulated by an external user. Finally, it does not involve a signed vs. unsigned type mismatch.

Appending the value digits for each of the twenty-two attributes forms a string that classifies a buffer overflow, which can be referred to during results analysis. For example, the sample program shown above is classified as "0000000000000000000100." The single "1" in this string represents a "Magnitude" attribute indicating a one-byte overflow. This classification information appears in comments at the top of each test case file, as shown in the example below:

```
/* Taxonomy Classification: 0000000000000000000000 */

/*
 * WRITE/READ                  0   write
 * WHICH BOUND                 0   upper
 * DATA TYPE                   0   char
 * MEMORY LOCATION             0   stack
 * SCOPE                       0   same
 * CONTAINER                   0   no
 * POINTER                     0   no
 * INDEX COMPLEXITY            0   constant
 * ADDRESS COMPLEXITY          0   constant
 * LENGTH COMPLEXITY           0   N/A
 * ADDRESS ALIAS               0   none
 * INDEX ALIAS                 0   none
 * LOCAL CONTROL FLOW          0   none
 * SECONDARY CONTROL FLOW 0        none
 * LOOP STRUCTURE              0   no
 * LOOP COMPLEXITY             0   N/A
 * ASYNCHRONY                  0   no
 * TAINT                       0   no
 * RUNTIME ENV. DEPENDENCE 0       no
 * MAGNITUDE                   0   no overflow
 * CONTINUOUS/DISCRETE         0   discrete
 * SIGNEDNESS                  0   no
 */
```

While the Zitser test cases were program pairs consisting of a bad program and a corresponding patched program, this evaluation uses program quadruplets. The four versions of each test case correspond to the four possible values of the Magnitude attribute. One version represents a patched program (no overflow), while the remaining three indicate buffer overflows of one, eight, and 4096 bytes denoted as minimum, medium, and large overflows.

3. TEST SUITE

A full discussion of design considerations for creating test cases is provided in [11]. Goals included avoiding tool bias; providing samples that cover the taxonomy; measuring detections, false alarms, and confusions; naming and documenting test cases to facilitate automated scoring and encourage reuse; and maintaining consistency in programming style and use of programming idioms.

Ideally, the test suite would have at least one instance of each possible buffer overflow that could be described by the taxonomy. Unfortunately, the vast number of attribute combinations this requires makes this impractical. Instead, a "basic" set of test cases was built by first choosing a simple, baseline example of a buffer overflow, and then varying its characteristics one at a time. This strategy results in taxonomy coverage that is heavily weighted toward the baseline attribute values. Variations were added by automated code-generation software written in Perl that produces C code for the test cases to help insure consistency and make it easier to add test cases.

Four versions of 291 different test cases were generated with no overflow and with minimum, medium, and large overflows. Each test case was compiled with gcc, the GNU C compiler [7], on Linux to verify that the programs compiled without warnings or errors (with the exception of one test case that produces an unavoidable warning). Overflows were verified using CRED, a fine-grained bounds-checking extension to gcc that detects overflows at run time [16], or by verifying that the large overflow caused a segfault. A few problems with test cases that involved complex loop conditions were also corrected based on initial results produced by the PolySpace tool.

4. EXAMPLE TEST CASE USAGE

As an example of how to use these diagnostic test cases, each test case (291 quadruplets) was used one at a time with five static analysis tools (ARCHER, BOON, PolySpace, Splint, and UNO). Tool-specific Perl programs parsed the output and determined whether a buffer overflow was detected on the line immediately following the comment in each test case. Details of the test procedures are provided in [11]. No annotations were added and no modifications were made to the source code for any tool.

5. RESULTS AND ANALYSIS

All five static analysis tools performed the same regardless of overflow size (this would not necessarily hold for dynamic analysis). To simplify the discussion, results for the three magnitudes of overflows are thus reported as results for "bad" test cases as a whole.

Table 2 shows overall performance metrics computed for each tool. These metrics do not indicate performance expected in real code for detecting new vulnerabilities. They only indicate overall performance across all test cases and are preliminary to more diagnostic analysis with individual test cases. The detection rate indicates how well a tool detects the known buffer overflows in the bad programs, while the false alarm rate indicates how often a tool reports a buffer overflow in the patched programs. The confusion rate indicates how well a tool can distinguish between the bad and patched programs. When a tool reports a detection in both the patched and bad versions of a test case, the tool has demonstrated "confusion." The formulas used to compute these three metrics are shown below:

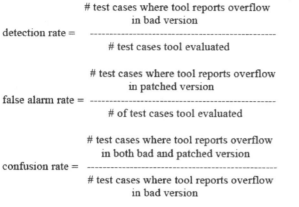

$$\text{detection rate} = \frac{\text{\# test cases where tool reports overflow in bad version}}{\text{\# test cases tool evaluated}}$$

$$\text{false alarm rate} = \frac{\text{\# test cases where tool reports overflow in patched version}}{\text{\# of test cases tool evaluated}}$$

$$\text{confusion rate} = \frac{\text{\# test cases where tool reports overflow in both bad and patched version}}{\text{\# test cases where tool reports overflow in bad version}}$$

As seen in Table 2, ARCHER and PolySpace both have detection rates exceeding 90%. PolySpace's detection rate is nearly perfect, missing only one out of the 291 possible detections. PolySpace produced seven false alarms, whereas ARCHER produced none. Splint and UNO each detected roughly half of the overflows. Splint, however, produced a substantial number of false alarms, while UNO produced none. Splint also exhibited a fairly high confusion rate. In over twenty percent of the cases where it properly detected an overflow, it also reported an error in the patched program. PolySpace's confusion rate was substantially lower, while the other three tools had no confusions. BOON's detection rate across the test suite was extremely low.

Table 2. Overall Performance on Basic Test Suite (291 cases)

Tool	Detection Rate	False Alarm Rate	Confusion Rate
ARCHER	90.7%	0.0%	0.0%
BOON	0.7%	0.0%	0.0%
PolySpace	99.7%	2.4%	2.4%
Splint	56.4%	12.0%	21.3%
UNO	51.9%	0.0%	0.0%

It is important to note that it was not necessarily the design goal of each tool to detect every possible buffer overflow. BOON, for example, focuses only on the misuse of string manipulation functions, and therefore is not expected to detect other overflows. It is also important to realize that these performance rates are not necessarily predictive of how the tools would perform on buffer overflows in actual, released code. The basic test suite used in this evaluation was designed for diagnostic purposes, and the taxonomy coverage exhibited is not representative of that which would be seen in real-world buffer overflows.

Figure 1 presents a plot of detection rate vs. false alarm rate for each tool. Each tool's performance is plotted with a single data point representing detection and false alarm percentages. The diagonal line represents the hypothetical performance of a random guesser that decides with equal probability if each commented buffer access in the test programs results in an overflow or not. The difference between a tool's detection rate and the random guesser's is only statistically significant if it lies

more than two standard deviations (roughly 6 percentage points when the detection rate is 50%) away from the random guesser line at the same false alarm rate. In this evaluation, every tool except BOON performs significantly better than a random guesser. In Zitser's evaluation [20], only PolySpace was significantly better. This difference in performance reflects the simplicity of the diagnostic test cases.

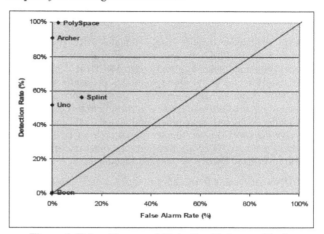

Figure 1. False Alarm and Detection Rates per Tool

Execution times for the five tools were measured as the total time to run each test case, including tool startup time, and are provided in Table 3. PolySpace's high detection rate comes at the cost of dramatically long execution times. ARCHER demonstrated both the second highest detection rate and the second highest execution time. Splint and UNO, with intermediate detection rates, had the two fastest execution times. BOON's slightly longer execution time did not result in a higher detection rate.

Table 3. Tool Execution Times

Tool	Total Time (secs)	Average Time per Test Case (secs)
ARCHER	288	0.247
BOON	73	0.063
PolySpace	200,820 (56 hrs)	172.526
Splint	24	0.021
UNO	27	0.023

6. Detailed Tool Diagnostics

The following paragraphs discuss each tool's performance in detail, especially compared to the tools' design goals.

ARCHER is designed to be inter-procedural, path-sensitive, context-sensitive, and aware of pointer aliases. It performs a fully-symbolic, bottom-up data flow analysis, while maintaining symbolic constraints between variables (handled by a linear constraint solver). ARCHER checks array accesses, pointer dereferences, and function calls that take a pointer and size. It is hard-coded to recognize and handle a small number of memory-related functions, such as malloc [19].

ARCHER provided a 91% detection rate with no false alarms. Most of its twenty-seven missed detections are easily explained by its limitations. Twenty of these were inter-procedural and these include fourteen cases that call C library functions, including the relatively common memcpy(). The other inter-procedural misses include cases involving shared memory, function pointers, recursion, and simple cases of passing a buffer address through one or two functions. Of the remaining seven misses, three involve function return values, two depend on array contents, and two involve function pointers and recursion.

These diagnostic results may explain ARCHER's poor performance in [20]. In this previous evaluation, that used model programs containing real code, ARCHER detected only one overflow. Of the thirteen model programs for which ARCHER reported no overflows, twelve contained buffer overflows that would be classified according to this evaluation's taxonomy as having inter-procedural scope, and nine of those involve calls to C library functions. To perform well against a body of real code, C library functions and other inter-procedural buffer overflows need to be detected accurately.

BOON's analysis is flow-insensitive and context-insensitive for scalability and simplicity. It focuses exclusively on the misuse of string manipulation functions, and the authors intentionally sacrificed precision for scalability [18].

In this evaluation, BOON detected only two out of fourteen string function overflows, with no false alarms. The two detected overflows involve the use of strcpy() and fgets(). BOON failed to detect the second case that calls strcpy(), all six cases that call strncpy(), the case that calls getcwd(), and all four cases that call memcpy(). Despite the heavy use of C library string functions in [20], BOON achieved only two detections in that prior evaluation as well. These results suggest that more complex analyses are required than provided in BOON to detect both real-world and simple buffer overflows.

PolySpace is the only commercial tool included in this evaluation. Although details of its methods and implementation are proprietary, its approach uses techniques described in several published works, including: symbolic analysis, or abstract interpretation [2]; escape analysis, for determining inter-procedural side effects [4]; and inter-procedural alias analysis for pointers [3].

PolySpace missed only one detection in this evaluation, which was a case involving a signal handler. PolySpace's detection rate was not nearly as high in Zitser's evaluation [20]. Presumably, the additional complexity of real code led to approximations to keep the problem tractable, but at the expense of precision. PolySpace reported seven false alarms across the test cases and many false alarms in Zitser's evaluation. In both evaluations, the majority of false alarms occurred for overflows involving calls to C library functions.

Splint employs "lightweight" static analysis and heuristics that are practical, but neither sound nor complete. Like many other tools, it trades off precision for scalability. It implements limited flow-sensitive control flow, merging possible paths at branch points. Splint uses heuristics to recognize loop idioms and determine loop bounds without resorting to more costly and accurate abstract evaluation. An annotated C library is provided, but the tool relies on the user to properly annotate all other functions to support inter-procedural analysis. Splint exhibited high false alarm rates in the developers' own tests [6,

12]. The basic test suite used in this evaluation was not annotated for Splint because it is unrealistic to expect annotations for most applications of static analysis tools.

Splint exhibited the highest false alarm rate of any tool. Many of the thirty-five false alarms are attributable to inter-procedural cases; cases involving increased complexity of the index, address, or length; and more complex containers and flow control constructs. The vast majority, 120 out of 127, of missed detections are attributable to loops. Detections were missed in all of the non-standard for() loop cases (both discrete and continuous), as well as in most of the other continuous loop cases. The only continuous loop cases handled correctly are the standard for loops, and Splint produces false alarms on nearly all of those. In addition, it misses the lower bound case, the "cond" case of local flow control, the taint case that calls getcwd, and all four of the signed/unsigned mismatch cases.

While Splint's detection rate was similar in this evaluation and the Zitser evaluation [20], its false alarm rate was much higher in the latter. Again, this is presumably because code that is more complex results in more situations where precision is sacrificed in the interest of scalability, with the loss of precision leading to increased false alarms. Splint's weakest area is loop handling. Enhancing loop heuristics to more accurately recognize and handle non-standard for loops, as well as continuous loops of all varieties, would significantly improve performance. Reducing the false alarm rate is also important.

UNO is an acronym for uninitialized variables, null-pointer dereferencing, and out-of-bounds array indexing, which are the three types of problems it is designed to address. UNO is not inter-procedural with respect to out-of-bounds array indexing and does not model function pointers, function return values, or computed indices [8].

UNO produced no false alarms in the basic test suite, but did miss nearly half of the possible detections (140 out of 291), most of which would be expected based on the tool's description. This included every inter-procedural case, every container case, nearly every index complexity case, every address and length complexity case, every address alias case, the function and recursion cases, every signed/unsigned mismatch, nearly every continuous loop, and a small assortment of others. It performed well on the various data types, index aliasing, and discrete loops. UNO exhibited a similar low detection rate in Zitser's evaluation [20].

7. CONCLUSIONS

A new taxonomy was used to construct a corpus of 291 small C-program test cases that can be used to evaluate static and dynamic analysis buffer overflow detection tools. This corpus is available at http://www.ll.mit.edu/IST/corpora.html. These test cases provide a benchmark to measure detection, false alarm, and confusion rates of tools, and can be used to find areas for tool enhancement. Evaluations of five tools validated the utility of this corpus and provide diagnostic results that demonstrate the strengths and weaknesses of these tools. Some tools provide very good detection rates (e.g. ARCHER and PolySpace) while others fall short of their specified design goals, even for simple, uncomplicated source code. Diagnostic results provide specific suggestions to improve tool performance (e.g. for Splint, improve modeling of complex loop structures; for ARCHER, improve inter-procedural analysis). They also demonstrate that the false alarm and confusion rates of some tools (e.g. Splint) need to be reduced.

The test cases we have developed can serve as a type of litmus test for tools. Good performance on test cases that fall within the design goals of a tool is a prerequisite for good performance on actual, complex code. Additional code complexity in actual code often exposes weaknesses of the tools that result in inaccuracies, but rarely improves tool performance. This is evident when comparing test case results obtained in this study to results obtained by Zitser [20] with more complex model programs.

The test corpus could be improved by adding test cases to cover attribute values currently underrepresented, such as string functions.

8. ACKNOWLEDGMENTS

We would like to thank Rob Cunningham and Tim Leek for discussions, and Tim for help with getting tools installed and running. We also thank David Evans for his help with Splint, David Wagner for answering questions about BOON, Yichen Xie and Dawson Engler for their help with ARCHER, and Chris Hote and Vince Hopson for answering questions about C-Verifier and providing a temporary license.

9. REFERENCES

[1] CERT (2004). CERT Coordination Center Advisories, http://www.cert.org/advisories/, Carnegie Mellon University, Software Engineering Institute, Pittsburgh, PA

[2] Cousot, P. and Cousot, R. (1976). Static determination of dynamic properties of programs, *Proceedings of the 2nd International Symposium on Programming,* Paris, France, 106--130

[3] Deutsch, A. (1994). Interprocedural may-alias analysis for pointers: beyond *k*-limiting, *Proceedings of the ACM SIGPLAN'94 Conference on Programming Language Design and Implementation*, Orlando, Florida, 230--241

[4] Deutsch, A. (1997). On the complexity of escape analysis, *Proceedings of the 24th ACM SIGPLAN-SIGACT Symposium on Principles of Programming Languages,* Paris, France, 358--371

[5] Etoh, H. (2004). GCC extension for protecting applications from stack smashing attacks, http://www.trl.ibm.com/projects/security/ssp/

[6] Evans, D. and Larochelle, D. (2002). Improving security using extensible lightweight static analysis, *IEEE Software,* 19 (1), 42--51

[7] GCC Home Page (2004). Free Software Foundation, Boston, MA, http://gcc.gnu.org/

[8] Holzmann, G. (2002). UNO: Static source code checking for user-defined properties, Bell Labs Technical Report, Bell Laboratories, Murray Hill, NJ, 27 pages

[9] ICAT (2004). The ICAT Metabase, http://icat.nist.gov/icat.cfm, National Institute of Standards and Technology, Computer Security Division, Gaithersburg, MD

[10] klog (1999). The frame pointer overwrite, *Phrack Magazine,* 9 (55), http://www.tegatai.com/~jbl/overflow-papers/P55-08

[11] Kratkiewicz, K. (2005). Evaluating Static Analysis Tools for Detecting Buffer Overflows in C Code, Master's Thesis, Harvard University, Cambridge, MA, 285 pages, http://www.ll.mit.edu/IST/pubs/KratkiewiczThesis.pdf

[12] Larochelle, D. and Evans, D. (2001). Statically detecting likely buffer overflow vulnerabilities, *Proceedings of the 10th USENIX Security Symposium*, Washington, DC, 177--190

[13] Moore, D., Paxson, V., Savage, S., Shannon, C., Staniford, S., and Weaver, N. (2003). The Spread of the Sapphire/Slammer Worm, http://www.caida.org/outreach/papers/2003/sapphire/sapphire.html

[14] PolySpace Technologies (2003). PolySpace C Developer Edition, http://www.polyspace.com/datasheets/c_psde.htm, Paris, France

[15] PSS Security Response Team (2003). PSS Security Response Team Alert - New Worm: W32.Blaster.worm, http://www.microsoft.com/technet/treeview/default.asp?url=/technet/security/alerts/msblaster.asp, Microsoft Corporation, Redmond, WA

[16] Ruwase, O. and Lam, M. (2004). A practical dynamic buffer overflow detector, *Proceedings of the 11th Annual Network and Distributed System Security Symposium,* San Diego, CA, 159--169

[17] Security Focus (2004). The Bugtraq mailing list, http://www.securityfocus.com/archive/1, SecurityFocus, Semantec Corporation, Cupertino, CA

[18] Wagner, D., Foster, J.S., Brewer, E.A., and Aiken, A. (2000). A first step towards automated detection of buffer overrun vulnerabilities, *Proceedings of the Network and Distributed System Security Symposium*, San Diego, CA, 3--17

[19] Xie, Y., Chou, A., and Engler, D. (2003). ARCHER: Using symbolic, path-sensitive analysis to detect memory access errors, *Proceedings of the 9th European Software Engineering Conference/10th ACM SIGSOFT International Symposium on Foundations of Software Engineering,* Helsinki, Finland, 327--336

[20] Zitser, M. (2003). Securing Software: An Evaluation of Static Source Code Analyzers, Master's Thesis, Massachusetts Institute of Technology, Cambridge, MA, 130 pages

[21] Zitser, M., Lippmann, R., and Leek, T. (2004). Testing static analysis tools using exploitable buffer overflows from open-source code, *Proceedings of the 12th ACM SIGSOFT International Symposium on Foundations of Software Engineering*, Newport Beach, CA, 97--106

ABM: A Prototype for Benchmarking Source Code Analyzers

Tim Newsham[*]
Waipahu, Hawaii USA
newsham@lava.net

Brian Chess
Fortify Software
Palo Alto, California USA
brian@fortifysoftware.com

ABSTRACT

We describe a prototype benchmark for source code analyzers. The prototype uses a combination of micro- and macro-benchmarking to measure the vulnerabilities a tool is capable of detecting and the degree to which it is able to distinguish between safe code and vulnerable code. We describe the design and implementation of our prototype, then discuss the effect that the our experience with the prototype has had on our future goals. Our prototype, along with sample output from a number of source code analysis tools, is available for download from http://vulncat.fortifysoftware.com.

1. INTRODUCTION

Static source code analysis provides a mechanism for reducing the amount of tedious work involved in inspecting a program for security vulnerabilities. As source code analysis grows in popularity, more potiential users of the technology are faced with the need to evalute the pros and cons of an increasing number of tools. A formal benchmark for comparing source code analyzers would provide several benefits: A benchmark would help consumers choose the best tool for their needs. It would pinpoint weaknesses in existing analyzers. It would quantify the strengths and weaknesses of competing analysis techniques and allow engineers to make measured tradeoffs. Benchmarking could also play a pivotal role in directing future research and development efforts.

We recognized the need for good benchmarking data for source code analyzers and resolved to create a benchmark. We chose to begin by constructing a prototype to test out and refine our ideas. Starting with a prototype allows us to understand what problems we know how to solve and gives us a platform to explore design decisions. An obvious goal of this work is to provide a foundation for the construction of a future benchmark.

---

[*]Under contract with Fortify Software.

We call our prototype the Analyzer BenchMark or ABM for short. The ABM benchmark is comprised of 91 micro-benchmark test cases and a single macro-benchmark test case. The purpose of each micro test case is to evaluate a tool against a very specific scenerio in a controlled way. The purpose of macro test cases is to capture properties of "real-world" programs, like size and complexity, that are absent from the micro test cases.

Our goal is to develop a framework that can be applied to any programming language or platform, but for the purposes of creating a prototype, all of the test cases target C-code source code analyzers running under Unix and Win32. We have applied the prototype to six different analyzers running in Redhat9 Linux and Windows XP. Our benchmark focuses on measuring the analysis strength of source code analyzers and does not concern itself with issues such as memory or time efficiency. Applying the ABM benchmark to source code analyzers results in quantifiable answers to the questions "What kind of vulnerabilities does this analyzer search for?" and "How effective is this analyzer at finding these vulnerabilities?".

Related work

We are not the first to attempt to measure the performance of source code analyzers. In his thesis [6] and accompanying article [7], Misha Zitser evaluates the performance of several source code analyzers for detecting buffer overflows. Zitser uses a test suite based on known vulnerabilities in real-world code. Zitser's test cases are derived from widely used applications but not comprised of the actual application code because many of the analyzers he measured were not capable of ingesting the large amount of code contained therein. Zitser's test suite is now available from the MIT Lincoln Laboratory in their publically available corpora [2].

Zitser describes the construction of "approximately 50 pairs" of small test cases. Each pair is made up of a small program with a single instance of a buffer overflow and a second matched program that is similar but does not contain the defect. To construct his test cases, Zitser first created a fairly detailed taxonomy of test case characteristics. He then hand-constructed the test pairs and classified them using his taxonomy. Although he describes the construction of his micro-benchmark test suite in detail, Zitser did not publish any results obtained from using the suite.

Zitser's micro-benchmark work was continued and extended by Kendra Kratkiewicz. In her thesis [1] Kratkiewicz extends the taxonomy created by Zitser and uses her taxonomy to guide the automatic generation of a micro-benchmark suite of 591 quadruplets. Each quadruplet consists of four programs: one with no buffer overflow and three with successively larger buffer overflows. Kratkiewicz's use of quadruplets allows the effect of the magnitude of a buffer overflow to be analyzed. Her thesis describes the results of using this benchmark to compare the performance of several analyzers in detecting buffer overflows.

The SAMATE project at NIST [3] was created with the objective of "identification, enhancement and development of software assurance tools." [3] Part of the project's mandate is to support tool evaluation and, towards this end, they plan to create a system for benchmarking software analysis tools. This work is still in the planning stages and we are not aware of any results at this time.

□o□tr□□t□o□□

We believe our work makes several important contributions to source code analyzer benchmarking. First, we are constructing a standard benchmark. Prior efforts focused on constructing a benchmark for the author's use in measuring particular tools. We intend our benchmark to be used by others including end-users and research and development teams from academia and industry.

Second, we wish to benchmark a large number of analyzers. This goal forces us to pay attention to engineering issues such as ease of retargetting. Our benchmark is carefully automated with a build environment that has small, isolated analyzer-specific components. We use a normalization mechanism to reduce the amount of analyzer-specific code in our benchmarking process.

Third, we are interested in benchmarking all vulnerability types and do not limit our focus to a single class of vulnerabilities. This choice has resulted in a classification system that is more flexible than those used previously.

Fourth, we are interested in benchmarking across a wide set of platforms and languages.

Fifth, we see weakness in the grading mechanisms used by Zitser and Krakiewicz, which expect that each test case can have at most one reported vulnerability. Our benchmark uses a more sophisticated grading process that does not make such an assumption.

Finally, we see value in both micro-benchmarking and macro-benchmarking and use both to measure the performance of source code analyzers.

With the remainder of this paper we discuss the composition of the ABM prototype benchmark, why we made certain choices, and our plans for expanding from a prototype to a full benchmark proposal. Examples of benchmark results are provided to clarify discussion, but, due to space constraints, complete results are not given. We direct curious readers to http://vulncat.fortifysoftware.com for more results.

□□ □□□□□□ □□□□□

If a benchmark is going to gain wide adoption, it must meet a number of requirements:

First, the benchmark must be fair, objective and transparent. A benchmark that is not fair and objective will be rejected by the source code analysis community. Our benchmark should generate transparent results that can be independently reproduced, scrutinized and verified so that matters of fairness can be publicly decided.

Second, the benchmark must be able to accomodate change.

The relevance of different vulnerabilities, platforms and languages will evolve over time. This evolution is driven both by technical factors (such as the discovery of new types of attacks) and social factors (such as increased emphasis on privacy rights). The widespread adoption of source code analysis tools is in its very infancy, virtually ensuring future change. In order to be successful our benchmark must be flexible and extensible. The framework should allow for the introduction of new languages, platforms and metrics.

The benchmark must also be applicable to a wide range of analysis techniques. Without good coverage of important platforms or languages, people will look elsewhere in order to find a becnhmark that is relevant to their needs and intrests. This means that, at a minimum, the benchmark must support the most popular languages and operating environments.

The benchmark must generate an easy-to-understand score. The majority of consumers of benchmark results will not be experts in source code analysis, and they will look to the benchmark for a simple way to compare competing tools. Some will use the scores to make important purchasing decisions. It is important that these scores be interpreted correctly and not be prone to marketing spin. In order to be relevant, the scores must also be based on measurements that are important in real-world programs.

Finally, the benchmark should generate a wealth of data about each tool measured. The need for this information is two-fold. First, the data will provide transparency by allowing the results of the benchmark to be scrutinized and independently verified. Second, the data will allow for detailed analysis of the strengths and weaknesses of each tool. Consumers will be able to use the data to focus on details that are most relevant to them. This data will also be useful in focusing future source code analysis research and development efforts.

Beyond these requirements we have some pragmatic goals for our benchmark. We would like the benchmark to be easy to use. We wish to create a benchmark that is easy to retarget for new source code analysis tools. To the greatest extent possible we want to automate the application of the benchmark, making it easy to carry out the benchmarking process. We believe that automation has the additional advantage of increasing the objectivity of a benchmark. We also want the benchmarking results to be easy to view, interpret and consume.

□□ □□□ □□□□□□ □R□

We chose to begin our project by creating a prototype. Our goal in starting with a prototype is to allow us to figure out what aspects of the design we actually understood and provide a platform to experiment with the aspects that we did not. For this purpose we chose to restrict the scope of our project significantly, focussing on static analyzers for Java and C code running under Linux and Windows XP. We decided that we should build a modestly sized suite of micro-benchmark test cases, with the understanding that the coverage of the suite would suffer for it. We also chose to begin with a single macro-benchmark test case. For maximum flexibility, all of our micro test cases would be constructed manually, and our macro test case would come from a widely adopted open source program.

The decision to use both micro- and macro-benchmarking was not an easy one. A macro-benchmark is made up of

Attribute	Parent	Keywords
Platform	General	Port Unix Win32
Program size	General	Size0...Size9
Program complexity	General	Complex0...Complex9
Vulnerability class	General	BufferOverflow Api Taint Race
Overflow location	BufferOverflow	Stack Heap
Overflow API	BufferOverflow	AdHoc AdHocDecode AdHocCopy Read Gets Strcpy Sprintf Memcpy
Overflow cause	BufferOverflow	Unbounded NoNul IntOverflow BadBound
API type	Api	MemMgmt Chroot
MemMgmt type	MemMgmt	DoubleFree Leak
Taint type	Taint	Unsafe InfoLeak FormatString
Race type	Race	Filename

Table 1: Measured attributes, their dependencies and the set of keywords used to describe them.

Keyword	Description
Port	Portable across all platforms.
Unix	Contains UNIX-specific code.
Win32	Contains Win32-specific code.
Size0...Size9	Description of the program size from small to large.
Complex0...Complex9	Description of the program complexity from simple to complex.
BufferOverflow	Contains a buffer overflow vulnerability.
Api	Contains a vulnerability caused by misusing an API.
Taint	Contains a vulnerability caused by misuse of tainted data.
Race	Contains a vulnerability cause by a race condition.
Stack	The overflow occurs in a buffer located on the stack.
Heap	The overflow occurs in a buffer located on the heap.
AdHoc	The overflow is caused by an ad hoc buffer manipulation.
AdHocDecode	The overflow is caused by an ad hoc buffer decode operation.
AdHocCopy	The overflow is caused by an ad hoc copy operation.
Read	The overflow is caused by use of the read() function.
Gets	The overflow is caused by use of the gets() function or a similar related function.
Strcpy	The overflow is caused by use of the strcpy() function or a similar related function.
Sprintf	The overflow is caused by use of the sprintf() function or a similar related function.
Memcpy	The overflow is caused by use of the memcpy() function or a similar related function.
Unbounded	The overflow was caused because no bounds check was made.
NoNull	The overflow was caused because a NUL character was expected but not found.
IntOverflow	The overflow was caused because of an integer overflow or underflow when computing bounds.
BadBound	The overflow was caused because an incorrect bounds check was performed.
MemMgmt	A memory management API was misued.
Chroot	The chroot() function was misued.
DoubleFree	Allocated memory was freed multiple times.
Leak	Allocated memory was never freed.
Unsafe	Tainted data was passed to an unsafe function.
InfoLeak	Sensitive data was revealed.
FormatString	Tainted data was used as a format string to a function in the printf family of functions.
Filename	A race was caused by accessing a file multiple times by its filename.

Table 2: Descriptions for each keyword.

larger test cases drawn from source code in use in "real-world" applications. These test cases are large, complicated, and provide several challenges to benchmark analysis. Macro-benchmark cases contain an entanglement of many factors that are not easily seperated for independent measure. A micro-benchmark is comprised of a set of small synthetic test cases in which each test case can be carefully designed to isolate characteristics. Tests can include control subjects to increase the realiability of any measurements made.

The precision of the micro-benchmark test cases comes at a cost: it is "real-world" applications that interest programmers, not synthetic test cases. A micro-benchmark may fail to capture some salient feature of important applications, such as size or complex interactions between features. Even when micro-benchmarks do provide useful results, their accuracy may be called into question unless they can be validated against data from important applications. For these reasons we chose to create a blend of micro-benchmarks and macro-benchmarks.

☐☐☐ ☐e☐t ☐a☐e ☐ttr☐☐te☐

BAD case	OK case	Keywords
ahscpy1-bad.c	ahscpy1-ok.c	Port Size0 Complex0 BufferOverflow Stack AdHocCopy Unbounded
chroot1-bad.c	chroot1-ok.c	Unix Size0 Complex0 Api Chroot
fmt1-bad.c	fmt1-ok.c	Port Size0 Complex0 Taint FormatString
fmt2-bad.c	fmt2-ok.c	Unix Size0 Complex0 Taint FormatString
fmt3-bad.c	fmt3-ok.c	Unix Size0 Complex1 Taint FormatString
	fmt4-ok.c	Port Size0 Complex0 Taint FormatString
	fmt5-ok.c	Port Size0 Complex0 Taint FormatString
into1-bad.c		Port Size0 Complex0 BufferOverflow Heap AdHoc IntOverflow
into2-bad.c	into2-ok.c	Port Size0 Complex0 BufferOverflow Heap AdHoc IntOverflow
mem1-bad.c	mem1-ok.c	Port Size0 Complex0 Api MemMgmt Leak
mem2-bad.c	mem2-ok.c	Port Size0 Complex1 Api MemMgmt Leak
race1-bad.c	race1-ok.c	Unix Size0 Complex0 Race Filename
race2-bad.c	race2-ok.c	Unix Size0 Complex0 Race Filename
snp1-bad.c	snp1-ok.c	Port Size0 Complex0 BufferOverflow Stack Sprintf BadBound
snp2-bad.c	snp2-ok.c	Port Size0 Complex0 BufferOverflow Stack Sprintf BadBound
tain1-bad.c	tain1-ok.c	Port Size0 Complex0 Taint Unsafe
tain2-bad.c	tain2-ok.c	Unix Size0 Complex0 Taint Unsafe

Table 3: A sampling of test cases and their attribute keywords.

To guide the creation of synthetic test cases we looked at computer security vulnerabilities arising from programming mistakes in C source code. We created a formal taxonomy of vulnerability attributes covering a wider range of vulnerability types than covered in previous benchmarks. While our taxonomy is not complete we believe it captures many of the kinds of program attributes that are important to source code analyzers. This taxonomy defines a problem space for our test cases that we were able to use for both choosing which test cases to create and to measure the coverage of the resulting test suite. The taxonomy also proved useful in automating the analysis of the results.

While creating our taxonomy, we observed that some program attributes are only relevant to some types of vulnerabilities. We support attributes in this irregular taxonomy by using a heirarchical system of keywords. For each attribute we enumerate a set of keywords that describe that attribute. Each attribute also has a parent keyword upon which it is dependent. When an attribute's parent keyword is present, exactly one of the keywords for that attribute must be specified. At the top of this dependency heirarchy is the keyword "General" which is always implicitly present. The attributes we measure are shown in Table 1 and the keywords used described in Table 2.

Each test case is described by a string of keywords for each relevant attribute. For example, the string "Port Size0 Complex1 BufferOverflow Heap Gets Unbounded" describes a small portable test case containing a buffer overflow on the heap using the gets() function, which does not perform any bounds checking.

This system of keywords is very flexible. Attributes that are specific to features of a particular language or operating system can be introduced without interfering with other unrelated attributes. Keywords and attributes can even be used to describe non-technical details about a test case such as the source of contributed material. Finally the system of keywords is well-defined (although some of the keywords currently in use are not). This simplifies the verification of well-formed test case descriptions.

▢▢▢ ▢e▢t ▢▢▢fe

We used our taxonomy to guide our creation of ABM micro-benchmark test cases. The intent is to have broad coverage of combinations of attributes in our taxonomy. We consciously chose to limit the number of test cases in our prototype benchmark allowing the benchmark coverage to suffer a little in order to focus on other details such as grading and analysis. We sketched out aproximately what types of test cases we wanted to include and constructed the test cases manually. Constructing a small number of test cases allowed us to explore some alternate test case designs during prototyping and allowed us to focus more quickly on other areas of the benchmark design such as grading and analysis.

The benchmark test suite is composed of 91 C test cases with a somewhat even coverage of attributes in our taxonomy. We are currently in the process of adding test cases for Java. Table 3 lists a sampling of 31 of the 91 test cases and their attributes. Whenever possible, test cases were constructed in matched pairs of OK and BAD test cases. Each BAD test case has code with a vulnerability in it. Corresponding OK cases are similar to BAD cases but do not share the vulnerability. OK cases are generally constructed by patching BAD cases to remove the vunlerability while retaining functionality. These OK cases share the same attribute keywords even though they do not contain a vulnerability.

Kratkiewicz [1] used test case quadruplets rather than pairs to measure the effects of buffer overflow magnitude. We did not take this approach because the magnitude attribute is specific to buffer overflow vulnerabilities. The effect of magnitude can still be measured by providing additional test case pairs that cover buffer overflows of varying mangitude.

Each test case contains annotations specifying where a bug may be present. Test cases with vulnerabilities are tagged with a comment "/* BAD */" at any line that may be considered to contribute to the vulnerability described by the test case's keywords. Those cases without vulnerabilities are tagged with a comment "/* OK */" at any line that could have contributed to the vulnerability if it had been present.

Each test case is also annotated with information about valid and invalid inputs. These annotations allow for au-

```
 1 /*
 2 Description: Printf is called with a user supplied
   format string.
 3 Keywords: Port Size0 Complex0 Taint FormatString
 4 ValidArg: "'NormalString\n'"
 5 InvalidArg: "%s"*100
 6 */
 7
 8 #include <stdio.h>
 9
10 void
11 test(char *str)
12 {
13     printf(str);                /* BAD */
14 }
15
16 int
17 main(int argc, char **argv)
18 {
19     char *userstr;
20
21     if(argc > 1) {
22         userstr = argv[1];
23         test(userstr);
24     }
25     return 0;
26 }
```

Figure 1: The test case fmt1-bad.c.

tomated testing of the resulting binaries. Some of the test cases we constructed were dependent on implementation details, such as compiler layout and padding, and were not vulnerable when using our compiler of choice. We felt these test cases were still important and did not want to simply discard them. As a result, some of our test cases fail automatic validation. It is also important to note that an incorrect test case may still pass validation if the validation inputs are not picked properly. Thus, we were able to use automated testing as an aid in validating our test suite but could not rely on it completely.

An example of a test case in the suite is shown in Figure 1. Annotations in the comments at the head of the file give a formal and informal description of the test case. They also provide test strings for automated verification of the test case. An annotation at line thirteen denotes the occurance of a vulnerability.

For our macro-benchmark test case we chose the Apache web server [4]. Our choice was influenced by several factors. Apache is well known, accepted, and mature. It is freely available in source form and runs on a wide range of platforms. Typical deployments of Apache require that it be exposed to security threats from the entire internet. Apache provides us with a relatively large and complex program that is representative of the types of programs that people would want to analyze with a source code analyzer.

☐☐☐ ☐rad☐☐☐

To benchmark a tool with the ABM suite, we run the tool being benchmarked against each test case in the suite and gather the results for grading. The entire process is automated with a system of makefiles. The tool is invoked once

```
N: fmt1-bad
L: fmt1-bad.c 13 FormatString format printf If
   format strings can be influenced by an
   attacker, they can be exploited. Use a
   constant for the format specification.
```

Figure 3: The normalized results of Flawfinder's analysis of fmt1-bad.c.

for each test case. The result of each analysis is normalized into a standard format, and a grading program compares the normalized tool output against the annotations in the test case. Finally, the graded results are combined into a benchmark result. This process is illustrated in Figure 2.

In order to benchmark a tool, the benchmark framework must be able to invoke the analyzer, and there must be a method for converting the results of the analysis into a standardized format. Most of the benchmark process is dictated by makefile rules shared by all tools. Tool-specific rules are contained in a separate makefile for each analyzer. Because some test cases are platform specific, each analyzer-specific makefile must specify which set of test cases to analyze. They must also specify how to invoke the analyzer and what file extension to use when saving the results. These tool-specific makefiles are typically less than 40 lines long.

We use a normalized output format to avoid putting analyzer-specific code in the grading process. The normalizer emits a line for each vulnerability reported by the analyzer. Each vulnerability is first mapped to the most specific matching keyword in our taxonomy. In some cases a vulnerability may be mapped to several keywords. The normalizer emits a single line for each combination of keyword, file name, and line number. To make it easier to verify that our normalizer is behaving as expected, we include the analyzer's original description of each vulnerability in the normalized output. The amount of code necessary to normalize an analyzer's output is highly dependent on the output format of an analyzer. So far we have constructed normalizers for six analyzers ranging in size from 59 to 137 lines of python code.

Figure 3 shows an exerpt of the normalized results from the Flawfinder [5] analyzer. The line starting with "N:" describes the test case source (fmt1-bad). The line starting with "L:" describes an instance of a FormatString vulnerability at line 13. The text following the FormatString keyword on this line is not used and is provided to aid manual review of the results. The remainder of the file contains results for other test cases.

We use an automated system to grade the normalized analysis results. Grading results manually would be tedious and error-prone and would place an artificially low bound on the practical size of our test suite. Manual grading would likely be less objective or at least less transparent than an automated process. Fortunately grading a test case's analysis results is a straightforward process of matching up the normalized results with the source code if the source code is properly annotated.

To grade the normalized results, each reported vulnerability is matched against the corresponding line in the annotated test case. Any reported vulnerability which does not appear as an attribute keyword for the test case is noted and ignored. Likewise, vulnerabilities matching attribute

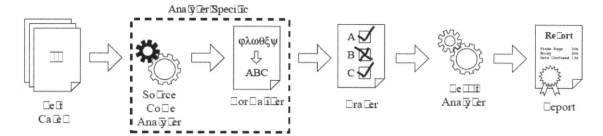

Figure 2: The ABM benchmarking process. Test cases are analyzed by the source code analyzer to be measured. The results are then normalized and graded before a report is generated. The invocation of the source code analyzer and the normalization of its results are the only analyzer-specific steps in this process.

```
fmt1-bad
Printf is called with a user supplied format string.
Port Size0 Complex0 Taint FormatString
13 BAD FormatString *MATCH* format printf If format
   strings can be influenced by an attacker, they can
   be exploited.  Use a constant for the format
   specification.

Raw results:
PASS fmt1-bad Port Size0 Complex0 Taint FormatString
```

Figure 4: The graded results of Flawfinder's analysis of fmt1-bad.c.

keywords but at lines that are not annotated as BAD or OK are noted and ignored. When a matching vulnerability occurs on a line with a BAD or OK annotation, it is noted as having matched. An analyzer is given a passing grade on a test case if it matches any of the BAD lines and does not match any of the OK lines. Upon completion, the grader emits a list of passing and failing test cases and their associated annotation keywords.

Notice that our grading process can ignore many reported vulnerabilities. Each test case is constructed to measure the analysis of a single type of vulnerability and the grader ignores any information about other reported vulnerabilities. Although it may appear that valuable information is discarded, this is not necessarily the case. Discarded information is not lost as long as there is another test case in the suite to measure the behavior. We believe that this approach of carefully focused measurment increases the reliability and leads to better analysis.

Figure 4 shows an exerpt of the graded results from the Flawfinder [5] analyzer. The group of lines at the top of the figure describe the grading process, starting with the test case name and the formal and informal descriptions of the test case. Following the description is a line representing the reported FormatString vulnerability at line 13. This line is indicated as a match since the test case is a FormatString test case. The Flawfinder tool passed this test case since there was a match for a "BAD" line. Had it failed, failure would be indicated in the output. These first lines are not used directly but are provided to ease human review of the grading process. The grader emits a table of graded results at the end of its output with a line for each graded test case. This is illustrated in the figure with a line that indicates that

Flawfinder passed the fmt1-bad case.

Grading the macro-benchmark test cases is even simpler than grading micro-benchmark cases. As with the micro-benchmark test cases, the results from the macro-benchmark are first normalized. The benchmark cases were chosen in part for their maturity and it is assumed that there are relatively few vulnerabilities left in the code. For the purpose of grading, we assume that all reported vulnerabilities are false-positives. This assumption introduces error; there are undoubtedly vulnerabilities in the macro-benchmark that have not yet been identified or fixed. However, the macro-benchmark provides good insight into the amount of output that a tool is likely to produce for a real-world program. Over time it is expected that a few bonafide vulnerabilities will be discovered in macro-benchmark test cases. We intend to maintain our current test cases and augment them with annotations as this occurs.

Analysis

The analysis phase makes use of the graded benchmark results to generate a report of meaningful measurements about an analyzer. The goal of the analysis is to measure the coverage and strength of an analyzer. An analyzer's coverage is a measure of the relevance of an analyzer to a variety of code defects. An analyzer with broad coverage is designed to detect a broad range of vulnerabilities whereas an analyzer with narrow coverage can only detect a small class of vulnerabilities. An analyzer's strength is a measure of the quality of analysis over diverse and sometimes difficult coding constructs. An analyzer with high strength can detect vulnerabilities in both simple and complicated code. Equally important, an analyzer with high strength is able to differentiate between vulnerable and non-vulnerable instances of similar code. An analyzer with low strength may not be able to detect a vulnerability in complex code or may incorrectly identify vulnerabilities where they do not exist.

In order to understand analysis of the results, it is necessary to first understand the meaning of passed and failed test cases. For "BAD" cases, a success indicates a "true positive" detection of a vulnerability while a failure indicates a "false negative" or that the analyzer incorrectly indicated that the vulnerability was not present. For "OK" cases, a success indicates a "true negative" or that the analyzer correctly indicated that no vulnerability was present, while a failure indicates a "false positive" detection of a vulnerability.

The simplest measure of an analyzer is given by a tally

	BAD tests			OK tests			Total			Discriminates		
	pass	total	perc	pass	total	perc	pass	total	perc	pass	total	perc
All	26	48	54%	23	43	53%	49	91	54%	4	22	18%
Unsafe	2	2	100%	0	2	0%	2	4	50%	0	2	0%
InfoLeak	0	2	0%	0	0	- %	0	2	0%	0	0	- %
FormatString	3	3	100%	3	5	60%	6	8	75%	3	3	100%
fmt1	1	1	100%	1	1	100%	2	2	100%	1	1	100%
fmt2	1	1	100%	1	1	100%	2	2	100%	1	1	100%
fmt3	1	1	100%	1	1	100%	2	2	100%	1	1	100%
fmt4	0	0	- %	0	1	0%	0	1	0%	0	0	- %
fmt5	0	0	- %	0	1	0%	0	1	0%	0	0	- %

Table 4: Exerpts of benchmark results for the Flawfinder scanner.

of the passing test cases. This measure imparts a rough measure of the analyzer but does not provide much insight into the analyzer's strengths or weaknesses. A slightly better measure is derived by partitioning the test cases into "OK" and "BAD" cases. This provides a measure of true positives and negatives, or, conversely, false positives and false negatives. The number of true positives gives some indication of how well the analyzer does the job advertised while the number of false positives gives a measure of how much additional noise it produces.

By partitioning the test cases according to vulnerability classes the coverage of an analyzer can easily be measured. An analyzer is said to cover a vulnerability class if it can report vulnerabilities in that class. If there are any true positives in the class (ie. there is at least one "BAD" test case that passed) then clearly the vulnerability class is covered.

Measuring an analyzer's strength is a little more complex. Some indication of an analyzer's strength is given by the number of false positives and false negatives that are reported. We can gain further insight into an analyzer's performance by partitioning a set of test cases based on a particular attribute. For example, by partitioning the set of BufferOverflow test cases according to program size, the effects of size on buffer overflow detection can be isolated.

One effect that is not easily isolated in this way is the ability of an analyzer to discriminate between vulnerable and non-vulnerable code. We introduce a new measure to quantify this component of an analyzer's strength. The *discrimination* of an analyzer is a tally of how often an analyzer passed an "OK" test case when it also passed a matching "BAD" test case. Together with the true negative and true positive tallies, discrimination gives a good indication of an analyzer's strength. An analyzer that finds many instances of a vulnerability but falsely reports the presence of this vulnerability where it is not present will score well when true-positives are measured but will not get a good true-negative or discrimination score.

Besides isolating the effect of defect variations, analyzing partitions based on keywords has an additional advantage – it allows us to make level comparisons of diverse analyzers. For example, the results of benchmarking an analyzer that runs only on Win32 platforms cannot directly be compared with the results from an analyzer that runs only in UNIX. However, by isolating the portable test cases (those described by the Port keyword) some amount of comparison can be made.

The ABM analyzer generates a report by generating ta-

bles of successively more detailed partitions of the data set. This process is straightforward because every test case is described by a sequence of keywords. Subsets of test cases are made by matching selected attribute keywords. These subsets are then scored for tallies of passed test cases, true positives, true negatives, and discrimination. Each tally is reported as an absolute count and as a percentage.

Table 4 shows an excerpt of the analyzed results from benchmarking the Flawfinder [5] source code analyzer. These results can be viewed in their entirety at http://vulncat.fortifysoftware.com. The line labelled "All" shows the accumulated results for all the micro-benchmark test cases. It shows that Flawfinder found 54% of the vulnerabilities, and properly did not report any vulnerabilities for 53% of the non-vulnerable test cases. When it was able to detect a vulnerability, it was able to discriminate it from non-vulenerable code 18% of the time. The next three lines show Flawfinder's performance for three classes of Taint vulnerabilities. Finally the last five lines show the individual test case pairs used to measure FormatString vulnerabilities. The fmt1-bad.c test case presented earlier is represented by the "BAD tests" column of the "fmt1" row.

Because of their nature, the macro-benchmark test cases are not as easy to analyze and do not provide as much information. The only analysis we perform is a counting of false-positives by attribute keyword. There is one subtlety in this process: we accumulate attribute counts up to their parent keywords. For example if there are five reported FormatString vulnerabilities and two reported InfoLeak vulnerabilities these counts are accumulated and reported as seven Taint vulnerabilities. The reason for this accumulation is to ease comparison of the results from different analyzers: some analyzers may report vulnerabilities deeper in the attribute taxonomy than other analyzers.

☐☐ ☐☐☐☐R☐ ☐ ☐R☐

We have built a prototype benchmark for source code analyzers, but our work is not yet done. A primary goal of this project has been to guide the development of our full benchmark. While what we have implemented is important, we consider what we have learned about what we must now implement an equally important contribution of our work.

We are currently in the process of adding Java test cases to the ABM suite. Although unexciting from a technical point of view these new test cases are critical to our goal of providing a standard cross-platform benchmark. Details about the Java test cases are available at http://vulncat.fortifysoftware.com.

The most glaring deficiency of the current benchmark is its coverage. This is partly due to our desire to keep the number of test cases manageably small in our prototype. A next-generation benchmark will require a micro-benchmark test suite one or two orders of magnitude larger. A hand-written test suite would clearly not be practical and we anticipate generating test cases programatically as was done in [1].

A larger macro-benchmark test suite will also be needed. The process of incorporating more macro-benchmarks is tedious but fairly straightforward.

Test case generation will be guided by a classification system. Our initial taxonomy was successful but somewhat simplistic. Its classification of complexity and size lacks formal definition. The ABM test suite has particularly poor coverage of large or complex programs. A formal classification of size and complexity will give us a better foundation for addressing this deficiency. To ensure consistent and unbiased coverage of the taxonomy's attribute space we intend to formalize the process by which we pick test cases. The process of constructing matched OK cases also suffers from a lack of formal structure which we hope to address by augmenting the taxonomy with alternate patch strategies.

The taxonomies created and employed by Zitser [6] and Kratkiewicz [1] to describe programs with buffer overflows are considerably more detailed than ours. In the future we plan to incorporate attributes from their work into our taxonomy and expand our taxonomy to cover details particular to vulnerabilities other than buffer overflows.

The area of result analysis is ripe for future research. As with any benchmark, we anticipate that the availability of raw data will stimulate others to find new ways of extracting important information. There are two areas that we would like to pursue further in the future. Currently the result analysis places equal importance on each test case. This artificially weights the aggregated results according to the number of test cases in each category. We hope to address this by investigating weightings that more properly reflect the importance of test case properties in real-world situations. We hope that comparisons with macro-benchmark results will prove useful in this effort.

A second area of future interest is to provide better synergy between the micro- and macro-benchmarking components. As currently implemented our micro-benchmark and macro-benchmark cases are used to measure very different things. The relation between their results is not clearly apparent in the results. We hope that future analysis will allow the two suites to complement each other and corroborate each other's results.

A subtle issue that has been glossed over earlier in this paper is the handling of macro-benchmark results across disparate platforms. Even though the test case we chose compiles on a wide range of platforms, the source code used in the build process is not identical for all platforms. The build environment selects certain platform specific files appropriate for the platform. Conditional compilation selects certain segments of code within files that are used by all platforms. This makes comparisons of results obtained on different platforms troublesome. We are currently investigating stronger analysis techniques to remedy this.

Beyond the technical, there is a lot of work remaining in getting our benchmark adopted. We hope to work with the community to get feedback on our methodologies and address any early concerns. We plan to support the bench-mark's adoption by promoting its fair use and the dissemination of results. We plan to continue benchmarking more analyzers, and we will make both the benchmark and results for a wide range of analzers available for download from http://vulncat.fortifysoftware.com.

R R

[1] K. Kratkiewicz. Evaluating static analysis tools for detecting buffer overflows in c code. Master's thesis, Harvard University, March 2005.

[2] MIT. Corpora. http://www.ll.mit.edu/IST/corpora.html, August 2005.

[3] NIST. Samate (nist software assurance metrics and tool evaluation). http://samate.nist.gov/, August 2005.

[4] The Apache Software Foundation. The apache http server project. http://httpd.apache.org/, August 2005.

[5] D. A. Wheeler. Flawfinder. http://www.dwheeler.com/flawfinder/, August 2005.

[6] M. Zitser. Securing software: An evaluation of static source code analyzers. Master's thesis, Massachusetts Institute of Technology, August 2003.

[7] M. Zitser, R. Lippmann, and T. Leek. Testing static analysis tools using exploitable buffer overflows from open source code. In *SIGSOFT '04/FSE-12: Proceedings of the 12th ACM SIGSOFT twelfth international symposium on Foundations of software engineering*, pages 97–106, New York, NY, USA, 2004. ACM Press.

A Benchmark Suite for Behavior-Based Security Mechanisms

Dong Ye, Micha Moffie and David Kaeli
Computer Architecture Research Laboratory
Northeastern University, Boston, MA 02115
{dye,mmoffie,kaeli}@ece.neu.edu

▢▢▢▢R▢▢▢

This paper presents a benchmark suite for evaluating behavior-based security mechanisms. Behavior-based mechanisms are used to protect computer systems from intrusion and detect malicious code embedded in legitimate applications. They complement signature-based mechanisms (e.g., anti-virus software) by tackling zero-day attacks whose signatures have not been added yet to the signature database, as well as polymorphous attacks that have no stable signatures.

In this work we present a benchmark suite of eight programs. All of these programs are legitimate applications, but we have designed them to be infected by malicious software. An evaluation framework is designed to infect, disinfect, build, and run the benchmark programs. This benchmark suite aims to help evaluate the effectiveness of various behavior-based defense mechanisms during different development stages, including prototyping, testing, and normal operation. We use this benchmark suite to evaluate a simple behavior-based security mechanism and report our findings.

▢▢ ▢▢▢R▢▢▢▢▢▢▢

▢▢▢▢e▢a▢▢or▢▢a▢ed ▢e▢▢r▢▢▢e▢▢a▢▢▢▢▢

Many host-based intrusion prevention systems [29, 34, 38] employ behavior-based analysis to protect an application running on a server from being hijacked. Most of these applications are known or highly suspected to horde security vulnerabilities, such as buffer overflows and format strings [21]. These systems use various methods to examine the actions taken by a program by inspecting library API activity and system calls. Actions that appear malicious, such as attempting a buffer overflow or opening a network connection in certain contexts, will trigger an alarm by the monitoring agents.

Over the past few years, spyware has become a pervasive problem [13, 16]. Many infections occur when spyware is piggybacked on top of popular software packages. Saroiu et al. [16] found that spyware is packaged with four of the ten most popular shareware and freeware software titles from C|Net's http://download.com/. Commercial security software vendors [28, 35, 30, 37] have developed a number of security products addressing this problem. All of these companies have emphasized that they detect spyware by observing system behavior and detecting abnormal activity from the norm.

Signature-based intrusion detection and anti-virus solutions fail to expose this class of exploitation and do not adapt well to even small changes in an exploit. A signature is a regular expression known a priori that matches the instruction sequence of the exploitation or the network packets presented in a specific attack [39]. Therefore, zero-days attacks that have not had a signature extracted yet, as well as polymorphous attacks, pose a great danger to these signature-based mechanisms. Behavior-based mechanisms aim to overcome these shortcomings and complement signature-based mechanisms with more adaptive and proactive protection. Instead of looking for fixed signatures in instruction sequences and network packet payloads, behavior-based approaches focus on detecting patterns at a higher level of abstraction. Ideally, the patterns are the inherent behavior associated with malicious activities and distinct from the normal behavior of legitimate programs. Evading a behavior-based protection mechanism normally requires a change in the logic of the malicious activity itself.

Gao et al. [6] investigated the design space of system-call-based program tracking, which is the technology behind many host-based anomaly detection and prevention systems. A detailed system call trace can be recorded and characterized to better understand the typical behavior of the program. By establishing a profile of normal behavior, an intrusion into the process will be detected when the system-call behavior deviates from this normal profile.

Edjlali et al. [4] presented a history-based access-control mechanism to mediate accesses to system resources from mobile code. Their idea was to maintain a selective history of the access requests made by individual programs and to use this history to differentiate between safe and potentially dangerous requests. Each program is categorized into one of several groups, whereas each of these groups contains a different profile of resource requests. The behavior of each program during the entire execution is also constantly monitored. The decision of whether to grant a resource request that the program makes depends on both its preassigned identity and its historical behavior during this execution, as well as additional criteria, such as the location where the program was loaded or the identity of its author/provider.

1.2 Security metrics and measurement

As behavior-based mechanisms become more commonly used, and the rules and analytics engine underlying these mechanisms become more sophisticated, we need a methodology to evaluate these security mechanisms. The evaluation could be (and, ideally should be) used both for testing these mechanisms during code development, and for the validation and product rankings.

Developing metrics to define security properties remains an ongoing research topic [5]. A number of approaches have been proposed to measure the value of a security product or technology, and to assess the level of security attained by the whole system [20, 32].

Kajava et al. [11] considered a range of criteria to qualify and quantify the degree of security attained. They summarized three major classes:

- *Risk analysis* is the process of estimating the possibility of individual exploitations, their impact on the system, and as well as the cost to mitigate the risk. Risk analysis considers the trade-off between cost and the level of protection, and is thought to be a good basis for any security evaluation [3].

- *Certification* involves decomposing the system into different classes based on design characteristics and security mechanisms. Standards organizations and commercial companies provide certification services to measure the level of confidence that can be assigned to the security features offered by a product [41, 31], or the degree of conformance of a security process to the established guidelines (e.g., ITIL [14], CMM [10] and COBIT [1]).

- *Penetration testing* provides statistics about the probability that an intrusion attack will be successful. For example, the WAVES project [42] standardizes the practice of penetration testing for Web applications.

There have also been efforts to employ multiple orthogonal criteria to quantify the value of the perceived security enhancement, and the cost associated with the enhancement. Gordon et al. [7] proposed a framework to use the concept of *insurance* to manage the risk of doing business in the Internet era. They also described how to evaluate and justify security-related investments. The criteria they used for their security evaluation includes the three elements just discussed.

There still remains no widely accepted way to measure and rank security properties. The difficulty of finding a common ground for evaluating various security mechanisms suggests that further work is needed before we can adopt an unified evaluation methodology for different categories of security mechanisms.

The goal of this paper is to describe a new benchmarking methodology to evaluate behavior-based security mechanisms. We present a benchmark suite composed of eight applications that are typically found in workstation/desktop environments. These applications are infected with a variety of malicious codes, that in turn, represent a broad spectrum of exploits. We demonstrate the utility of our benchmark suite by applying it to a simple behavior-based security mechanism. The rest of paper is organized as follows. We discuss the rationale of our benchmarking methodology for evaluating behavior-based security mechanisms in section 2. We then describe the suite of benchmarks we have created in section 3. In section 4, we use this benchmark suite to evaluate a simple behavior-based security mechanism and analyze the results. In section 5, we summarize the paper and discuss future directions for our work.

2. A CASE FOR BENCHMARKING BEHAVIOR-BASED SECURITY MECHANISMS

Benchmarking has been used widely in the field of computer architecture and system software development to evaluate the performance of a particular design or implementation. The basic idea behind benchmarking is to create a common ground of comparison for a certain category of targets. Normally a suite of applications is constructed to serve as this common ground. These applications reflect typical workloads running on a selected category of computer systems (e.g., servers) or a selected category of application software (e.g., database). The value of different design mechanisms is measured by obtaining performance metrics while running the suite. Benchmarking promotes the practice of quantitative analysis [8]. There have also been efforts to use benchmarking to evaluate properties other than performance, such as dependability [12].

One of the key challenges addressed by most security-related mechanisms is that they need to address a moving target. The activities and scenarios that may do harm to the system are unpredictable, and tend to change their form. It would seem that a benchmarking methodology might not be a good choice for evaluating security mechanisms, since there is no stable workload that can be used.

In spite of the differences between their various approaches, all the behavior-based mechanisms make a common claim that they can differentiate the behavior of the malicious code from the normal behavior of the program. Malicious behaviors are limited to several general categories, such as resource abuse, information tampering, and information leakage [16]. More and more of these attacks are being motivated to obtain financial gains [17]. This indicates that the malicious behavior that these mechanisms are trying to single out is limited, and is relatively stable. For these cases, benchmarking can be very useful. A benchmark suite that consists of representative workloads infected with representative malicious activities can provide a good test of behavior-based security mechanisms.

Our benchmarking approach diverges from the penetration testing either performed by third-party auditors and certification service providers [41, 31], or embodied in software packages which are composed of a set of penetration cases [42]. These differences include:

- The main purpose of penetration testing is to find security vulnerabilities in the targeted programs, while the goal of our benchmarking technology is to find out whether the analytics and rules behind behavior-based mechanisms are sufficient.

- Penetration testing can be very implementation specific. Whenever a exploit of a newly discovered vulnerability appears, this new penetration scenario must be added to the set of test cases. On the contrary, the collection of malicious behavior included in our benchmark suite is much less dependent upon individual exploits. Unless the entire strategy behind an exploit is different from those included in the benchmark suite, there is no need to update the benchmark suite with every newly discovered exploit.

- Last, our benchmarking methodology is complementary to commonly used audit and certification services. Designers and developers can benefit from our benchmark suite because it is more cost-effective and convenient to use to test new ideas and prototype products during the entire development cycle.

The anti-virus community has already tested the idea of benchmarking. Basically they combine the signatures of all the known (and some not widely known) exploits and see how many of them different anti-virus products can find. In a test performed by Virus Bulletin [40], 100% of their signatures were detected by all the tested anti-virus software. It should be apparent that it would be difficult to produce a meaningful comparison here. A 100% detection rate suggests that benchmarking may not be a good way to evaluate detection accuracy (i.e., effectiveness) of anti-virus technology.

Using our approach, we emphasize that it is behavior-based mechanisms that we propose to evaluate using benchmarking. Different types of security mechanisms may need different methods to be properly evaluated.

□ THE SECS□EC BEHAVIORA□ BENCHMARK SUITE

□.1 C□m□□nents □□t□e □enc□mar□ suite

We have developed a benchmark suite called *SecSpec*. The benchmark programs included in the suite, as well as the malicious code, are written in Java. The choice of language should not limit the scope of applying the benchmarking methodology, though the implementations of malicious behavior may need to be ported to another language and a new set of benchmark programs may need to selected.

We target a typical workstation/desktop computing environment when choosing the component programs for the benchmark suite. We include four types of applications and consider two particular programs from type.

Browsers: Jbrowser [24] and JXWB [26] are two simple and functional web browsers. They are simple because they do not possess elaborate features such as client-side plug-ins.

Editors: Jedit [33] and Jexit [25] are two full-blown editors. The feature richness of these two applications pose a great challenge to behavior-based security mechanisms.

Instant Messengers: BIM [23] and SimpleAIM [27] are two simple AOL instant messaging clients. SimpleAIM is console-based and BIM is GUI-based. Instant Messaging (IM) has become a serious application in both enterprise and personal desktop environments, and is also a favorite medium for spyware distribution [15].

Games: Computer games are a major channel for viruses to infect both enterprise and home desktops. Even games developed for mobile phones can be be infected with viruses [2]. We include two simple games, Tetris [36]

and AntiChess [22], to cover this category of applications.

In our suite, we cover five categories of malicious code. We arrive at this categorization based on the behaviors they present. Each category of malicious behavior includes one or more implementations. Table 1 lists our categorization of these malicious behaviors.

We have placed the implementations of the malicious behavior inside a single source file for easy maintenance. Different types of malicious behavior are implemented in separate functions. The execution of a particular malicious behavior is simply a call to the corresponding function(s). Specially-formatted comments are placed in the source code of the benchmark programs. These special comments are placeholders for the invocation of malicious behavior. To infect (or disinfect) the benchmark programs, we simply uncomment (or comment) these placeholders.

Malicious behavior type	Implementation(s)
1. Direct information leakage	Read local file and email out.
2. Indirect information leakage	Copy local file to user's webpage directory.
	Copy local file to /tmp.
	Change file permission bits.
3. Information tampering	Update .hosts file in home directory.
4. Direct resource abuse	Write a huge file to current directory.
	Crash a process.
5. Indirect resource abuse	Download remote code, put in the system startup folder or update system startup script.

Table 1: Categorization and implementation of malicious behavior

□.2 □□acement □□ma□ici□us c□de inside □enc□-mar□ □r□□rams

The location of malicious behavior inside a benchmark impacts the accuracy of behavior-based security mechanisms. When invoking malicious code at different locations, the malicious behavior will appear in different contexts. If we place the invocation of the malicious code such that it presents a similar library API call or system call profile as in the original application, the behavior-based mechanism will face a bigger challenge to do its job well. Previous studies [18, 43, 6] have demonstrated the viability of the mimicry attacks against host-based intrusion prevention systems. They engineered the attack code to confuse the detection agent by limiting the usage of library APIs and system calls to those that are also used by the application.

This could lead to a practice of choosing the location of the placeholders inside the benchmark program according to the similarity between the malicious code and the context of the benchmark program around the placeholders. However, we have focused on capturing more general application behavior instead of worrying about mimicing a specific low-level library API and system call profile. Our goal is not to defeat these security mechanisms, but instead, to evaluate their effectiveness. We want to measure the robustness of the logic and rules sets underlying these mechanisms when encountering potentially confusing information. We call this practice orthogonality-directed placement. The less orthogonal the malicious behavior and the surrounding context of benchmark are relative to one another, the larger the challenge that this benchmark suite poses to behavior-based mechanisms.

Different placement schemes demand different levels of understanding of benchmark programs. The minimum level of understanding is to make sure the insertion of placeholders does not break the original code. We have experimented with two placement schemes:

Random placement: Beyond the minimum requirement of not breaking benchmark programs, our random placement makes sure that the malicious code will appear in at least two types of locations: at a location where it will definitely appear on the execution path; and at a location where it may or may not appear on the execution path, depending on some particular run time events. We position the placeholders in the startup or termination section to emulate the first scenario and in the user interface event handling section to emulate the second scenario.

Orthogonality-directed placement: This requires us to compute the degree of similarity of the program behavior and the malicious behavior. Our approach is to classify both the benchmark programs and malicious code to obtain four general categories of behavior: network oriented, file system oriented, mixed or neither. We then mix them together according to the extent of overlap between behaviors in these four categories.

Among the four types of benchmark programs, we classify IM clients as network-oriented, editors as file system-oriented, browsers as mixed, and games as neither. Among the five types of malicious behaviors, we classify indirect information leakage, information tampering, and direct resource abuse as file system oriented, direct information leakage and indirect resource abuse as mixed.

		\multicolumn{5}{c}{Malicious behavior}				
\multicolumn{2}{c}{Benchmark programs}	1	2	3	4	5
Browsers	Jbrowser [24]	Δ				
	JXWB [26]	Δ				
Editors	Jedit [33]		Δ	Δ	Δ	
	Jext [25]		Δ	Δ	Δ	
IMs	BIM [23]					Δ
	SimpleAIM [27]					Δ
Games	AntiChess [22]	Δ	Δ	Δ	Δ	Δ
	Tetris [36]	Δ	Δ	Δ	Δ	Δ

Table 2: Placement of malicious code in applications

An example of an orthogonality-directed placement would look like Table 2. Note that the numbering of the malicious behavior corresponds to the numbering given in Table 1. All of the placeholders are inserted manually.

□.□ User inter□ace □□t□e □enc□mar□ suite

The user interface to the benchmark suite is provided via the Apache Ant build tool [19]. We provide four build targets for each benchmark program:

1. Infect: Insert malicious code into a benchmark program by uncommenting the placeholders in the source code.

2. Disinfect: Restore a benchmark program to the clean version by commenting out these placeholders.

3. Jar: Build a single jar file of a benchmark program, including all the class files, supporting files, as well as the library package that implements the malicious behavior.

4. Run: Run a benchmark program, generating the command line and running the benchmark program.

□ E□□ERIMENTATION

□.1 A Hist□ry-Based Access C□ntr□□

To test our benchmark suite, we have implemented a history-based access control mechanism based on the work done in [4]. This is an example of a behavior-based security mechanism.

The basic idea of this mechanism is that a running program is constantly categorized into a series of contexts according to the resource requests it makes during execution. Each context includes a number of Java permissions [9] which could permit access to the guarded resource. This series of contexts is the historical profile of the program and determines whether the future resource request should be granted or rejected.

The relationship between different contexts are either cooperative or non-cooperative. A policy file explicitly specifies the cooperative relationship. Permission to a new resource request can be granted only under one of the following two scenarios:

- The program's historical profile already includes a context that contains this permission,

- The context that needs to be added to grant this permission must be held in a cooperative relationship with the program's historical profile.

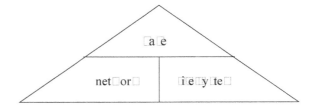

Figure 1: Contexts provided in a history-based access control mechanism.

We have implemented a simple version of the history-based access control. More sophisticated mechanisms can be implemented in a similar way. However, this simple mechanism helps us to locate where the problem is when this it succumbs to an exploit.

The mechanism we implemented has three contexts: base, network, and file system, as shown in Figure 1. The base context includes the most restrictive permissions, network and file system grant all network-related and all file system-related permissions, respectively, which are thought of as resources susceptible to attack.

When a resource access request is made, the base context is searched first for permissions that could imply allowing this access. Whenever a permission in the base context can service the need, two things will happen: the base context will be added to this program's historical profile; and the search process stops, even if permission in either the network or the file system context may also allow this access.

Figure 2 shows an outline of the policy file for this simple history-based access control mechanism. Note the priority of the `base` context over the `network` and `file_system` contexts is indicated by the fact that the specification of the `base` context precedes the other two in the policy file.

□.2 E□a□uati□n

We carried out our experiment in two stages: (1) first profiling clean benchmarks; (2) testing the security mechanism against infected benchmarks.

During the profiling stage, a clean version of each benchmark is run once. We have modified the security manager to intercept all resource requests. Permissions that are required to run a clean benchmark are granted and recorded. We then create the policy file for the history-based access control mechanism. We organize the gathered permissions into the base context, and try to make some too permissive permission more fine-grained, in order to minimize the risk exposure of the base context. We make sure the clean version of each benchmark can run without having to be categorized into either a network or file system context.

During the testing stage, we run the infected version of each benchmark. The security manager is loaded upon the startup of the JVM and uses the policy file established from the profiling stage to apply history-based access control.

Table 3 shows our experimental results. In this experiment, we randomly placed the five types of malicious behavior inside each benchmark program.

Attack stopped√/missed×		Malicious behavior				
Benchmark programs		1	2	3	4	5
Browsers	Jbrowser [24]	×	×	×	×	×
	JXWB [26]	×	×	×	×	×
Editors	Jedit [33]	×	×	×	×	×
	Jext [25]	×	×	×	×	×
IMs	BIM [23]	√	√	√	√	√
	SimpleAIM [27]	√	√	√	√	√
Games	AntiChess [22]	√	×	×	×	√
	Tetris [36]	√	×	×	×	√

Table 3: Malicious behaviors inside the benchmark suite stopped or missed by the history-based access control. A √ indicates the failure of this instance of attack (being stopped); A × indicates the success of this attack (being missed).

Before running this experiment, we anticipated that holes in Java permission could cause trouble for our security mechanism. Also, we suspected that the permissions gathered in the profiling stage are not fine-grained enough (i.e., we may be too permissive). The analysis of our testing results confirmed our suspicions. In addition, we uncovered an instance of sloppy coding practices in terms of security.

1. The permissions inside the contexts of this history-based mechanism are not sufficiently fine-grained.

   In the two games, the security mechanism stopped all network-based attacks, yet failed to detect any file system-based attacks. The problem is that the base context cannot identify all of the file system access requests during the testing stage. Therefore, the program has to be categorized as file system context to continue running. Once the file system context is added into the historical profile of the program, any file system-based attack can succeed in this program.

   One possible remedy would be to add a fine-grained file system permission into the file system context. Another choice would be to profile the program more extensively so that every possible file system access permission required by the clean version of the program could be added into the base context. However, this second approach has two shortcomings: Complete coverage during profiling is not always realistic; and we may not be able to to profile every program before deployment.

   The two browsers are wide open to any attack. The network-related and file system-related permissions included in the base context are sufficient for all the attacks to succeed.

   Although we characterized editors as file system oriented, the Jext program needs network access to provide the functionality of viewing a URL and editing the file denoted by the URL. The execution of this functionality during the profiling stage has already granted some network access permissions to the base context. As such, all network-based attacks in our benchmark suite can also succeed.

2. The information provided by Java is insufficient. It appears that the history-based access control mechanism did a perfect job in protecting the two IM clients. However the interpretation of the logging messages indicates these two mixed attacks (i.e., direct information leakage and indirect resource abuse) were stopped only because of the portion that needs file system access. The portions of these two attacks that have access to the network were not stopped by the mechanism.

   This time we do not believe the problem lies in the coarseness of the network access permissions. After all, it is impossible to specify every possible instance of a network connection. This suggests other information, such as the producer of the destination address of a network connection (binary or console input)) should be collected and analyzed to detect potential malicious behavior.

3. It may not be wise to count on other programs to fully appreciate and correctly utilize the security capabilities of a high-level system like Java. Java provides a good interface to mediate access to various resources: permission-based capabilities, as well as a security manager mechanism that intercepts each request to a resource to check granted capabilities. New security mechanisms such as this history-based access control mechanism can be readily implemented in this

```
context base
{
    permission java.net.SocketPermission "vanders.ece.neu.edu", "resolve";
    permission java.net.SocketPermission "localhost:*", "connect,listen, resolve";
    permission java.net.NetPermission "specifyStreamHandler", "";
    permission java.io.FilePermission "/home/student/dye/.jedit/-", "read,write,delete";
    permission java.lang.reflect.ReflectPermission "*", "";
    permission java.awt.AWTPermission "*", "";
    permission java.lang.RuntimePermission "*", "";
    permission java.util.PropertyPermission "*", "read,write";
    permission java.util.logging.LoggingPermission "control", "";

    ....
};
context file_system
{
    permission java.io.FilePermission "<<ALL FILES>>", "read,write,execute,delete";
};
context network
{
    permission java.net.SocketPermission "*", "connect,listen,accept,resolve";
};
CooperatingContexts
{
    file_system
    base
};
CooperatingContexts
{
    network
    base
};
```

Figure 2: Skeleton of the policy file for the history-based access control mechanism.

infrastructure. However, this mechanism can be rendered powerless if the application is not well-formed. For instance, a library function call inside Jedit simply requests `java.security.AllPermission` upon program startup. Once this permission is granted, our security mechanism (based on Java permissions and Java security manager) cannot offer any help. This is the real reason why our security mechanism cannot protect this program against any attack, even though the case looks exactly the same as in the cases of the two browsers and the Jext.

This suggests that when we have little confidence in the code quality of an application, behavior-based security mechanisms may have to gather lower-level information to discern the behavior, even though a more convenient higher-level infrastructure is available.

We should note that these problems all apply to a wider range of security mechanisms. We expect to expose more design problems if similar benchmarking processes are applied to more sophisticated mechanisms.

□ CONC□USION AND FUTURE □ ORK

In this paper, we have presented a benchmarking methodology to evaluate the effectiveness of behavior-based security mechanisms. We have developed a benchmark suite and designed an evaluation framework. We exercised our suite by applying it to a simple history-based access control mechanism. We discussed the findings of our experiment. The experience and the results suggest that benchmarking is a viable approach to evaluate the effectiveness of behavior-based security mechanisms.

In the future, we plan to implement a set of benchmarks using other mainstream languages such as C and C++. This will allow us to evaluate some commercial behavior-based security mechanisms. In the long term, we plan to explore more sophisticated algorithms for malicious code placement. We also plan to look into whether we can use binary instrumentation to insert malicious code in binary form directly into an application.

□ REFERENCES

[1] Information Systems Audit and Control Association. Control Objectives for Information and Related Technology (COBIT).

[2] BBC. Game Virus Bites Mobile Phones. `http:`

//news.bbc.co.uk/1/hi/technology/3554514.stm.

[3] Jeff Crume. *Inside Internet Security: What Hackers Don't Want You to Know*, chapter 4, pages 38–50. Addison-Wesley, 2000.

[4] Guy Edjlali, Anurag Acharya, and Vipin Chaudhary. History-based Access Control for Mobile Code. In *Proceedings of the 5th Conference on Computer & Communications Security*, pages 103–118, 1998.

[5] Marshall D. Abrams et al. Position Papers. In *Proceedings of the 1st Workshop on Information-Security-System Rating and Ranking*, pages 35–40, 2001.

[6] Debin Gao, Michael K. Reiter, and Dawn Song. On Gray-Box Program Tracking for Anomaly Detection. In *Proceedings of the 13th USENIX Security Symposium*, pages 103–118, 2004.

[7] Lawrence A. Gordon, Martin P. Loeb, and Tashfeen Sahail. A Framework for Using Insurance for Cyber-Risk Management. *Communications of the ACM*, 46(3), March 2003.

[8] John L. Hennessy and David A. Patterson. *Computer Architecture: A Quantitative Approach*. Morgan Kaufmann, 2002.

[9] Permissins in the Java™ 2 SDK. http://java.sun.com/j2se/1.4.2/docs/guide/security/.

[10] Information Technology—Systems Security Engineering—Capability Maturity Model (SSE-CMM). ISO/IEC 21827.

[11] Jorma Kajava and Reijo Savola. Towards Better Information Security Management by Understanding Security Metrics and Measuring Processes. In *Proceedings of the European University Information Systems (EUNIS) Conference*, Manchester, U.K., 2005.

[12] Philip Koopman and Henrique Madeira. Papers. In *Proceedings of Workshop on Dependability Benchmarking*, 2002.

[13] David Moll. Testimony on Spyware in Congress. http://commerce.senate.gov/hearings/testimony.cfm?id=1496&wit_id=4255.

[14] U.K. Office of Government Commerce. IT Infrastructure Library (ITIL).

[15] Paul F. Roberts. Instant Messaging: A New Front in the Malware War. http://www.eweek.com/article2/0,1759,1818611,00.asp.

[16] Stefan Saroiu, Steven D. Gibble, and Henry M. Levey. Measurement and Analysis of Spyware in a University Environment. In *Proceedings of the 1st ACM/USENIX Symposium on Networked Systems Design and Implementation (NSDI)*, pages 29–31, San Francisco, CA, USA, 2004.

[17] Bruce Schneier. Attack Trends: 2004 and 2005. *ACM Queue, Special Issue on Security: A War Without End*, 3(5), June 2005.

[18] Kymie M. C. Tan, John McHugh, and Kevin S. Killourhy. Hiding Intrusions: From the Abnormal to the Normal and Beyond. In *IH '02: Revised Papers from the 5th International Workshop on Information Hiding*, pages 1–17, London, UK, 2003. Springer-Verlag.

[19] Apache Ant. http://ant.apache.org/.

[20] Common Criteria Evaluation & Validation Scheme (CCEVS). http://niap.nist.gov/cc-scheme. National Institute of Standards and Technology.

[21] National Vulnerability Database. http://nvd.nist.gov/.

[22] AntiChess. http://sourceforge.net/projects/antichess/.

[23] BIM. http://sourceforge.net/projects/bim-im/.

[24] Jbrowser. http://sourceforge.net/projects/jbrowser/.

[25] Jext. http://sourceforge.net/projects/jext/.

[26] JXWB. http://sourceforge.net/projects/jxwb/.

[27] SimpleAIM. http://sourceforge.net/projects/simpleaim/.

[28] WebSense. http://ww2.websense.com/.

[29] Cisco Security Agent 4.5. http://www.cisco.com/.

[30] NOD32. http://www.eset.com/.

[31] ICSA Labs. http://www.icsalabs.com/.

[32] Information Technology Security Evaluation Criteria (ITSEC). http://www.itsec.gov.uk/. Commission for the European Communities.

[33] Jedit. http://www.jedit.org/.

[34] McAfee Entercept 5.1. http://www.networkassociates.com/.

[35] PC Tools. http://www.pctools.com/.

[36] Tetris. http://www.percederberg.net/home/java/tetris/tetris.html.

[37] QRadar. http://www.q1labs.com/.

[38] Sana Security Primary Response 3.0. http://www.sanasecurity.com/.

[39] Snort. http://www.snort.com/.

[40] Virus Bulletin. http://www.virusbtn.com/.

[41] Checkmark. http://www.westcoastlabs.org/.

[42] WAVES (Web Application Vulnerability and Error Scanner). http://www.openwaves.net/.

[43] David Wagner and Paolo Soto. Mimicry Attacks on Host-Based Intrusion Detection Systems. In *CCS '02: Proceedings of the 9th ACM Conference on Computer and Communications Security*, pages 255–264, New York, NY, USA, 2002. ACM Press.

Testing and Evaluation of Virus Detectors for Handheld Devices

Jose Andre Morales, Peter J. Clarke, Yi Deng
School of Computing and Information Sciences
Florida International University
Miami, Fl 33199
{ jmora009, clarkep, deng } @cis.fiu.edu

ABSTRACT

The widespread use of personal digital assistant and smartphones should be securing these devices a high priority. Yet little attention has been placed on protecting handheld devices against virus. Currently available antivirus software for handheld devices is in ... At this stage, the opportunity exists for the evaluation and improvement of current solutions. By pinpointing weaknesses in the current antivirus software, improvement can be made to properly protect these devices from all threats made of virus. This research evaluates four currently available antivirus solution for handheld devices. A formal virus transformation that provides transformation traceability is presented ... the modification of source code of a known virus for handheld devices. The testing techniques ... are detailed herein. Our testing showed the ... research identify the virus. The virus will be undetected and capable of spreading, infecting and causing damage.

Categories and Subject Descriptors

D.2.5 [Software Engineering]: Testing and Debugging; D.2.8 [Software Engineering]: Metrics — *performance measures;* D.4.6 [Operating Systems]: Security and Protection — *Invasive Software*

General Terms

Measurement, Performance, Reliability, Security, Verification.

Keywords

Anti-virus, malware, black-box testing, virus, mirror, handheld, pda, windows mobile, smartphone, windows ce

1. INTRODUCTION

On June 15, 2004, the first computer virus infecting handheld devices was identified [25]. The first virus to infect handheld devices running the Windows Mobile operating system was released July 17, 2004 [21]. This was the beginning of a new era for the virus and antivirus community. At the time there were little if any antivirus solution available. An overwhelming majority of users were vulnerable to any possible virus attack. In a reactionary effort, security companies released antivirus solution for the infected devices that only protected against the specific virus. Still to day many handheld devices do not have some form of antivirus software installed.

This research evaluates current antivirus solution for handheld devices with the objective of identifying problems in their detection mechanism. To achieve this objective we introduce a formal model to represent virus transformation and we use the model in the generation of test cases. This model provides detailed traceability of the transformation process of any virus. The transformed virus can be precisely ordered by creation time and transformation type. The approach taken was to create test cases that are modifications of an already identified virus and load them into the handheld running the antivirus software. That is, we wanted to test the detection accuracy of the antivirus software against virus modification. Specifically, the test were designed with the goal of producing a false negative, which occurs when an infected object is not detected as infected, by the virus detector. Testing virus detector for production of false negative has been extensively performed in [1, 2] and while we documented ... therefore this research focused only on testing handheld devices. A high false negative rate would reveal virus detection weakness in the software. The test environment consisted of a Pocket PC running the Microsoft Windows Mobile operating system and the antivirus software. The tested antivirus software is specifically designed for this platform and are currently available to the public.

To our knowledge, this research is the first to evaluate current antivirus solution for the Windows Mobile platform and for handheld devices in general. The main goal and contribution by this research can help play the foundation for future study and for virus detection for handheld devices. The result of this ...

[1] Smartphones and personal digital assistant will be collectively referred to as handheld devices or handhelds throughout this paper.

...or can be a public vulnerability database, such as the National Vulnerability Database [19]. This research also provides insight on the application of testing methodologies to a new platform in the emerging area of handheld devices. *Currently there is no standard set of test cases for virus detectors on this platform.* Testing related organizations like icar.co and antitest.org also have not yet addressed this issue. The test cases created here can be applied to the development of a standard set of test cases for this platform and other devices.

In the next section we overview the terminology used in the paper. Section 3 describes related work on testing virus detectors. Section 4 describes a model for virus transformation and the test categories used to generate the test cases. Section 5 describes the test suite performance and Section 6 covers results. Finally we conclude in Section 7.

2. BACKGROUND

2.1 Computer Viruses   A computer virus is defined as a program that copies a possibly evolved version of itself [2]. Computer viruses have become very sophisticated in detection avoidance, as well as spreading and causing damage. A highly populated taxonomy of viruses exist with each classification having its own challenges for successful detection and removal [2]. Today viruses are regarded as a real global threat and likened to a real weapon namely those bent on creating large scale interruption of everyday life [1, 10].

2.2 Virus Detectors   The problem of virus detection was studied by Cohen which showed that detecting a virus is not decidable [2]. Many detection algorithms have been presented [2], each with its advantages and disadvantages. Virus detection can be classified as one of two forms *signature based* and *behavior based* [2]. Signature based detectors work by searching through objects for a specific sequence of bytes that uniquely identify a specific version of a virus. Behavior based detectors identify an object as being viral or not by scrutinizing the execution behavior of a program [23]. Behavior based detection is used by many including the authors as a key to the future of virus detection [3, 15, 17] because of its ability to detect unknown viruses.

Handheld Devices   A handheld device can be described as a pocket sized device with computing capabilities. Two types of handheld devices are relevant to this paper the personal digital assistant, also called a pda, and the smartphone. A pda is a digital personal organizer that includes a contact list, calendar event, voice recorder, notes, and more. A smartphone can be described as a cellular phone integrated with a pda. Both of these types of handheld share common limitations like limited screen size, variable battery life, small storage space, operating systems installed with finite resources and reduced processing capabilities [8, 27]. These limitations may not allow for antivirus software to be as powerful as those found in laptop or desktop PCs. Signature databases and detection functionalities are limited in size and scope. This can possibly result in more viruses being able to easily spread and avoid detection in an environment with weak security. Some handheld device security issues have been previously addressed in [5, 6, 7, 13, 29].

Evolution of Virus Detectors   The evolution of virus detectors has to move parallel with the release of viruses in a reactionary manner [12]. A new virus with new techniques...

...were identified, antivirus researchers are then to include the new tactic in their software [18, 2]. This evolution has produced a learning curve, with virus authors an antivirus researcher as both teacher and student. Antivirus companies need to develop security solutions for these devices that defend against the types of virus seen in the past without having to go through the same learning curve for a second time.

2.4 Software Testing   In this paper we use a black-box approach to test the antivirus solution for handheld devices. Black-box testing is an approach that generates test data solely from the application specification [1]. Since the software under test is proprietary, we employ the end-user view of the software as our specification. This specification is *the detection of objects infected with a virus.* There are several techniques used to generate test cases based on the specification of a software type [30]. Two of these techniques are *input space partitioning, and random testing [30].* Partition testing uses domain analysis to partition the input-output behavior space into domains such that any two test points chosen in a domain generate the same output [20]. Random testing involves the selection of test points in the input space via a probability distribution over the input space [1]. To generate the input data for our test cases we use a combination of input space partitioning and random selection of test points. Due to the limited access to the specification of the antivirus software, we informally apply partition testing and random testing. We intentionally apply these techniques using the results of previous studies in testing antivirus software.

3. RELATED WORK

This research is motivated by the work done by Christodorescu and Jha [1]. Their research proposed methods of testing malware detectors based on program obfuscation [2]. They previously identified ways to test the resilience of commercially available antivirus software for PCs. Christodorescu and Jha addressed obfuscation in their work [1] the resistance of malware detectors to obfuscation is known as malware [2] can a virus author identify the algorithm used in a malware detector based on obfuscation of the malware. The approach they used to answer the detection involved the generation of test cases using program obfuscation, the development of a signature extraction algorithm, and the application of their methodology to three commercial virus scanners. The results of their work indicate that the commercial virus scanners available for PCs are not resilient to common obfuscation transformation. We use a similar approach to test the virus detection ability for handheld devices. Unlike the work by Christodorescu and Jha [1], we are limited by the number of viruses available for handheld devices. This limitation is based on the fact that virus authors have still only started to write viruses targeting handheld devices. We experiment using similar transformation on the source code of the malware to generate test cases.

Mar[ ] present a comprehensive methodology line for testing anti-malware software for the area of worms. Mar claims that many of the approaches used to test anti-malware software in research do not translate into appropriate testing strategies for malware in the wild than those in choice. He further states that the focus of testing for the area of worms should be to create tests that are able to act appropriate. That is, tests that focus on known-good and non-accepted, viral infection and false positive testing of the anti-malware...

software project. Although this article is targeted for data security managers and professional testers, the outline procedure that should be taken when performing anti-virus software testing in any environment. The work done by Mar... ...a...e...a reference guideline for this research. Other relevant research on the ...ffect of testing virus detector can be found in [9, 11]...

5 TESTING AND EVALUATION

In this section we present a formal model for the transformation of virus and show how this model is used to generate the test cases for ...or...tly. ...escription ...o each of the six test categories are also given.

5.1 Formal Model of Virus Transformations

As previously stated, a virus we define as a program that copies a policy... ...erion of site [2]. A virus $v \in V$ where V is the set of all possible viruses, entering its detection and transformation stage R_i where one or more policy ...e... copies of v, written v', are produced and copied to the location ....ation [1]. Success... transformation occurs when v' has preserved the original intended detection behavior XB of v (see equation [2])... ...h ...we have the following:

$$R_i (p_j, v, s) \equiv p_{ij} (v, s) = v' \qquad [1]$$

R_i is the currently running transformation instance. $p_{ij} \in P$ is the specific type of transformation where $P = \{..., ..., B, L, C\}$ for ...e...a...p...B...ean ...titution ...e...ection [2] for ...cription of ... the ...a...e ...i...ho...a...a...e representing the number of transformation that have occurred, the current value of i in the ith transformation to have taken place. j ...ho... the value representing the number of times the jth occurrence, a specific transformation type p has occurred, in ...p...an... $j \ge 3$ that ...ean...that the transformation type p has been used in 3 transformation up to this point. v is the vir... to be transformed, s is an element that provides p the detail for a specific transformation. For example i... p... B then ...ay contain the line number to ...titute and the new line to ...or substitution (see section [2] for detail... s for each transformation type. v' is the transformed version of v. When R_i occurs, the operation ...ay in dependent from every other occurrence of R. The vir... as an input by R_i... ay be the ...a...e i... it is the vir... currently executing that in one of R_i. The output of R_i, written v', is always a possible version of v. The number of v' that is produced ...als to the value of i. In each occurrence of R, the only input that may change is the information held in s. Thus the output v' of two occurrence of R may be the ...a...e if s is unchanged in both operation and the ...a...e transformation type p is ...e...

$$If (XB(v') = XB(v)) \; Then \; R_i (p_j, v, s) = Success$$

$$Else \; R_i (p_j, v, s) = Failure \qquad [2]$$

v' can be identify be written as v_{ijk} where k is the ... y... or the transformation type ...e... in a specific transformation R_i. k is a...le to differentiate the ...a...e of j for each transformation type p. ...hi... i... nece...ary to illustrate that there are ...ltiple instance of j, one for each transformation type p that i... ...e... each j has it... o... value representing the j number of times p has been used. Therefore, if $i = 2$ and $k = C$, we ...no... that this is the ...econd time a compression is ...ed. A vir... v that is in the ...one ...e...ection of site... during this ...e...ection [5] transformation occurred. The transformation type... ...e... here [1] ...titution of ...or...ce code, [2]...

compression, [3]... insertion of ...tra... ...o...rce code and [4] ...a...e renaming. Using the notation above, we can for...ate this ta... ...o...o...:

$$R_1 (B_1, v, s) \equiv B_{11} (v, s) = v_{11B}$$

$$R_2 (C_1, v, s) \equiv C_{21} (v, s) = v_{21C}$$

$$R_3 (C_2, v, s) \equiv C_{32} (v, s) = v_{32C}$$

$$R_4 (H_1, v, s) \equiv H_{41} (v, s) = v_{41H}$$

$$R_5 (L_1, v, s) \equiv L_{51} (v, s) = v_{51L}$$

...e...can...ee from this notation that placing the output v' in order of creation i... ...i...ple. ...he notation facilitate identifying each vir...v' by or... of creation an input transformation type. ...ote that vir... v_{21C} an... v_{32C} ...ay have been transformed the ...a...e or ...i...erently from one another. ...hi... i..., a... previously note... ...ependent on the information held in s.

A vir... detector written D, is a software program meant to detect an... re...o...e vir... before infecting a computer sy...te... [2]. ...hen... detection is co...plete only one of two outcome can re...lt. ...he detection ...a... ...ucce...s... or there ...a...a fai...re. A ...ucce...s... detection i...plie... the correct identification of a vir... infected o...ect O_v. ...hi... i...plie... that the o...ect O is infected with a vir... v. ...hat i..., the ...e...ence o...it representing v i... contained within the ...e...ence o...it representing the o...ect O. ...hi... vir... code or the ...e...ence o...it ... o... the o...ect O. ...he o...ect co...ld ...e...a...i...e, ...an a...re in... ...e...ory, or ...o...e other information ...tore... in a computer sy...te... A...o...ect O are a...ed the non-vira... ...efore detection ...tart... ...e... e...pre...s this i... ...ea...a...o...o...:

$$v \; is \; a \; subsequence \; of \; O \; iff \; O \; is \; infected \; with \; v \qquad [3]$$

$$if \; v \; is \; a \; subsequence \; of \; O \; then \; O \; transforms \; to \; O_v \qquad [4]$$

$$D(O) = Success \; implies \; v \; is \; a \; subsequence \; of \; O \qquad [5]$$

A fai...e... detection pro...ce one of two o...tco...e a fa...e positive, FP, or a fa...e negative, FN. A fa...e positive occur... when a non-vira... o...ect i... detected a... ...eing vira... A fa...e negative occur... when a vir... infecte... o...ect i... not detected a... ...eing vira... A fa...a...a o...nt to ...a...e positive i... to ...e...a...re, ...t ...a...e negative ...o... the ...o...ce ...a...ay... ...herefore...

$$D(O) = FP \; falsely \; implies \; v \; is \; a \; subsequence \; of \; O \; for \; some$$
$$virus \; v \qquad [6]$$

$$D(O_v) = FN \; D \; fails \; to \; recognize \; that \; v \; is \; a \; subsequence \; of \; O$$
$$for \; a \; specific \; virus \; v \qquad [7]$$

...ote [7] a...e... that the o...ect i... a...ready infected with a vir... th...i...ti...ying the ...e...o...the ...y... o...o... O_v.

5.2 Test Categories

...he te...t ca...e generate..., ...ing a non-...trict approach to ...inp...t ...pace partitioning an... ...ran...o... te...ting, can ...e cla...ified in si... categorie... ...here are tran...po...ition of ...o...rce code, in...ertion of ...tra... ...o...rce code, ...titution of ...o...rce code, ...a...e renaming an... co...pre...ion of the ...ir...ect... ...a...e. ...he ... categorie... were cho...en... ...e... to the ...acilitation ...each one give... ...ir... detector to pro...ce a ...a...e negative [1]... ...he...e categorie... are a...o characteri...tic of poly...orphi... [18, 2] an... ...eta...orphi... [2], po...er...l technique... ...e...... y vir... a...thor... ...e...t ca...e i...ple...entation of each category are pre...ente... in ...ection 5.2. ...

1. Transposition of Source Code. Transposition is the rearrangement of statements in the source code. This alters the virus code by reorganizing its physical appearance, yet still preserves the original intended execution behavior. Transposition can be done randomly or in specific areas. The whole body of the source code or only pieces of it can be transposed as long as the original intended execution behavior is preserved. Applying 1 we have:

$$R_i(T_j, v, s) \equiv T_{ij}(v, s) = v_{ijT} \qquad (8)$$

where p indicates transposition and s provides the line number of the source code to transpose. Transposition can result in changing the area of source code that is used as the signature by the virus detector. This results in a change in the byte sequence of the detectable portion of the virus. The transposition can also result in an increase in the byte size of the virus executable. This is due to the addition of code that preserves the original intended execution behavior. The rearrangement and transposition of source code as possible cause of a virus detector producing a false negative.

2. Insertion of Trash Source Code. This category inserts new code into the original source code. This new code consists of instructions that do nothing to change, alter or affect the intended behavior of the original source code. It does, in some cases, change the byte size of the detectable portion of the virus. By changing the byte size of the detectable, some virus detectors may produce a false negative more easily. This occurs in the case where the detector uses the length of the entire virus as part of the detection process. Such a change in this length could result in the detector misreading the virus. Note that the newly inserted code does not is inconsequential as long as it does not change the original intended behavior of the source code. Using rule 1, trash source code insertion is presented as:

$$R_i(H_j, v, s) \equiv H_{ij}(v, s) = v_{ijH} \qquad (9)$$

where p denotes trash insertion. s shows the trash code to be inserted and the source code location of where to insert them.

(Substitution of Source Code) Here, some lines of source code is replaced with different lines of source code. The lines of source code used for replacement are not copied from other areas of the code only. The replacement lines can be the same size as the original. They can also be deliberately shortened or lengthened. This is done to manipulate the overall byte size of the virus executable. The lines that are to be replaced cannot be in an area that can disrupt the original intended execution behavior. This implies that this process cannot be random. Careful selection of lines to replace can assure preservation of execution behavior. Applying 1 produces as below:

$$R_j(B_j, v, s) \equiv B_{ij}(v, s) = v_{ijB} \qquad (10)$$

p specifies substitution and s retains which line to replace and the line to replace them with. A virus detector can produce a false negative under this category for one of two possible reasons. First, the substitute lines can change the source code used as a signature by the detector for a given virus. Second, a size issue before, if the byte size is not preserved it could cause the detector to identify it as benign. This occurs in cases where the length of the virus is used in detection.

(Label Renaming) This category involves the substitution of a label name in the source code for a new name. A label is synonymous with a procedure or function name in a high level language. The label is a pointer to an address space where the instructions to execute are located. A label therefore points to a set of instructions that are always executed when the label is referenced. The new label can accept the label byte file as the original one and also can be purposely changed to a different file. In addition, the corresponding call to the label is also updated to ensure original intended execution behavior. The label name is chosen for substitution should be those that reference blocks of instructions essential to the virus execution such as inducing a file to infect, opening a file for infection and infecting the file. A virus detector can produce a false negative in this category only when a signature includes a label or a call to a label that has been modified. If no labels are included in the virus signature and the length of the entire virus is not used for detection, the possibility of a false negative is greatly reduced. This category is presented as below through 1:

$$R_i(L_j, v, s) \equiv L_{ij}(v, s) = v_{ijL} \qquad (11)$$

where p L signifies label renaming and s should a list to the label name to replace and then the new name to replace them with.

(Compression of a Virus Executable) This category is the compression of the original virus executable. Compression is done by a commercial product or private software belonging to the virus author. The original intended execution behavior is fully preserved. When a virus transforms it can come into a new version of itself that is then compressed. This new version makes no modification to alter the execution and it is originally intended. A virus detector can produce a false negative under this category by failing to match the virus signature. The compression may create a new byte sequence in achieving an overall byte size reduction. This in turn may cause the source code used for the virus signature to become completely modified and thus detection is also not possible. Virus compression can be simply presented as below:

$$R_i(C_j, v, s) \equiv C_{ij}(v, s) = v_{ijC} \qquad (12)$$

p C represents compression and s should the file name for the compressed version.

TEST IMPLEMENTATION

As of the writing of this paper there were only two known viruses for the Windows Mobile platform, WinCE.InfoJack.A and Backdoor.BraDor.A [21, 22]. Of the two viruses there were only able to conduct testing with one of them, WinCE.InfoJack.A. Although the source code for both of these is readily available to the public [21, 22], it is the only one whose available source code can be assembled and executed. The test virus consists of 531 lines of source code. This virus was created as a proof of concept by the virus author Matter Grey of the virus writer group 29A. It exploited some of the vulnerabilities already present in the Windows Mobile platform. It is written in the ARM processor assembly language.

.1 Testing Environment

Four commercially available antivirus products for the Windows Mobile platform were tested – Norton, Avast!, Kaspersky, and

Airscanner.com. ▯▯The ▯han▯he ▯▯▯e▯ice ▯▯e▯▯or▯e▯ting ▯a▯a▯ ▯o▯hi▯a▯2032S▯▯oc▯et▯C▯r▯nning ▯ in▯o▯▯Mo▯i▯e▯2002▯ ▯er▯ion▯3.0.11171, ▯▯i▯11178▯▯ith ▯▯▯phone ▯▯nctionality▯ pro▯i▯e▯ ▯y Sprint ▯CS. ▯▯he ▯centra▯ proce▯▯ing ▯nit i▯ the A▯M▯ proce▯▯or ▯SA1110. ▯▯he ▯▯perating ▯Sy▯te▯ ▯o▯the ▯C ▯▯e▯▯a▯ ▯▯in▯o▯▯▯▯er▯ice pac▯ ▯2. Be▯ore ▯a▯▯ini▯tering the ▯te▯t ca▯e▯ a ▯contro▯ te▯t ▯a▯ ▯gi▯en. ▯▯he ▯origina▯ ▯ir▯▯ ▯a▯ ▯▯e▯ ▯or▯ ▯etection ▯to a▯▯▯re each anti▯ir▯▯ pro▯ect ▯properly i▯enti▯ie▯ it. ▯▯

Each of the ten test cases were allowed to fully execute to assure that infection of the system was occurring. Thus showing the original intended execution behavior of the virus had been preserved after modifications was made.

▯.2 Descri▯ti▯n ▯▯▯ Test ▯Cases▯

▯he ▯te▯t ca▯e▯ ▯ere intro▯▯ce▯ to the ▯han▯he ▯▯▯e▯ice ▯ia the ▯ ▯synchroni▯ation ▯▯nctionality ▯ro▯▯a▯C. ▯▯he ▯er▯ion ▯▯e▯ here▯ ▯a▯ ▯Micro▯o▯t ▯Acti▯eSync ▯▯er▯ion ▯3.7.1 ▯▯▯i▯▯▯▯03▯▯▯he ▯ anti▯ir▯▯ ▯o▯t▯are per▯or▯e▯ a ▯co▯▯▯ete ▯ir▯▯ ▯can ▯ith e▯ery▯ te▯t. ▯▯Be▯ore ▯te▯ting ▯co▯▯ence▯ the ▯anti▯ir▯▯ ▯o▯t▯are ▯a▯ ▯ chec▯e▯ ▯or ▯▯p▯ate▯ ▯ro▯ the ▯▯o▯t▯are co▯pany ▯▯▯e▯▯ite ▯ inc▯▯▯ing the ▯ate▯t ▯ir▯▯ ▯ignat▯re ▯ata▯a▯e. ▯▯▯e to the ▯page ▯ ▯i▯it▯o▯ ▯thi▯ ▯paper ▯▯e are ▯▯na▯▯e to ▯ho▯ the ▯co▯▯▯ete ▯co▯e ▯ ▯i▯ting ▯▯or the te▯t ca▯e▯ ▯▯o▯e▯er, ▯▯e ▯ho▯ ▯re▯e▯ant ▯▯eg▯ent▯ o▯ ▯ co▯e ▯or ▯e▯era▯ te▯t ca▯e▯ ▯

1. ▯Trans▯▯siti▯n ▯▯▯S▯urce ▯C▯de▯

Test ▯Case ▯1.1 ▯▯▯▯ ▯e ▯too▯ ▯a ▯▯et ▯o▯ ▯▯oc▯▯ ▯o▯ ▯▯o▯rce ▯co▯e ▯an▯ in▯erte▯ ▯a ▯▯e ▯to ▯each ▯o▯ ▯the▯e ▯▯oc▯▯. ▯▯he ▯area ▯o▯ ▯the ▯▯o▯rce ▯ co▯e ▯cho▯en ▯or ▯thi▯ ▯i▯ ▯the ▯area ▯▯here the ▯act▯a▯ ▯▯i▯e ▯in▯ection▯ ta▯e▯ ▯▯▯ace, ▯th▯▯ a▯▯▯ring ▯pro▯a▯▯e ▯e▯ec▯tion ▯o▯ the ▯tran▯po▯e▯▯ ▯o▯rce ▯co▯e. ▯▯hen ▯▯ith the ▯▯▯e ▯o▯ ▯▯ranch ▯▯tate▯▯ent ▯each ▯▯a▯e▯e ▯ ▯▯oc▯ ▯▯ranche▯ ▯to the ▯ne▯t ▯▯oc▯ ▯in ▯▯e▯ ▯th▯▯ pre▯er▯ing the ▯ origina▯ ▯e▯ec▯tion ▯or▯er. ▯▯A▯ a ▯▯ina▯ ▯▯tep, ▯a▯▯ the ▯▯oc▯▯ ▯▯ere▯ rearrange▯ ▯an▯ ▯ta▯en ▯o▯t ▯o▯ ▯it▯ ▯origina▯ ▯phy▯ica▯ ▯or▯er. ▯▯he ▯ ▯o▯▯o▯ing ▯i▯ ▯an ▯i▯▯▯e▯entation ▯o▯ ▯thi▯ ▯▯tarting ▯at ▯▯ine ▯308 ▯o▯ the ▯ ▯ir▯▯ ▯▯o▯rce ▯co▯e ▯▯▯

Original Source Code	Modified Source Code
	section19
ldr r8, [r0, #0xc]	ldr r8, [r0, #0xc]
add r3, r3, r8	add r3, r3, r8
str r3, [r4, #0x28]	str r3, [r4, #0x28]
	bl section20
sub r6, r6, r3	section21
sub r6, r6, #8	mov r10, r0
	ldr r0, [r10, #0x10]
mov r10, r0	add r0, r0, r7
ldr r0, [r10, #0x10]	ldr r1, [r4, #0x3c]
add r0, r0, r7	bl _align_
ldr r1, [r4, #0x3c]	bl section22
bl _align_	
	section20
	sub r6, r6, r3
	sub r6, r6, #8
	bl section21

Test ▯Case ▯1.2 ▯ ▯hi▯ ▯in▯o▯▯e▯ ▯▯anip▯▯ation ▯o▯ ▯a ▯▯a▯▯e ▯he▯▯ ▯in ▯ ▯ario▯▯ ▯regi▯ter▯ ▯at a ▯gi▯en ▯▯o▯ent ▯▯▯ring ▯the ▯e▯ec▯tion. ▯▯In ▯ a▯▯e▯▯▯y ▯▯ang▯age, ▯regi▯ter▯ are ▯▯e▯ e▯ten▯i▯e▯y to ▯ho▯▯ ▯▯a▯▯e▯ ▯

an ▯a▯▯re▯▯e▯. ▯▯he ▯▯anip▯▯ation ▯o▯ the ▯▯a▯▯e ▯▯a▯ ▯▯one ▯▯ia ▯ a▯▯ition ▯an▯▯or ▯▯▯traction ▯o▯ ▯a ▯▯a▯▯e ▯in ▯a ▯partic▯▯ar ▯regi▯ter. ▯▯▯ Mo▯ing ▯the ▯▯a▯▯e ▯to ▯other ▯regi▯ter▯ ▯▯a▯ ▯a▯▯o ▯▯▯e▯. ▯▯▯here ▯i▯▯ ▯a ▯▯a▯e▯ ▯ten▯e ▯piece ▯o▯ ▯▯o▯rce ▯co▯e that ▯too▯ ▯a ▯▯a▯▯e, ▯▯o▯i▯ie▯ it ▯▯ia ▯2 ▯to ▯5 ▯in▯tr▯ction▯ ▯an▯ ▯▯ini▯he▯ ▯▯y ▯▯▯acing ▯▯ac▯ the ▯origina▯ ▯ ▯a▯▯e ▯in the ▯origina▯ ▯regi▯ter. ▯▯hi▯ ▯tran▯▯or▯ation ▯pre▯er▯e▯ the ▯ ▯e▯ec▯tion ▯or▯er ▯o▯ the ▯▯ir▯▯ ▯an▯ ▯the ▯intence ▯▯a▯▯e ▯the ▯▯i▯ ▯in ▯the ▯ regi▯ter ▯at a ▯gi▯en ▯in▯tant ▯in ▯e▯ec▯tion. ▯▯he ▯▯o▯▯o▯ing ▯i▯ an ▯ i▯▯▯e▯entation ▯▯tarting ▯at ▯▯ine ▯80 ▯o▯ the ▯▯ir▯▯ ▯▯o▯rce ▯co▯e▯▯

Original Source Code	Modified Source Code
	mov r0, r5
mov r0, r5	mov r1, r4
mov r1, r4	add r0, r0, #2
mov lr, pc	add r0, r0, #4
ldr pc, [r11, #-20]	add r1, r1, #6
cmp r0, #0	sub r0, r0, #6
bne find_files_iterate	sub r1, r1, #4
	sub r1, r1, #2
	mov r4, r1
	mov r5, r0
	mov lr, pc
	ldr pc, [r11, #-20]
	cmp r0, #0
	bne find_files_iterate

2. ▯Inserti▯n ▯▯▯Tra▯▯S▯urce ▯C▯de▯

Test ▯Case ▯2.1 ▯ ▯hi▯ ▯in▯o▯▯e▯ ▯a ▯copy ▯o▯ ▯an ▯origina▯ ▯▯ing▯e ▯▯ine ▯o▯▯ co▯e. ▯▯he ▯▯ine ▯▯a▯ ▯pa▯te▯ ▯▯ac▯ into the ▯▯o▯rce ▯co▯e ▯▯i▯e ▯i▯▯e▯iate▯y▯ ▯o▯▯o▯ing the ▯origina▯ one. ▯▯▯hi▯ ▯▯i▯▯ not ▯change the ▯▯eha▯ior ▯ ▯eca▯▯e the ▯▯ine ▯o▯ ▯▯o▯rce ▯co▯e ▯cho▯en ▯con▯i▯t▯ o▯ the ▯in▯tr▯ction ▯ ▯CB ▯▯hich ▯▯e▯ine▯ ▯a ▯▯yte ▯▯ith a ▯▯tring ▯▯a▯▯e. ▯▯hi▯ ▯in▯ertion ▯on▯y ▯ increa▯e▯ the ▯▯yte ▯▯i▯e ▯o▯ the ▯▯i▯e ▯▯y the ▯▯i▯e ▯o▯ the ▯▯ine ▯o▯ ▯co▯e. ▯▯▯

Test ▯Case ▯2.2 ▯ ▯In ▯thi▯ ▯te▯t, the ▯▯a▯e ▯in▯tr▯ction ▯a▯ ▯in ▯te▯t ca▯e ▯2.1 ▯ ▯▯a▯ ▯in▯erte▯ ▯right ▯a▯ter ▯▯i▯e▯ ▯▯ine ▯o▯ ▯▯o▯rce ▯co▯e. ▯▯he ▯▯i▯e ▯▯ine▯▯ ▯▯ere ▯not ▯in ▯▯▯cce▯▯i▯e ▯or▯er ▯an▯ ▯▯ere ▯iterate▯y ▯cho▯en ▯to ▯co▯er the ▯ ▯▯ho▯e ▯▯o▯y ▯o▯ the ▯▯o▯rce ▯co▯e. ▯▯ach ▯cho▯en ▯▯ine ▯repre▯ente▯ ▯an ▯ e▯▯entia▯ ▯part ▯o▯ the ▯e▯ec▯tion ▯▯e▯▯ence ▯▯▯ch a▯ ▯▯in▯ing ▯a ▯▯i▯e to ▯ in▯ect ▯an▯ ▯▯crea▯ing the ▯▯tac▯ ▯pointer. ▯▯he ▯in▯ertion ▯▯i▯▯ ▯not ▯a▯▯ect ▯ the ▯intence ▯e▯ec▯tion ▯o▯ the ▯co▯e ▯an▯ ▯increa▯e▯ the ▯▯i▯e ▯▯▯ ▯yte ▯ ▯i▯e▯▯y ▯▯ength ▯o▯ the ▯in▯ert ▯▯ine ▯▯▯▯tip▯ie▯ ▯▯y ▯▯i▯e. ▯▯▯

DCB "just looking "

Inserted after each of the following lines

Line 18 mov r11, sp
Line 64 ldr pc, [r11, #-24] ; find first file
Line 228 cmp r0, #0
Line 303 ldr r6, [r4, #0x28] ; gimme entrypoint rva
Line 361 mov lr, pc

[Su□stituti□n □□□S□urce □C□de□

Test □Case □□1□ □ere □□e □e□replace □□line 51□□o □the □□ir□□□□o□rce □code□

DCB "This is proof of concept code. Also, i wanted to make avers happy."

With

DCB "This is foorp fo tpecnoc code. Also, i wanted to make avers happy."

□he □□□□titi□tion □pre□er□e□ □the □length □o□□the □original □line □□hile □□a□ing □a □□o□i□ication □to □a □□□ection □o□□it. □□hi□□□a□□□one □to □□a□e □a □□o□i□ication □that □□i□ not □a□□ect □the □□yte □□ile □o□□the □□ir□□. □□hi□□□titi□tion □□i□ not □a□□ect □the □inten□□e □□e□ection □o□□the □□ir□□□inall□y, □it □i□ □orth □noting □that □the □□or□at □o□□the □t□□o □line □□i□□ in□□ee□□i□entica□□□ith □re□pect □to □□pace □□an□ □character □a□ign□ent□.□□□

Test □Case □□2□ □□hi□ te□t □i□ □i□ilar □to □te□t □ca□e 3.1. □□□e □replace□ □the □□a□e □line 51□□o □the □□ir□□□ource □code □□ith □an □al□o□t □i□entical □□one. □□□hi□ □ne□□□line □al□o □ha□ □a □□o□i□ication □to □a □□□ection □o□□it. □□he □□o□i□ication □□a□ not □the □□a□e □a□ □that □o□□the □□ir□t □te□t. □□hi□ □□o□i□ication □□a□e □the □length □o□□the □line □□a□er □than □the □original □an□□□th □□a□□□ecrea□e□ □the □□o□era□□ □□yte □□ile. □□□A□□o □the □character □□an□ □□pace □a□ign□ent □□a□ not □pre□er□e□. □□□he □□o□□□□ing □i□ □the □per□or□e□ □line □□□titi□tion□□

DCB "This is proof of concept code. Also, i wanted to make avers happy."

Changed to

DCB "This is poc code. Also, i wanted to make avers happy."

Test □Case □□□□ □□ere □□e □again □□□titi□te □line 51□□o □the □□ir□□ □□o□rce □code □□□ith □a □□ne□ □one. □□□he □□ne□□□line □□o□□code □□a□ □□a□i□al□y □□o□i□ie□ □□hile □□ti□□ □pre□er□ing □the □a□ility □to □□a□e □□e□ □the □□o□urce □code. □□□he □line □□i□e □□or □replace□ent □□a□ □the □□a□e □□ength □a□ □the □original □line □□t □□pace □an□ □character □a□ign□ent □□ere □□p□rpo□e□y □not □pre□er□e□. □□he □□o□□□□ing □i□ □the □act□a□□□□titi□tion□□

DCB "This is proof of concept code. Also, i wanted to make avers happy."

Changed to

DCB "dkfjvd dkfje dkfdsfg kd934,d kdick 3949rie jdkckdke 345r dlie4 vhg"

□□a□e □Renamin□□□

□he □□a□e□ □that □□ere □□□□or □□□□titi□tion □□ere □□p□rpo□e□y □□ept □the □□a□e □□yte □□ile □an□ □a □□o□a □□i□erent □□□ile □in □the □te□t. □□A□□o □the □corre□□pon□ing □□ca□□□or □□ranche□ □to □the □□e□a□e□ □□ere □al□o □□o□i□ie□ □to □en□□re □original □□e□ection □□e□ha□ior. □□□he □□□a□e□na□e□ □cho□en □□or □□□titi□tion □re□erence□ □□□oc□□□□o□in□tr□ction□ □□e□entia□ □to □the □□ir□□□e□ection □□□ch □□a□□□in□□ing □a □□ile □to □in□ect, □opening □a □□ile □□or □in□ection □an□ □in□ecting □the □□ile.

Test □Case □□1□ □□hi□ te□t □□a□ □a □□□i□p□e □re□er□a□ □o□□□□or□a□e□ □na□e □□□o□n □□thro□gho□t □the □□□o□rce □code. □□□he □□yte □□ile □□a□ □pre□er□e□. □□A□□o □character □a□ign□ent □□a□ □pre□er□e□ □□□□o □o□□the □□□a□e□, □appearing □in □line□ 79 □an□ 397 □o□□the □□ir□□□o□rce □code □□ere □rena□e□ □□a□ □□o□□o□□□

Line Number	Original Source Code	Modified Source Code
79	find_next_file	next_file_find
397	open_file	file_open

Test □Case □□2□ □□n □thi□ □te□t, □the □□□a□e □na□e□ □□ere □p□rpo□e□y □□a□e□ □□onger □th□□increa□ing □the □□yte □□ile. □□n □thi□ □te□t □the □character □□an□ □□pace □a□ign□ent □□ere □not □pre□er□e□. □□□□o □o□□the □□□a□e□□, □□ocate□ □at □□ine□ 79 □an□□□82 □o□□the □□ir□□□o□rce □code □□ere □rena□e□ □□a□ □□o□o□□□

Line Number	Original Source Code	Modified Source Code
79	find_next_file	next_file_to_find_for_use
482	ask_user	user_ask_question_to_continue

□C□m□re□ssi□n □□□□a □Virus □E□ecuta□□e□

Test □Case □□□1□ □Co□□pre□□ion □o□□the □□ir□ □□□e□□ecta□□e □□a□ □□one □□□y □co□□pre□□ing □the □□e□□ecta□□e □□er□ion □o□□the □original □□ir□□□□□ing □co□□□ercia□□y □a□a□ia□□e □□o□□t□are. □□□he □□o□t□are □□□oc□□et □□A□□□28 □□□a□□cho□en □□or □thi□ □□ta□□□□□hi□ □choice □□□a□□□a□e □□a□e□ □on □the □e□□perience □o□□□□□ing □the □□o□t□are □an□ □there □i□ □a □□er□ion □a□ai□a□□e □□or □□□in □□o□□□Mo□i□e. □□□he □co□□pre□□e□ □□ile □□□a□□p□ace□ □into □the □□han □the □□□e□□ice □□an □□opene□ □to □□ie□ □it□ □content□. □□□hen □the □□ir□□ □□can □□a□□per□or□e□. □□□hi□ □□a□□□one □to □□in□□o□□t □i□ □the □anti□ir□□ □□o□t□are □□o□□□□not □on□y □□etect □the □□ir□□ □in □co□□pre□□e□ □□or□ □□□□t □□al□o □□e□ete □it □□or □at □a□□□□in□□□□□□□□eep □it □□ro□□□□e□ecting.□□

□ TEST □RESU□TS□

□a□□□e □□1 □□ho□□□□re□u□t□ □o□□□app□ying □the □te□t □□e□criteria □a□o□e. □□Co□□□n □1 □i□ □the □te□t □categorie□. □□Co□□□n □2 □i□ □the □in□i□i□a□te□t □in □the □□or□er □□e□crib□□in □Section 5. □□Co□□□□n □3 □thro□gh □□contain □the □in□i□i□a□te □te□t □re□u□t□ □□or □the □anti□ir□□ □□o□t□are □□□e □in □the □te□t □□e□ection. □□□he □□a□t □ro□ □□ho□□ □the □□a□e □negati□e □rate □o□□each □o□□the □□o□t□are □te□te□. □□A □□a□□e □o□□0 □repre□ent □□□etection □□ai□□re, □□th□□the □□ir□□ □□a□ □not □□etected □□an□ □□e□ete□ □□an□ □□a □□ti□□□capa□□e □o□□□e□ection. □□A □□a□□e □o□□1 □repre□ent □□□etection □□ucce□□ □an□ □□e□□tion □o□□the □in□ected □□ile. □□A □□a□□e □o□□2 □□enote□ □□□ucce□□□□ □□etection □□□t □not □□e□□tion, □thi□ □□a□□e □□a□□a□□e □□or □the □□pecia□ □ca□e □o□□co□□pre□□ion. □□C□ear□y □a □□a□□e □o□□0 □i□ □a □□a□□e □negati□e. □□□

□□orton □ha□ □the □highe□t □□□a□□e □negati□e □rate □□ith □□A□a□t □ha□ing □the □□□o□e□t. □□□□ot □inc□□□ing □□canning □the □original □□ir□□, □a □total □n□□□er □o□□□0 □te□t□ □□ere □per□or□e□ □□□the□e, 23 □te□t□ □□ere □□ucce□□□ □□□etection □□□ea□ing □17 □□□a□i□□re□. □□□hi□ □i□ □an □o□era□□ □2.5□□ □□a□□e □negati□e □rate, □□ery □high □an□ □□nacceptab□□e. □□□n □the □te□t □□or □co□□pre□□ion □o□□□□o□rce □code, □a □□pecia□ □note □□ho□□□□e □ta□en □regar□ing □the □□□eha□ior □o□□the □□ir□□. □□□he □co□□pre□□ion □□o□t□are □apparent□y □create□ □a □te□porary □copy □o□□the □content□ □o□□a □co□□pre□□e□ □□ile □□hen □the □□ile □are □□ie□e□. □□□he □□ir□□ □□can □□etect □an□ □□e□ete □thi□ □te□porary □copy, □ho□□e□er, □the □original □□ir□□ □□ile □□can □□ti□□□□e □□e□ected □□ro□ □□□□ithin □the □co□□pre□□e□ □□ile □□ile□. □□□ith □the □co□□pre□□ion □□o□t□are □□oe□ □not □a□□o□ □the □anti□ir□□ □□o□t□are □to □□e□ete

Table 1 Virus Scanner Test results and False negative percentage by software		Norton	Avast	Kaspersky	AirScanner.com
Original virus		1	1	1	1
Transposition	Test 1.1	0	1	0	0
	Test 1.2	0	1	1	0
Trash Insertion	Test 2.1	0	1	1	1
	Test 2.2	0	0	0	0
Substitution	Test 3.1	1	1	1	1
	Test 3.2	0	1	1	1
	Test 3.3	1	1	0	0
Label Renaming	Test 4.1	1	1	1	1
	Test 4.2	1	1	1	1
Compression	Test 5.1	2	2	2	2
False Negative %		(0)	20%	(0)	50%

Table 2 False negative percentage by individual Test and Category		Successful Detection	Failed Detection	Per Test False Negative %	Test Category False Negative %
Transposition	Test 1.1	1	3	75%	(2.50%)
	Test 1.2	2	2	50%	
Trash Insertion	Test 2.1	3	1	25%	(2.50%)
	Test 2.2	0		100%	
Substitution	Test 3.1		0	0%	25%
	Test 3.2	3	1	25%	
	Test 3.3	2	2	50%	
Label Renaming	Test 4.1		0	0%	0%
	Test 4.2		0	0%	
Compression	Test 5.1	0		100%	100%

the content to a compressed file. We count this as a virus free because the virus definition is still in the file than the same file, even though it was detected, and can still be detected. Table 2 shows the false negative rate. Column 1 and 2 similar to Table 1, Column 3 and 4 show successful and failed detection, and Column 5 and 6 show false negative rate by individual test and test category.

Compression has the highest false negative rate followed by transposition of source code and insertion of trash source code. In the initial test results, the second test of trash insertion caused all the antivirus software to produce a false negative, yet the first test only caused one false negative. This shows the insertion of trash source code within an actual line of instruction code is enough to cause the detector to incorrectly identify the file as a virus. The transposition test category, the virus test caused the most false negatives. The insertion of branch statements in the source code results in a different physical appearance while maintaining the same detection behavior proves to be very effective in avoiding detection.

In the substitution of source code category the false negative produces in test to hint that a slight decrease in the byte size of

the virus detectable may cause the virus to go undetected. In test three of the same category, even purposely adding space and character alignment different than the original line of source code while keeping the byte size the same which cause those false negative to occur.

In the label renaming category preserving and purposely changing the byte size of the label will not affect the virus detector. This implies that changing the byte size may have the affect to avoiding detection if the byte size reduction is done in certain areas of the source code. Also one can infer that a file may not be exactly the virus signature when a byte size reduction cause a false negative, the modified area might be of critical importance to the detector deciding if the code is a virus or not. During the test case creation, we were not aware if the signature used by a detector was modified. Many of the successful detection could have occurred because the transformation did not affect the virus signature. Overall, with a 2.5% false negative rate, there is clearly room for improvement.

□ CONCLUSION

We have presented a technique to testing than the malware on a worm or malware virus transformation. The result shows multiple

73

□a□□in c□rrent □ir□□□etector□ □or han□he□□□e□ice□. □he te□t□ □e□to high □a□□e negati□e rate□ □or each anti□ir□□pro□□ct an□ □an□ e□tre□e□y high o□era□□ □a□□e negati□e rate o□ □2.5□. □he□e re□□□t□ □□gge□t that c□rrent □ir□□□etector□ are p□re□y □i□p□e □ignat□re□ □a□e□ □etection. □ □he □ or□ a□□ □o□e□ □ho□□ ho□□ □etai□e□ tracea□i□ity o□ the □ir□□ tran□□or□ation can □e □one. □□□t□re □or□ inc□□□e the □etai□e□ □t□□y o□ □a□□e negati□e pro□□ction in any o□ the gi□en te□t□. Byte □i□e change□, □□□tit□tion an□ tran□po□ition o□ □o□rce co□e an□ co□pre□□ion re□□ire □□rther □t□□y to i□pro□e □ir□□□etection □n□er the□e con□ition□. C□rrent□y □e ha□e a great archi□e o□ □□no□□ □e□ge o□ □ir□□e□ □or C. □hi□ in□or□ation can □e □□e□ to pro□□ce □ophi□ticate□ □ir□□ □canner□ □or han□he□□□e□ice□ gi□en their □i□itation□. □□ea□□y, thi□ □□i□□ occ□r □e□pe□itio□□y an□ pree□pti□e□y to □he□p □a□oi□ in□ection□ o□ □□t□re □ir□□e□ □or han□he□□□e□ice□.

□ ACKNO□ □EDGEMENTS

□hi□ □□a□ □□pporte□ in part □y the □ationa□ Science □o□n□ation □n□er □rant □o. □□□□-0317□92. □□he □ie□□ an□ conc□□□ion□ containe□ herein are tho□e o□ the a□thor□ an□ □ho□□□ not □e interprete□ a□ nece□□ari□y repre□enting the o□□icia□ po□icie□ or en□or□e□ent□ either e□pre□□e□ or i□p□ie□ □y the a□o□e agencie□. □he a□thor□ than□ □on□a□o Argote-□arcia, □on□tantin Be□no□o□ an□ Mihai Bar□□e□c□ □or their contri□□tion□ to thi□ re□earch.

□ REFERENCES

[1] Chri□to□ore□c□ M. an□ □ha□ S. □e□ting Ma□□are □etector□. □nternationa□ Sy□po□i□□ on So□t□are □e□ting an□ Ana□y□i□ □SS□A□ 200□.

[2] Cohen □. A □hort co□r□e on co□p□ter □ir□□e□. □ i□ey □ro□e□□iona□ Co□p□ting, 199□.

[3] Conry-M□rray A. Beha□ior B□oc□ing Stop□ Un□no□n Ma□icio□□ Co□e. □et□or□ Maga□ine, □□ne 2002.

□□ □enning □. Cy□erterrori□□. □e□ti□ony □e□ore the Specia□ □□er□ight □ane□ o□ □errori□□ Co□□ittee on Ar□e□ Ser□ice□, US □o□□e o□ □epre□entati□e□, 23 May 2000.

[5] □ogie S. □oc□et□C A□□e□□ □o □rotect an□ □e□troy. B□ac□ □at USA 200□.

□□ □o□ey S. an□ □□□igan □. Are □an□he□□ □ir□□e□ a □hreat□ Co□□□nication□ o□ the ACM, □an□ary 2001, □o□. □□, □o. 1.

[7] □or□ □. □he □ rong St□□□, □□□□ Sec□rity □□ □ri□acy, 200□.

[8] □rancia □. □□□e□e□ Sy□te□ □rogra□□ing. □o□rna□ o□ Co□p□ting Science□ in Co□□ege□, □ec 2001, □o□.17 □□□e 2.

[9] □or□on S. an□ □o□ar□ □. Anti□ir□□ So□t□are □e□ting □or the □e□ Mi□□enni□□. □rocee□ing□ o□ □ationa□ □n□or□ation Sy□te□□ Sec□rity Con□erence □□SSC□ 2000.

[10] □or□on S. an□ □or□ □. Cy□erterrori□□□ Sy□antec Sec□rity □e□pon□e □ hite □aper, 2003.

[11] □or□on S. an□ □or□ □. □ea□ □or□□ Anti-□ir□□ □ro□□ct □e□ie□□ an□ □□a□□ation – □he c□rrent □tate o□ A□□air□. □rocee□ing□ o□ the 199□ □ationa□ □n□or□ation Sy□te□□ Sec□rity Con□erence.

[12] □BM □e□earch. □ir□□ □i□e□ine. http://□□□.re□earch.i□□.co□/anti□ir□□/ti□e□ine.ht□.

[13] Mac□ey □., □o□e□ □. an□ □ohn□on B.C. Sec□ring yo□r han□he□□ □e□ice□. □he □SSA □o□rna□, Apri□ 200□.

[1□] Mar□ A. A g□i□e□ine to anti-□a□□are-□o□t□are te□ting. □□ropean □n□tit□te □or Co□p□ter Anti-□ir□□ □e□earch □□CA□□ 2000 Be□t □aper □rocee□ing□, pp.218-253.

[15] Me□□er □. Beha□ior □□oc□ing repe□□ne□ □ir□□e□. □et□or□ □or□□□ion, □an□ary 28, 2002.

[1□] Myer□ □. □. □he Art o□ So□t□are □e□ting. □ohn □ i□ey □□ Son□, □econ□ e□ition, □□ne 200□.

[17] □achen□erg C. Beha□ior B□oc□ing □he □e□t Step in Anti-□ir□□ □rotection. Sec□rity □oc□□, March 19, 2002. http://□□□.□ec□rity□oc□□.co□/in□oc□□/1557.

[18] □achen□erg C. Co□p□ter □ir□□-Anti□ir□□ Coe□o□□tion. Co□□□nication□ o□ the ACM, □an□ary 1997, □o□. □0 □o. 1.

[19] □ationa□ □□nera□i□ity □ata□a□e. http://n□□.ni□t.go□/.

[20] □ta□o□ S. C. □n□ran□o□ an□ partition te□ting. □n □rocee□ing□ o□ the ACM S□□S□□□ □nternationa□ Sy□po□i□□ on So□t□are □e□ting an□ Ana□y□i□ 1998 □□SS□A □98□ pp. □2-□8, C□ear□ater Beach □L, Mar 1998. ACM □re□□.

[21] □ei□ari C., □ogie S. an□ □atter/29A. □etai□□ □□erge on the □ir□t □ in□o□□ Mo□i□e □ir□□□. http://□□□.in□or□it.co□/artic□e□/artic□e.a□p□p□3370□9.

[22] □ei□ari C., □ogie S., □atter/29A an□ □□ea□□. □e□er□e □ngineering the □ir□t □oc□et □C □ro□an. http://□□□.a□□p□□i□hing.co□/artic□e□/artic□e.a□p□p□3□05□

[23] Schnei□er □. □n□orcea□□e Sec□rity □o□icie□. ACM □ran□action□ on □n□or□ation an□ Sy□te□ Sec□rity. □o□.2, □o. 1, □e□r□ary 2000, page□ 30-50

[2□] Singh □. an□ La□hotia A. Ana□y□i□ an□ □etection o□ Co□p□ter □ir□□e□ an□ □ or□□. An Annotate□ Bi□□iography. ACM S□□□LA□ □otice□, □e□r□ary 2002.

[25] Sy□antec Anti□ir□□ □e□earch Center. http://□ec□rityre□pon□e.□y□antec.co□/a□center/□enc/□ata/□y□□o□.ca□ir.ht□□

[2□] S□or □. □he Art o□ Co□p□ter □ir□□ □e□earch an□ □e□en□e, A□□i□on-□ e□□ey, 2005.

[27] □ahi□ □. an□ □i□argi□ □. □□□e□□e□ Sy□te□ □e□ign a□ Uni□ie□ □ar□□are/So□t□are □ntro□□ction. □ i□ey 2002.

[28] □ in□A□, http://□□□.□in-rar.co□/.

[29] □ ire□e□□ an□he□□ an□ S□artphone Sec□rity, Sy□antec Sec□rity □ hite □aper, http://□□□.□y□anctec.co□.

[30] □h□ □., □a□□ □. A. □. an□ May □. □. □. So□t□are Unit □e□t Co□erage an□ A□e□□acy. ACM Co□p□ting S□r□ey□, 29□□□, pp. 3□□□□27,1997. ACM □re□□

Eliminating Buffer Overflows,
Using the Compiler or a Standalone Tool

Thomas Plum
Plum Hall, Inc.
3 Waihona Box 44610
Kamuela, HI 96743 USA
+1-808-882-1255

tplum@plumhall.com

David M. Keaton

1630 30th Street #311
Boulder, CO 80301 USA
+1-303-782-1009

dmk@dmk.com

ABSTRACT

□e present a set of method (SSCC) for safe, secure C/C□□□ to eliminate buffer overflow (including with-pointer stores in C□ an□ C□), using a suite of compile-time, link-time, and run-time text, plu□ so□e design-time restriction□. A prototype i□ple□entation indicate□ that run-time overhead i□ □uch smaller than previou□ □ethod□. □he SSCC □etho□□ do not require change□ to e□isting data layout□ or object-code representation.

□he SSCC □etho□ are applicable to application□ written for the □ S□/□C 9899 1999 □C99□ standard□ 5 and the 1□882 2003 □C□□ standard□ □herein, the □Standard□□, ta□le ta□le□ to□t co□ercially-popular e□tension□ to tho□e standard□, and the earlier □S□/□C 9899 1990 □C90□ standard□ no□ e□entially out-o□-print□.

Cate□ries and Su□ect Descri□t□rs

□.2. □S□ftware En□ineerin□ □So□tware/□rogra□ □eri□ication□□ *assertion checkers, class invariants, reliability*□
□.3. □□r□grammin□ □an□ua□es □□roce□or□ *code generation, compilers, optimization;*

Genera□ Terms

□e□ign, □ □cono□ic□□ □elia□ility, □ Sec□rity, □ Standar□i□ation, □ Langua□e□, □eri□ication. □

Key□rds

Static □analy□i□, □yna□ic □analy□i□, □□ffer o□erflo□, □relia□ility, □ co□e □generation, co□piler, □opti□i□ation. □

1. INTRODUCTION

B□ffer o□erflo□□ in C and in C□□ are the □nderlying ca□e o□ □any □□lnera□ilitie□, acco□nting □or □p to 50□ o□ □ulnera□ilitie□ reporte□ □y C□□□/CC□1□□. Co□plete□y pre□enting the□e □lea□ne□□□ witho□t □acri□icing e□iciency □o □□□ contri□te□ po□iti□e□y to e□ery □o□tware □ec□rity a□□urance (SSA) approach □or C and C□□. Accor□ing to □o□ert Seacor□ □11□, □□□lnera□ility

report□ contin□e to gro□ at an ala□ing rate□... □o a□re□ the□ gro□ing n□□er o□ both □ulnera□ilitie□ and inci□ent□ it i□ increa□ing□y apparent that the pro□le□□ it □e attac□e□ at the □o□rce □y □orking to pre□ent the intro□ction o□ □o□t□are □ulnera□ilitie□ □□ring □o□t□are □e□elop□ent an□ ongoing □aintenance. □□

□□ are can □La□□□□ □arie□ the □itation□. A con□idera□le a□o□nt o□ □ork ha□ □een per□or□e□ on □itigating the □□□er o□er□o□ pro□le□ □ing □either □tatic analy□i□ or □yna□ic analy□i□. □10□ □o□e□er, in SSCC □e attac□ the □□□er-o□er□o□ pro□le□ □ing □tatic analy□i□ □or □□ie□ that can □e re□ol□e□ at co□pile-time□ and □in□-ti□e□, □pl□□ □e a □o□nt o□ □yna□ic analy□i□ □□ing high□y-opti□i□e□ co□e re□erence, □or □□ie□ that can on□y □e re□ol□e□ at r□n-time. □□□rther□ore, certain □e□ign-ti□e re□triction□ can help e□i□inate □□□er o□er□o□□, a□ □e□cri□e□ later in thi□ paper. □

Mo□ern □co□piler□ □or C an□ C□□ a□rea□y per□or□ □igni□icant□ □tatic □analy□i□ to in□er □tan□ progra□ □e□antic□ □or opti□i□ation□, e□pecially on □ector an□ □□□per-□cala□ hard□are. □□rther□ore, in □□□□ritten□ progra□□ the □array-□o□n□□ in□or□ation i□ a□rea□y □aintaine□ in □aria□le□ □e□ine□ □y the progra□□er. □□SSCC pro□i□e□ a □etho□ □or the □co□piler to □trac□ that □□o□n□□ in□or□ation an□ □eri□y at co□pile-ti□e, □in□-ti□e, or r□n-ti□e□ that □etch-an□-□tore operation□ are proper. □

□hene□er po□□i□le□ □e ha□e a□opte□ ter□inology an□ concept□ that □□o□□□ □e rea□ona□ly □a□i□iar to progra□□er□ an□ □co□piler i□ple□enter□. □C an□ C□□ are □ri□e□ □ith concept □hich are int□iti□e to the progra□□er □□t □co□plicate□ to repre□ent in a□□tract □athe□atical □logic□□ □an□ice-□er□a. □he progra□□er □ho □n□er□tan□□ the □concept□ □ehin□ SSCC □i□□ □e □etter prepare□ to achie□e the □□□□a□ety/□ec□rity goal□ o□ SSCC □hile □ini□i□ing r□n-ti□e o□erhea□. □□□e□□e the □athe□atical□ notation □□or □ha□□-open □inter□al □□Lo, □oo□ar□ □in contra□t to the□ c□o□e□ □inter□a□ □Lo, □i□□. □

□he SSCC □etho□ □i□□ generate □ata □diagno□tic □□e□□age□ in □any □ ca□e□ □here □□□er o□er□o□□ cannot □be □e□initi□e□y pre□ente□□. □o□e□er, the SSCC □etho□ □□ □o not i□po□e □□□y r□□e□ □or□ porta□ility con□i□eration□ □pon the co□□pilation. □Any □partic□lar□ tool□ can enhance the □□a□ic SSCC □etho□□□.

SSCC a□□o a□□lie□ to the □pro□□ction o□ □□o□t□are □or e□□e□□e□□ □y□te□□, □□t there are □ight□y □i□□erent □□e□ign criteria □in□ that□ arena. □□hi□ paper pri□ari□y a□□re□e□ the □application o□ the□ SSCC □etho□ □to ho□te□ □y□te□□, □□ch a□ application □□written □or□ Lin□□ or□ □in□o□□□ □or the □Mac□□.S. □

2. BACKGROUND

□e□e the de□inition □or □o□e □n a □enta□ter□ □□□

Bound □o□ an array □□the n□□□er o□ e□e□ent□ in the array. □

Lo □o□ an array □□the a□□re□□ o□ the □ir□t e□e□ent o□ the array.

Hi □o□ an array □□the a□□re□□ o□ the □a□t e□e□ent o□ the array.

Toofar □o□ an array □□the a□□re□□ o□ the □one-too-□ar □e□e□ent o□ the array, the e□e□ent □□□□t □a□t the ***Hi*** e□e□ent. □

Target-size □or ***Tsize*** □o□ an array □□a □e□a □□i□e o□ array□

□nce a pointer i□ a□□ociate□ □ith an o□□ect, the □a□a□eter□ □are □ □e□ine□ □or that pointer. □□□or an array o□□ect, the □□i□e o□ a □ pointer into that o□□ect i□ the □tota□ n□□□er o□ □□yte□ in the array □ that i□ acce□□e□ □y the pointer □i.e. the □□□o□n□ o□ the array ti□e□ □ the n□□□er o□ □□yte□ in □or□□i□e o□□each e□e□ent. □□rther□ore, □ the □a□e □e□inition□ are a□□□ie□ to pointer□ to non-array o□□ect□, □ con□i□tent □ith the e□□i□a□ence □et□een a non-array □an□ an array □ □ho□e ***Bound*** i□ 1. □□he ter□□ ***Lo***, □i□, an□ □oo□ar can a□□o □□e □ a□□□ie□ to integer □□□□cript □a□□e□ □□hen the conte□t a□□o□□□□

□e □□e □aria□□e□ to □e□ignate na□e□ o□□ect□ □inc□□□ing □□□- o□□ect□ □ec□are□ □ith □□e □terna□ □. □□e □□e □tate□ o□ an o□□ect □ e□c□□□i□e□y to re□er to r□n-ti□e □tate, an□ □attri□□te □o□ a □aria□□e □ to □e□ignate the co□□i□e-ti□e □□n□er□tan□ing o□ that □tate. □□ne □ i□□□e□ec□a□□e□□the □□□attri□□te. □□□n the □t□□ □□o□-contro□ □arc□ □ ro□□□i□□p 0□, □p□ ha□ the □□□attri□□te on the □□a□□e □o□ outco□□e □ arc □an□ the □not-□□□□n □□attri□□te on the □□tr□e □o□ outco□□e arc. □ □ther attri□□te□ □□e□ in SSCC are a □□o □□□□□□ □in □ir□in□irecta□□e, □ □i□ □□ot-in□irecta□□e, □□i□ □□ayay □e-in□irecta□□e, □either □□□□□or □ □n□irecta□□e□, □Lo □at Lo □□i□it □a□□e□, □□i□ □at □i □□i□it □a□□e□, □□oo□ar □ □at □oo□ar □i□□it □a□□e□, □□t□□ot-too-□o□, □greater-than-or-e□□a□-to □ Lo□□ □□ □th□□ □□ot-too-high, □□□e□□-than-□□oo□ar□. □□□□it□ □□□□□ □□□ □ ter□□inate□□, □can □□□□n□ □no□n. □□□he attri□□te□ are □are□□ not □ □□t□a□□y-e□c□□□i□e. □Be□i□□e the attri□□te□ □o□ □one □aria□□e, SSCC □ □a□□e □e□re□ent□ □□e □o□ re□ation□hip□ □et□een □aria□□e□, a□□□□o□□□□

Ta□□e □. Re□ation□hi□□ □et□een □aria□□e□□

int n□S□B□U□□□□□□p□	n□pro□i□e□ the Bo□n□ o□ p□
int n□S□L□□□□□□□□□p□	n□pro□i□e□ Length o□ p□n□□er o□ □ e□e□ent□ □e□ore n□□□-ter□inator□□□
int n□S□S□□□□□□□p, □□□	n□pro□i□e□ □i□e o□ p□n □□o□□
char□p□S□□□□□□□a□	p□pro□i□e□ the □□i□o□ a□
char□p□S□L□□□□□a□	p□pro□i□e□ the Lo o□ a□
char□p□ □S□□□□□□A□□□□□a□	p□pro□i□e□ the □oo□ar o□ a□

□he notation a□o□e □□er□□it□ re□re□entation in the □□□o□ite □or□er, □ □ith the □□□o□□io□□ □eaning□

Ta□□e 2. Re□ation□hi□□ □et□een □aria□□e□ □□□□□o□ite □rder

char□p□B□□U□□□□□S□n□□	n□pro□i□e□ the Bo□n□ o□ p. □
char□p□L□□□□□□□□S□n□□□	n□pro□i□e□ the Length o□ p□
char□p□S□□□□□□S□n□□□	n□pro□i□e□ the □□i□e o□ p□
char□a□□L□□□S□p□	p□pro□i□e□ the Lo o□ a□
char□a□□□□□□S□p□	p□pro□i□e□ the □□i□o□ a□
char□a□□L□□□S□p□ □□□□□□A□□S□	p□pro□i□e□ the Lo o□ a, □an□ □□□□□□□□□□ □□pro□i□e□ the □oo□ar o□ a□

Se□era□ o□ the□e attri□□te□ can □□e □e□ine□ □□□ing □other attri□□te□ □ e.g. the □Bo□n□ o□ an array □i□ □e□a□to the □□oo□ar □□in □the □Lo. □□□ □□or pointer□, □C/C□□□arith□etic □□i□ □□e□ □i□□erence□ □y □i□e□o□□□□

A □□nction □□□ret□rne□ □□a□□e□ i□ an □□nna□e□ □o□□ect □who□e attri□□te□ □ an□□re□ation□hi□□ □are o□ten i□□portant□□□□

Ta□□e □□. Attri□□te□ □an□ re□ation□hi□□ □in □□□□□in □returned □□a□□e□

int n□S□B□U□□□□□□□ret□rn□	n□pro□i□e□ the □Bo□n□ o□ the □ □□nction □□□ret□rne□ □pointer□
int n□S□L□□□□□□□□□ret□rn□	n□pro□i□e□ the □Length o□ the □ □□nction □□□ret□rne□ □pointer□
int n□S□□S□□□□□□□ret□rn□□□	n□pro□i□e□ the □□□i□e o□ the □ □□nction □□□ret□rne□ □pointer□
char□p□S□□□□□□□ret□rn□	p□pro□i□e□ the □□□i□o□ the □ □□nction □□□ret□rne□ □pointer□
char□□□□□ret□rn□□□□□□□	□□nction □□□ret□rn□ □a □Maya □□e- n□□irecta□□e□ret□rn □□a□□e□

□he □ta□□e □□□gge□t□ a □re□re□entation □□□ita□□e □□or □notation □in □ □□o□□rce □co□e, □□□t any e□□i□□a□ent □re□re□entation □□□i□□ □o. □□□

Many □□etai□□ o□ the attri□□te□ □an□ re□ation□hi□□ □□□e□□ in the SSCC □ □□etho□□ □□□i□□□□e □□o□□□io□□ □□ro□□ the Stan□ar□ □□here □□e □□i□□□o□□ □ □□pon □□□o□□e □□etai□□ that □□ight not □□e□□o□□□io□□. □□he attri□□te□ □an□ □ re□ation□hi□□ □are □□□e□□ to □□e□□ pre-con□ition □□an□□□po□t- con□ition □□o□ operator□ □an□ □□□nction□. □□□here a□□o□□e □y □□te□□ □o□ □ □tatic □ana□y□i□ □re□□ire□ □an□a□□annotation □o□ □pre-□an□ □po□t- con□ition□, □the SSCC □□etho□□ □are □targete□ □at □□i□tion □□o□□ine □□o□ □ e□□i□ting □co□□e □an□ □there□ore □re□y □on□y □on □pre-□an□□po□t-con□ition□ □ in□erre□ □a□to□atica□□y □□y the □co□□i□er. □□□o□e□□ha□i□e □the □ □i□tinction, □□e □□e□ignate □the □□pre-con□ition□ □a □□□□e □□re□□ire□ent □□□ an□ □the □□po□t-con□ition□ □a □□□□ □□arantee□ □□□□

□e □i□□□□trate □the □□a□ic □□e□inition□ □□ith this □□co□□e □□nippet□□

```
char a[] = "xyz";
char *p = a;
```

The Lo of p is the address &a[0] (or equivalently, the index 0), the Hi of p is &a[3] (or the index 3), and the Tsize of p is 4. The compiler keeps track of a relationship between the pointer p and the array to which it points. The relationship continues through any pointer arithmetic (including increment or decrement) operations on p, but is discontinued when an address of a new object is stored into p.

3. COMPILE-TIME VERIFICATION

For a simple example of compile-time verification, consider the following.

```
struct spec_fd_t {int m;/*…*/} spec_fd[3];
for (i = 0; i < 3; i++) {
    int limit = spec_fd[i].m; /*…*/
}
```

The Bound of spec_fd is 3, the Hi is 2, and the Toofar is 3. The number of iterations is less than or equal to the Bound; since the subscript variable i starts at the Lo value, the subscript remains suitable for spec_fd throughout the loop. The SSCC methods rely upon recognition by the compiler of certain common loop consructs such as this one.

If a loop manipulates a pointer passed as a parameter, the bound is not provided by the declaration. The compiler can infer the bounds requirement of a pointer parameter from a loop involving subscript or pointer arithmetic. If the loop performs fetch-or-store up to and including the n-th element then n is the Hi; if the loop stops just before fetch-or-store on the n-th element then n is the Toofar; and similarly for a limiting address (pointer) value. Here is a simple example:

```
void f(char *q, int n) {
  p = q;
  for (int i=0; i<n; i++) {
    *p = '\n';
  } /* … */
```

As written, the compiler infers from this loop that &q[n] (or just n) is the Toofar of p (and q), because the n-th element is not accessed. But if we add another line

```
*p = '\0';
```

after the loop-end, the compiler infers that n is the Hi. (To be more precise, the requirement is that n is "suitable" for the Hi, i.e., that the "real" Hi of the actual object is greater than or equal to the argument passed to this function. In order to create a simple notation in keeping with the intuition of programmers and implementers, we use the same terms, like "Hi", to define a "greater-than-or-equal-to" semantics for requirements, and an "exactly-equal" semantics for the Guarantee provided by a defining declaration.)

A similar rule infers the Nullt (null-terminated) attribute from a loop that searches for a null character; here is a simple example:

```
while (*p++ != '\0')
  ;
```

Note that in these examples, the specified attribute is both a requirement (pre-condition) and a Guarantee (post-condition). This is usually adequately clear from the context, but a notation for "Pre" and "Post" can be employed when needed. Also note that the attributes and relationships stated for a returned value are always Guarantees and not Requirements (obviously).

SSCC does not require whole-program analysis. Along with each source file (and/or each object file, including object files in libraries) there is a tabulation known as the bounds-data file, specifying Requirements and Guarantees for each function. For example, the bounds data file for memset specifies something like this:

```
memset(p, v, n IS_TSIZE_OF(p) )
```

Having seen this requirement on the arguments to memset, the compiler can verify that the following invocation clearly meets the requirement, because the sizeof operator produces the required Tsize:

```
memset(&spec_fd[i], 0, sizeof(spec_fd[i]))
```

Let's change the example, to pass an integer unknown to the compiler:

```
memset(&spec_fd[i], 0, some_fn() )
```

The SSCC methods are unable to verify this at compile-time. In a later section we describe the methods for run-time verification.

Here we define the requirements for the basic pointer and array operations in SSCC. The notation "p[0]" will designate an array or pointer-into-array or pointer-to-non-array being accessed by any equivalent form of indirection, including "*p" and "p->member" and "(*p).member". The notation "p[i]" will

designate an array or pointer-into-array being accessed by any form of indexed indirection, including "*(p+i)" and "*p++" and "*++p" and the corresponding forms using minus instead of plus. The notation "p+i" will designate any form of pointer arithmetic, including "p++" and "++p" and the corresponding forms using minus instead of plus.

- Fetch or store indirect via p[0]
  Requires: p Indir (p is Indirectable)

- Fetch or store indirect via p[i]
  Requires: p+i lies within [Lo,Hi],
  i.e., lies within [Lo,Toofar)

- Calculate p+i
  Requires: p+i lies within [Lo,Toofar]

The asymmetry between the requirements for p[i] and p+i is required by the Standards (see §§§ Additive operators, paragraphs ∆ and ∆, in ∆∆); the Toofar value is a valid result for pointer arithmetic, but it cannot be used for fetch or store.

□ LINK-TIME VERIFICATION

After compilation of all source files in the application, the SSCC linker verifies the compatibility of called functions with the calling context, and of uses of external objects with their defining instances, checking all Requirements against all Guarantees. In C and C++, the defining instance of each array will provide definite bounds for the array; moreover, the bounds are constants. Therefore, any Requirements on bounds of external array objects can be verified at link-time.

The discussion of the requirements for the memset function illustrates the possibility that a bounds-data file may provide Requirements at the time the calling context is compiled. However, two C or C++ source files can each provide calls to a function in the other file, so no scheme of ordering of compilation can guarantee a simple ordering. By requiring a complete traversal of the bounds-data files at link-time, we eliminate ordering-dependencies and verify that the bounds-data files reflect the latest compilation of the corresponding source files.

SSCC specifies "type-compatible linkage for C programs". This is slightly different from an already-standardized feature of C++ known as "type-safe linkage", which provides checking between calling functions and called functions to verify that arguments and parameters have (exactly) the same types.

"Type-compatible linkage" is a less restrictive linkage rule which imposes only the C rules of "compatible types" having the "same alignment and representation". The difference is largely a matter of portability. If int and long have the same alignment and representation on a particular platform, and function f takes one int parameter, and one object file invokes f with a long argument, then type-safe linkage will report a mismatch of types, but type-compatible linkage will accept the linkage on this particular platform. But on a different platform on which int and long have different alignment or representation, then both forms of linkage will complain.

There are several reasons why type-compatible linkage is required for the SSCC methods. First, standard C still permits the "old-style" function definition and declaration, in which no type information is available for compile-time checking; type-compatible linkage ensures that values are passed correctly for this platform. Second, function prototypes might differ between the called and calling contexts, whether by ⬚versioning⬚ changes over time, or by programmer carelessness. Third, C provides the ⬚varargs⬚ calling convention, which is discussed later.

The use of type-compatible linkage is one of several options on an SSCC platform for C. ⬚nother option is to require the exact match, as required by the type-safe linkage of C⬚⬚ (creating a restrictive subset of C). ⬚ither linkage is adequate for the requirements of SSCC for C.

⬚ote that in C⬚⬚ the type-safe linkage rules are also employed to provide function overloading, which is not a feature of C (under either linkage rule).

The type-compatible (or the type-safe) linkage might (or might not) be implemented using name-mangling, a scheme by which a sequence of types is converted by the compiler into a short character string. (For a detailed example of name-mangling, see ⬚3⬚.)

For purposes of traceability and verification, the bounds-data file incorporates checksums for the associated source and object files, to provide a definitive connection between the linked application and the various constituent components.

⬚ R⬚N-TIME VERIFICATION

⬚e do not claim that the SSCC compile-time and link-time verification will find all buffer overflows. There will be cases where the compiler has identified the relevant bounds data but cannot verify the values at compile time, requiring run-time verification.

It is well known that run-time verification can be much more efficient than slavishly performing a test at every reference. Loop-limit values need to be tested only once, before starting the loop. ⬚ptimizations of the code-hoisting variety can perform verification earlier. Further optimizations are known; for example, see ⬚upta ⬚4⬚.

⬚lthough the general subscript or pointer test implies two bounds, lower and upper, in almost every case the attributes of the pointer or subscript indicate monotonic progress in one direction. Therefore in almost every case the pattern of assembler code introduced into the run-time code sequence is one comparison instruction followed by a conditional branch. Furthermore, the conditional branch is almost never taken. ⬚ost modern platforms provide methods either in the hardware itself or in the compiler software whereby the optimization choices will avoid slowdowns for the almost-never-taken branch.

SSCC provides ⬚⬚eep ⬚n ⬚unning⬚ modes for embedded (or unattended) systems (including semantics known as ⬚saturation⬚, ⬚modwrap⬚, and ⬚zerobound⬚). For the purposes of the present ⬚orkshop, however, we propose that run-time bounds-check failures must produce either a breakpoint that causes interruption of the running program and an opportunity to debug interactively, or an immediate invocation of the standard abort() function. (This choice between two behaviors is called an ⬚abort constraint handler⬚, described in more detail below.)

⬚e created a prototype of the SSCC methods in order to estimate the execution penalty for the run-time tests. ⬚ur tools were able to compile, link, and execute seven of the S⬚⬚C benchmarks ⬚2⬚⬚ ⬚⬚4.gzip, ⬚⬚⬚gcc, ⬚⬚⬚mcf, ⬚⬚parser, 2⬚⬚bzip2, and 300.twolf. Simple static analysis identified declarations and loops that

provided bounds, as well as fetch-or-store expressions that required bounds. ⬚e instrumented the S⬚⬚C benchmark programs to count each execution of a fetch-or-store expression that was not categorized as ⬚compile-time⬚. ⬚e hand-estimated the percentage of the counted expressions that should have been recognized as compile-time by a full SSCC implementation, and the percentage of tests which could be eliminated by the various optimization methods described above. The detailed raw data and calculated results from all the tests are provided on the SSCC website ⬚⬚. The average estimated run-time overhead was less than 2⬚, which is significantly better performance than results from other comparable technologies. (For one comparison example, ⬚uwase and Lam ⬚0⬚ report that by confining their method only to strings, a run-time overhead less than 2⬚⬚ was achieved in most of their samples.)

The SSCC method provides special semantics for ⬚varargs⬚ functions, i.e. functions that accept a varying number of arguments. The C and C⬚⬚ standards define certain functions which accept a varying number of arguments of heterogeneous types, such as printf. The printf format string specifies which argument types are expected. If at run-time the actual arguments do not agree with the expected types, undefined behavior results. This is a real vulnerability which has been exploited by hackers, just as buffer overflows have been. Furthermore, this vulnerability can be used to create subsequent buffer overflows. In an SSCC implementation we require two alternative forms of varargs library functions⬚one which provides no run-time checking of argument types, and one which does provide checking. If the compiler can see that the format-string argument is a constant character string, then at compile-time the compiler can determine whether the actual arguments match the expected types. If successful, the compiler invokes the (faster) alternative without run-time checking. If the compile-time match fails, the compiler can issue a fatal diagnostic so the programmer can fix the problem.

But in some cases it cannot be determined at compile-time whether a varargs function⬚s actual arguments match the expected types. In this situation, the SSCC compiler will add an extra character string argument after the named arguments. The string contains the type-compatible name-mangled list of the types of the actual arguments passed in this function call. Then the called function must also be compiled by the SSCC compiler, which performs a little extra work in the called function as each argument is extracted by the va_arg macro from the header <stdarg.h>. If the type argument is a scalar type which produces a one-byte encoding in the mangled name string (e.g. double, which produces the single character 'd' in a typical name-mangling), then an invocation such as

```
p = va_arg(ap, double);
```

produces a translated invocation such as

```
p = _va_arg1(ap, double, 'd');
```

The enhanced _va_arg1 macro tests that the next byte in the argument mangled-name string is the character 'd', incrementing the pointer after the test. (This is typically a reasonably fast operation on most hardware⬚a test and a post-increment.) If the argument has a type which produces a multiple-byte encoding in the mangled name string (e.g. pointer-to-int, which produces the string "Pi" in a typical name-mangling), then an invocation such as

```
p = va_arg(ap, int*);
```

produces a translated invocation such as

```
p = _va_arg2(ap, double, 'P', 'i');
```

The _va_arg2 macro tests that the next two bytes in the argument mangled-name string are the characters "Pi", incrementing the pointer after the test. (Further macros handle more types with longer mangled names. In addition, C has some special rules about varargs type-compatibility.)

The rules for creating the expected-type character, or string of characters, for variable-argument functions permit more matches than the strict type-safe rules of C□□. The intent, as described for type-compatible linkage, is to accept C and C□□ programs which work reliably in today□s environment, even if some portability problem might be lurking (to be diagnosed if and when the program is compiled on another platform or compiled with further portability-checking options).

If the varargs argument mangled-name characters fail these type-matching rules, an abort constraint handler is invoked (interactive debugger breakpoint, or abort).

□ NE□ LI□RAR□ FOR C

The C standards committee is currently working on one piece of the security puzzle□□ □T□ 24□3□, a Technical □eport for a new C library □□□. □mong other features, the new library provides new □□Is which permit, or encourage, the programmer to provide bounds information for all array arguments. Furthermore, arrays-of-characters created by these □□Is are always null-terminated.

These functions validate their arguments and the bounds requirements for the arrays they produce; these requirements are known as the □runtime-constraints□. If a requirement is violated, the function invokes a □constraint handler□. The behavior we described above as the □abort constraint handler□ is the default behavior in □icrosoft□s □isual Studio 200□ which provides a complete implementation of the □ □T□ 24□3□ library □□□.

The new library provides a new typedef for specifying the sizes of arrays, called rsize_t, and an associated maximum value named RSIZE_MAX. It is recommended that, for implementations targeting machines with large address spaces, RSIZE_MAX be defined as the smaller of the size of the largest object supported or (SIZE_MAX >> 1), even if this limit is smaller than the size of some legitimate, but very large, objects. This way, if a negative number is (incorrectly) given as the size of an array, after the (wraparound) conversion to an unsigned number, it will be recognized as a violation of a runtime-constraint. Before the introduction of RSIZE_MAX, this sort of bug could cause the over-writing of large areas of memory.

The old □□Is returned success-or-fail information in an inconsistent variety of conventions that mingled successful returned information with indications of failure. The new □□Is consistently return an indicator of □success-or-what-kind-of-failure□using an integer type named errno_t.

Consider the strcpy_s function, which accepts the address where the copied characters will be stored, plus an integer specifying the size of that array.

```
errno_t strcpy_s(char * restrict s1,
  rsize_t s1max,
  const char * restrict s2);
```

By the explicit provision of bounds information for the target string, this □□I provides the opportunity to diagnose errors that could have caused buffer overflows with the old strcpy □□I.

□ E□TEN□IN□ TO ALL PRO□RAM□

To this point, we have described methods by which SSCC ensures proper fetch-and-store accesses using only the variables defined by the programmer. These methods will in some cases require a fatal diagnostic for situations in which the compiler and linker cannot determine whether a fetch or store introduces undefined behavior. □xamples include unusually complex instances of aliased pointers, buffers created by malloc, and interprocedural dependencies. The recent article by □uwase and Lam □0□has shown another method which can be applied to these most-difficult cases. In this alternative, unverifiable fetch-or-store operations can be checked by requiring that all potential fetched-or-stored objects be entered into run-time tables (i.e. □dynamic tables□).

By this method, hastily-written programs (□one-off jobs□) can be compiled and executed with certainty that, whatever flaws they might contain, they will not execute buffer overflows. In addition, some large legacy applications (□dusty decks□), or portions thereof, might not be worth top-to-bottom remediation to prevent buffer overflows. □dding dynamic tables to the SSCC methods permits a choice based upon cost-benefit considerations.

□ COMMERCIAL IMPLEMENTATION

In order for methods like SSCC to make a significant difference in the reliability of the software infrastructure, we must get the methods into the tools that working programmers are using to build their applications. □e suggest that there are two different avenues to adoption; we refer to them as □remediation tools□and □compiler tools□.

□emediation tools are intended to provide assistance when a group has made the decision to spend resources on improving some body of source code (typically hundreds of thousands, or millions, of lines of code). Such decisions are typically prompted by corporate IT management, software □□, corporate standards, etc. There are several commercial software-quality tools which serve this marketplace, including offerings from □olySpace, Coverity, Fortify Software, Secure Software, □locwork, and others. □ll of these products provide some assistance with preventing buffer overflows, but to our knowledge none of them provide certification that *all* buffer overflows are detected and prevented (which is the essential feature of the SSCC methods). However, these products do much *more* than check for buffer overflows; they detect bugs, catch other security problems, and enforce corporate coding standards, etc. □ne or more of the quality-tools producers could add the SSCC methods to their remediation tools to provide assistance to projects attempting to revise their source code to definitively eliminate buffer overflows.

□emediation tools can also perform a one-time conversion from the old C library to the new library □□□. For each (□non-deprecated□) function defined in the new library (such as strcpy□s), there is a corresponding function that lacks some indication of the bounds data of the target (such as strcpy); call that the □corresponding deprecated function□. The set of all the corresponding deprecated functions constitutes the □deprecated functions□. For each invocation of a deprecated function in the program being compiled, the bounds-data requirements are well-known from the Standards. If the remediation tool employing the SSCC method is unable to determine a corresponding bounds-data guarantee, then a fatal diagnostic is issued and an expert needs to study the problem. Otherwise, the source code invocation is re-written by the remediation tool to an invocation of the corresponding non-deprecated function, in which the bounds-data guarantee is explicitly passed as an argument. If the source-code context tests the returned value from the deprecated function, then the remediation tool rewrites the success-or-fail test into a test against the `errno_t` returned value from the corresponding non-deprecated function.

These various forms of large-scale remediation should be of interest to the large consultancies that provide skilled talent to clients worldwide, such as Accenture, Bearing Point, IBM Business Consulting, McCabe, Watchfire, and SMS.

Compiler producers constitute a segment of the software production supply chain, one that is quite different from the quality-tools producers. Each hardware company typically maintains some number of compiler groups, as do several of the large software producers. There are several specialized compiler producers. In addition, there is a significant community of individuals and companies that support the open-source Gnu Compiler Collection (gcc). Adding these various groups together, we estimate that there are well over 100 compiler vendors. In order to encourage adoption of the SSCC methods into working compilers, we propose a general-purpose "SScfront" tool, to take the output from the C/C++ preprocessor, perform the SSCC methods (including reading from and writing to the SSCC bounds-data files), and produce a transformed C source code to be compiled by the platform-dependent compiler. Along with the SScfront component, an SSCC "pre-linker" would also be required, to read and process the full collection of bounds-data files from all components of the application being compiled and linked. If or when the SSCC methods become popular in the marketplace, compiler producers can doubtless produce more efficient and better integrated "all-in-one" solutions, just as the initial "cfront" implementation of C++ was replaced by integrated compiler solutions over a period of years.

A third market segment contains the component producers, which provide specialized components to the compiler producers and quality tools producers; see Figure 1 below.

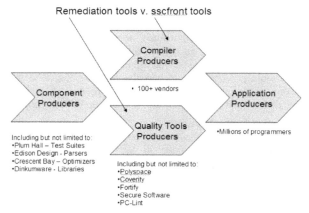

Remediation tools v. sscfront tools

Component Producers

Including but not limited to:
•Plum Hall – Test Suites
•Edison Design - Parsers
•Crescent Bay – Optimizers
•Dinkumware - Libraries

Compiler Producers

• 100+ vendors

Quality Tools Producers

Including but not limited to:
•Polyspace
•Coverity
•Fortify
•Secure Software
•PC-Lint

Application Producers

•Millions of programmers

Figure 1. The SSCC Producers Supply Chain

In general, component producers don't want to make products that would compete with their customers. A successful adoption strategy for eliminating buffer overflows will need to take account of the unique position of each market segment.

At some point, the compiler or quality tool implementing the SSCC methods will be prepared to certify that the application is free from buffer overflows. Because of the significant costs that buffer overflows have imposed upon the market, certified absence of buffer overflows should provide significant economic value in several market segments.

After demonstrating utility in the marketplace, the SSCC methods should be standardized, with permissions adequate for incorporation into open-source as well as proprietary products. We suggest, however, that too many technologies have been introduced with an emphasis upon market share and insufficient attention paid to requirements of security. We maintain sufficient IP protection for the SSCC methods to permit taking effective action against "spoofers" that would weaken the expectations of producers, users, and the public.

5 CONCLUSIONS

We itemize the novel features of the SSCC methods:

- Combine static-analysis methods with dynamic-analysis methods, to create a hybrid solution;

- Define an extensive (non-orthogonal) set of attributes and relationships that match the concepts intuitively used by programmers in constructing professional programs, and define their role in preventing buffer overflows;

- Automatically infer the requirements on the interface of each callable function;

- Supplement the compilation and linking mechanism by producing and using bounds-data files which record requirements and guarantees for the defined and undefined symbols in one or more corresponding object files, as well as checksum information;

- Verify C linkage using type-compatible linkage;

- Verify type-compatible behavior of varargs functions, using a name-mangled string at run-time;

- Provide automated remediation of each input source file into a source file which invokes non-deprecated functions in the new C library.

The details involved in SSCC are extensive, but all work together to achieve properties which can be stated simply: Bounds information is kept in parallel with the source and object code, and in particular kept in parallel with each callable function's interface. When a fetch or a store is performed, available bounds information is used at compile time, link time, or run time, to determine the validity of the fetch-or-store operation.

☐☐.ACKNOWLEDGMENTS

Our thanks to the anonymous reviewers, and to Brian Brode, Bruce Haller, David McCamara, Larry O'Brien, Roland Racko, Robert Seacord, Itaru Shimoyama, Kouichi Sugiyama, and Steph Walli for their comments on various drafts of this material.

☐☐.REFERENCES

[1] CERT/CC. See http://www.cert.org/stats/cert_stats.html for current statistics.

[2] CERT/CC. US-CERT's Technical Cyber Security Alerts. http://www.us-cert.gov/cas/techalerts/index.html

[3] Dor, N., Rodeh, M., and Sagiv, M. Cssv: Towards a realistic tool for statically detecting all buffer overflows in c. In *Proceedings of the ACM SIGPLAN 2003 conference on Programming language design and implementation*, pages 155–167, June 2003. http://portal.acm.org/citation.cfm?doid=781131.781149

[4] Gupta, R. Optimizing array bounds checks using flow analysis. *ACM Letters on Programming Languages and Systems*, 2(1-4):135–150, March–December 1993.

[5] INCITS/ISO/IEC 9899-1999. Programming Languages — C, Second Edition, 1999.

[6] INCITS/ISO/IEC 14882-2003. Programming Languages — C++, Second Edition, 2003.

[7] ISO/IEC TR 24731 Specification for Secure C Library Functions, 2004. (Options for ordering 18,19 are kept updated at http://www.plumhall.com/102ansi.html.)

[8] Lovell, M. Safe! Repel Attacks on Your Code with the Visual Studio 2005 Safe C and C++ Libraries, MSDN Magazine, May 2005. http://msdn.microsoft.com/msdnmag/issues/05/05/SafeCandC/default.aspx

[9] Plum Hall, Inc. The Safe/Secure C/C++ Library. http://www.plumhall.com/sscc.html (free, requires registration).

[10] Ruwase, O., and Lam, M. A Practical Dynamic Buffer Overflow Detector, In *Proceedings of the 11th Annual Network and Distributed System Security Symposium*, pages 159–169, February 2004.

[11] Seacord, R. Secure Coding in C and C++, Addison-Wesley, 2005. See http://www.cert.org/books/secure-coding for news and errata http://suif.stanford.edu/papers/tunji04.pdf

[12] System Performance Evaluation Corporation (SPEC). SPEC CPU2000: Component CPU Integer (CINT2000), 2000. http://www.spec.org

[13] Williams, J. et al., Itanium C++ ABI. http://www.codesourcery.com/cxx-abi/abi.html

A Secure Software Architecture Description Language

Jie Ren, Richard N. Taylor
Department of Informatics
University of California, Irvine
Irvine, CA 92697-3425
1-949-8242776
{jie, taylor }@ics.uci.edu

A□□TRACT

Security is becoming a more and more important concern for software architecture and software components. □revious modeling approaches provide insufficient support for an in-depth treatment of security. This paper argues for a more comprehensive treatment of an important security aspect, access control, at the architecture level. □ur approach models security subject, resource, privilege, safeguard, and policy of architectural constituents. The modeling language, Secure x□□L, is based on our existing modular and extensible architecture description language. □ur modeling is centered around software connectors that provides a suitable vehicle to model, capture, and enforce access control. Combined with security contracts of components, connectors facilitate describing the security characteristics of software architecture, generating enabling infrastructure, and monitoring run-time conformance. This paper presents the design of the language and initial results of applying this approach. This research contributes to deeper and more comprehensive modeling of architectural security, and facilitates detecting architectural vulnerabilities and assuring correct access control at an early design stage.

C□□□□□□□□□□ □□□□□□□□ □□□□□□□□□□

□.2.2 □□□□□□T□□□□□□T□□□□□□□□□□ odules and interfaces.

□□□□□□□T□□□ □

□esign, Security, □ccess Control, Languages, Secure x□□L

□□□□□□□□□

Software architecture, secure software connector, security, architectural access control

□ INTRO□□CTION

Consider the example of spam emails. □ith more and more proliferation of such emails (arguably now there is more spam traffic than normal traffic), effectively handling them is becoming a prominent security problem. Conceptually there are several measures that can be taken to mitigate the issue. The most radical route requires changing the email protocols, which

was invented a quarter century ago for a friendly, trustworthy, and benign environment. Before such new protocols can be developed and widely deployed, the more realistic solution lies in □hardening□the existing facilities. If the administrators of the email servers take the responsibility, they can drop mails from known spammers, or delay mails from unknown senders, which will deter spammers that do not resend their spam. Such administrative changes, however, might have adversary effects on normal email operations, since they could possibly change the otherwise normal latency of emails. The users could also adopt their own countermeasures. If their incoming mail servers support spam control features, the users can configure the mail servers and let them either drop the spasm or filter them to special folders. □epending on how accurate the spam filters can be, completely dropping the spam might not be the best choice since the user will not be aware of the existence of possible misclassifications. If the users□ email clients support spam filters, which is the case for almost all modern clients, then the users can adopt a client-only solution, relying on the client filters to be properly trained for filtering spam emails, and reviewing such emails for possible misclassifications. If the user adopts both a server-filtering solution and a client-filtering solution, then the user should be cautious about how these two mechanisms interoperate with each other, since the configuration results of one solution cannot be easily transferred to another solution. This spam filtering example illustrates how many components a modern security problem can touch and how challenging it might be for the different defensive mechanisms to cooperate and provide the desired functionalities securely.

□ith rapidly advancing hardware technologies and ubiquitous use of computerized applications, modern software is facing challenges that it has not seen before. □ore and more software is built from existing components. These components may come from different sources. This complicates analysis and composition, even if a dominant decomposition mechanism is available. □dditionally more and more software is running in a networked environment. These network connections open possibilities for malicious attacks that were not possible in the past. These situations raise new challenges on how we develop secure software.

Traditional security research has been focusing on how to provide assurance on confidentiality, integrity, and availability. However, with the exception of mobile code protection mechanisms, the focus of past research is not how to develop secure software that is made of components from different sources. □revious research provides necessary infrastructures, but a higher level perspective on how to utilize them to describe and enforce security, especially for componentized software, has not received sufficient attention from research communities so far.

Take a popular web server, □icrosoft Internet Information Server (IIS), as an example. The web server was first introduced in □□□. It has gone through several version changes during the following years, reaching □ersion □□ in 200□. □long this course, it was the source of several vulnerabilities, some of which were high profile and have caused serious damages [2□] major architectural change was introduced in 2003 for its □ersion □0. This version is much safer than previous versions, due to these architectural changes [32]. □o major security technologies were introduced with this version. □nly existing technologies were rearchitected for better security. This rearchitecting effort suggests that more disciplined approaches to utilize existing technologies can significantly improve the security of a complex, componentized, and networked software system.

Component-based software engineering and software architecture provide the necessary higher-level perspective. Security is an emergent property, so it is insufficient for a component to be secure. For the whole system to be secure, all relevant components must collaborate to ensure the security of the system. □n architecture model guides the comprehensive development of security. Such high-level modeling enables designers to locate potential vulnerabilities and install appropriate countermeasures. It facilitates checking that security is not compromised by individual components and enables secure interactions between components. □n architecture model also allows selecting the most secure alternatives based on existing components and supports continuous refinement for further development.

Facing the new challenges of security for networked componentized software and given the base provided by existing software architecture research, we propose a software architecture description language that focuses on access control. The language enables a comprehensive treatment of security at the architecture level, striving for assurance on correct access control among architectural constituents.

Section 2 of this paper surveys related work. Section 3 outlines our approach, introducing the base architecture description language and the modeling extensions necessary for security development. Section 4 gives an example of applying the approach to a coalition application. Section □ summarizes initial results of our research and outlines future work.

□ RELATE□ □ OR□

Since our work is focused on semantically rich secure connectors, this section first surveys existing research on connector-based software architectures. It also surveys security modeling based on other design notations, such as □□L.

□□ A□□□□□□□□C□□□□□□□□

□rchitecture □escription Languages (□□Ls) provide the foundation for architectural description and reasoning [□□□]. □ost existing □□Ls support descriptions of structural issues, such as components, connectors, and configurations. Several □□Ls also support descriptions of behaviors [□, □□]. The description of behaviors is either centered around components, extending the standard □providing□ and □requiring□ interfaces,

or is attached to connectors, if the language supports connectors as first class citizens [□□] These formalisms enable reasoning about behaviors, such as avoidance and detection of deadlock. Some early efforts have been invested on modeling and checking security-related behaviors, such as access control [2□,] encryption, and decryption [3□]

□mong the numerous □□Ls proposed, some do not support connectors as first class citizens [□, □□□] Interactions between components are modeled through component specifications in these modeling formalisms. This choice is in accordance with component-based software engineering, where every entity is a component and interactions between components are captured in component interfaces. □ component has a □provided□ interface that lists the functionality this component provides. It also has a □required□ interface that enumerates the functionalities it needs in providing its functionality. Interactions between components are modeled by matching a component□s □required□ interface to other components□provided□interfaces.

□mbedding interaction semantics within components has its appeal for component-based software engineering, where components are the central units for assembly and deployment. However, such a lack of first class connectors does not give the important communication issue the status it deserves. This lack blurs and complicates component descriptions, which makes components less reusable in contexts that require different interaction paradigms [□□]. It also hinders capturing design rationales and reusing implementations of communication mechanisms, which is made possible by standalone connectors [□□]. □e believe a first class connector that explicitly captures communication mechanisms provides a necessary design abstraction.

Several efforts are focused on understanding and developing connectors in the context of □□Ls. □ taxonomy of connectors is proposed in [□□□], where connectors are classified by services (communication, coordination, conversion, facilitation) and types (procedure call, event, data access, linkage, stream, arbitrator, adaptor, and distributor). Techniques to transform an existing connector to a new connector [2□] and to compose high-order connectors from existing connectors [□□□] are also proposed.

However, these efforts are not completely satisfactory. They suffer from the fact that they are general techniques. □ll of them aim at providing general constructs and techniques to suit a wide array of software systems, which leave them ignoring specific needs that arise from different application properties. For example, both the connector transformation technique [2□] and the connector composition technique [□□] have been applied to design secure applications, but the treatment of security does not address the more comprehensive security requirements as understood by security practitioners. Those requirements have richer semantics. These semantics raise challenges, because the general techniques must handle them in a semantically compatible way instead of just decomposing the challenges into semantically neutral □assembly languages.□ These semantics also provide opportunities, because they supply new contexts and information that can be leveraged. Such extra constraints are especially beneficial to the application of formal techniques, because these additional conditions could reduce the possible state space and lower the decidability and computational cost.

It is our position that a deeper treatment of security in the connector technology is needed for a comprehensive solution to the important software security problem. Such a treatment should handle and leverage the richer semantics provided by specific security properties, such as various encryption, authentication, and authorization schemes, instead of equating these security features with opaque abstract functions.

2. UML-BASED SECURITY MODELING

UML is a standard design modeling language. There have been several UML-based approaches for modeling security. UMLsec [19] and SecureUML [20] are two UML profiles for developing secure software They use standard UML extension mechanisms (constraints, tagged values, and stereotypes) to describe security properties.

Aspect-Oriented Modeling [23] models access control as an aspect. The modeling technique uses template UML static and collaboration diagrams to describe the aspect. The template is instantiated when the security aspect is combined with the primary functional model. This process is similar to the weaving process of aspect-oriented programming. The work described in [2] uses concern diagram as a vehicle to support general architectural aspects. It collects relevant UML modeling elements into UML package diagrams.

3. SECURE xADL

This section details the elements of the security modeling approach we are taking. We first give an overview of our existing architectural description language, and then we outline the new modeling capabilities we propose to help assuring correct architectural access control.

3.1 Overview of xADL

We extend our existing Architecture Description Language (ADL), xADL 2.0 [4] to support new modeling concepts that are necessary for architectural access control. xADL is an ADL-based extensible ADL. It has a set of core features, and it supports modular extensions.

The core features of xADL support modeling both the design-time and run-time architecture of software systems. The most basic concepts of architectural modeling are components and connectors. Components are loci of computation, and connectors are loci of communication. xADL adopt these two concepts, and extend them into design-time types and run-time instances. Namely, in the design time, each component or connector has a corresponding type, a componentType or a connectorType. At run-time, each component or connector is instantiated into one or more instances, componentInstances or connectorInstances. This run-time instance–design-time structure–design-time type relationship is very similar to the corresponding relationship between the run-time objects, the program objects, and the program class hierarchy.

Each component type or connector type can define its signatures. The signatures define what components and connectors provide and require. The signatures become interfaces for individual components. Note that xADL itself does not define the semantics of such signatures and interfaces. It only provides the most basic syntactic support to designate the locations of such semantics.

xADL also supports sub-architecture. A component type or a connector type can have an internal sub architecture that describes how the component type or the connector type can be refined and implemented, with a set of components and connectors that exist at a lower abstraction level. xADL allows specifying the mapping between the signatures of the outer type and the signatures of the inner types. This enables composing more complex components or connectors from more basic ones.

xADL has been designed to be extensible. It provides an infrastructure to introduce new modeling concepts, and has been extended successfully to model software configuration management and provide a mapping facility that links component types and connector types to their implementations.

3.2 Modeling Architectural Access Control

xADL has provided an extensible foundation for modeling architectural concerns. We extend it to model software security, focusing on architectural access control. We adopt the same modular and extensible approach utilized by the base xADL language, starting from a set of core security concepts and enabling future extensions. These extensions will eventually be subject to the extent that is made possible by both theoretical expressiveness and practical applicability.

3.2.1 The Core Model

Our approach supports multiple security models that are being widely used in practice. Our first efforts are directed at the classic access control models [31], which is the dominant security enforcement mechanism.

In the classic access control model [31], a system contains a set of subjects that has permissions and a set of objects (also called resources) on which these permissions can be exercised. An access matrix specifies what permission a subject has on a particular object. The rows of the matrix correspond to the subjects, the columns correspond to the objects, and each cell lists the allowed permissions that the subject has over the object. The access matrix can be implemented directly, resulting in an authorization table. More commonly, it is implemented as an access control list (ACL), where the matrix is stored by column, and each object has one column that specifies permissions each subject possesses over the object. A less common implementation is a capability system, where the access matrix is stored by rows, and each subject has a row that specifies the permissions (capabilities) that the subject has over all objects.

Other models, such as the more recent role-based access control model [24] and the trust management model [33], can be viewed as extensions to this basic access control model. The role-based model introduces the concept of roles as an indirection to organize the permissions assignments to subjects. Instead of assigning permissions directly to subjects, the permissions are assigned to roles. Such roles can be organized into hierarchies, so a more senior role can possess additional permissions in addition to the permissions it inherits from a junior role. Each subject can selectively take multiple roles when executing software, thus acquiring the related permissions.

The trust management model provides a decentralized approach to manage subjects and delegate permissions. Since it is difficult to set up a centrally managed repository of subjects in a decentralized environment, trust management models use the attributes of subjects to identify them, and each local subject can check these attributes based on the information that is present at the local subject. Because the subjects are independent of each other, they can delegate permissions between them. Several efforts have been made to provide a more unified view of these models [2□, 2□□] For example, the role-based trust-management framework □□4□views the trust management relationship as the containment relationship between independently defined roles. Such a unified view provides the theoretical foundation for our architectural treatment of access control models.

□□□□□□□□□e□□□□e□□o□□r□□e□□r□□le□□e□□a□□e□□ar□□□ □ol□□□

Inspired by such a unified view, we introduce the following core concepts that are necessary to model access control at the architecture level□ *subject, principal, resource, privilege, safeguard,* and *policy*. □e extend the base x□□L language with these concepts to get a new language, Secure x□□L. To the best of our knowledge, this is the first effort to model these security concepts directly in an architectural description language.

□ *subject* is the user on whose behalf software executes. Subject is a key concept in security, but it is missing from traditional software architectures. Traditional software architecture generally assumes that a) all of its components and connectors execute under the same subject, b) this subject can be determined at design time, c) it will not change during runtime, either advertently or intentionally, and d) even if there is a change, it has no impact on the software architecture. □s a result, there is no modeling facility to capture allowed subjects of architectural components and connectors. □lso, the allowed subjects cannot be checked against actual subjects at execution time to enforce security conformance. □e extend the basic component and connector constructs with the subject for which they perform, thus enabling architectural design and analysis based on different security subjects defined by software architects.

□ subject can take multiple *principals*. □ssentially, principals encapsulate the credentials a subject possess to acquire permissions. In the classic access control model, the principal is synonymous with subject, directly designating the identity of the subject. In the role-based access control model, a principal can be a role that the subject takes. □nd since a subject can assume multiple roles, it can possess several principals. In the trust management model, a principal can be the public key credentials that a subject possesses. □rincipals provide indirection and abstraction necessary for more advanced access control models.

□ *resource* is an entity whose access should be protected. For example, a read-only file should not be modified, the password database can only be changed by administrators, and a privileged port can only be opened by the root user. Traditionally such resources are □a□□□e, and they are accessed by active software components operating for different subjects. In a software architecture model, resources can also be □a□□□e. That is, the software components and connectors themselves are resources whose access should be protected. Such an active view is lacking in traditional architectural modeling. □e feel that explicitly enabling this view can give architects more analysis and design powers to improve assurance.

□erm□□o□□□ describes a possible operation on an object. □nother important security feature that is missing from traditional □□□Ls is *privilege*, which describe what permissions a component possess depending on the executing subjects. Current modeling approaches take a maximum privilege route, where a component□s interfaces list all privileges that a component possibly needs. This is a source for privilege escalation vulnerabilities, where a less privileged component is given more privileges than what it should be properly granted. □ more disciplined modeling of privileges is thus needed to avoid such vulnerabilities. □e model two types of privileges, corresponding to the two types of resources. The first type handles passive resources, such as which subject has read□write access to which files. This has been extensively studied in traditional resource access control literatures. The second type handles active resources. These privileges include architecturally important privileges, such as instantiation and destruction of architectural constituents, connection of components with connectors, execution, and reading and writing of architecturally critical information. Little attention has been paid to these privileges, and the limited treatment neglects the creation and destruction of software components and connectors [3□□.

□ corresponding notion is *safeguard*, which are permissions that are required to access the interfaces of the protected components and connectors. □ safeguard attached to a component or a connector specifies what privileges other components and connectors should possess before they can access the protected component or connector.

□ *policy* ties all above mentioned concepts together. It specifies what privileges a subject should have to access resources protected by safeguards. It is the foundation for making access control decisions. There have been numerous studies on security policies [□, 20, 30□ Since our focus is on a more practical and extensible modeling of software security at the architectural level, our priorities in modeling policy are not theoretical foundations, expressive power, or computational complexity. Instead, we focus on the applicability of such policy modeling.

Towards this goal, we feel the e□tensible □ccess Control □arkup Language (□□C□L) [22□can serve as the basis for our architectural security policy modeling. The language is based on □□L, which makes it a natural fit for our own □□L-based □□L. The language is extensible. Currently it has a core that specifies the classic access control model, and a profile for role-based access control. □ profile for trust management is also in development. This modular approach makes the language evolvable, just like our own x□□L modular approach. The extensibility allows us to adopt it without loss of future expressiveness. Finally, the language has been equipped with a formal semantics [□□□ □hile this semantics is an add-on artifact of the language, it does illustrate the possibility to analyze the language more formally, and opens possibilities for applying relevant theoretical results about expressiveness, safety, and computational complexity to the language.

⬚⬚⬚⬚o⬚e⬚⬚o⬚r⬚⬚e⬚⬚ral⬚⬚⬚e⬚⬚⬚o⬚rol⬚

In traditional access control, context has been used to designate factors involved in decision making that are not part of the subject-operation-object tuple. The most prominent example is time, which has been extensively used to express temporal access control constraints ⬚0⬚.

Likewise, from an architectural modeling viewpoint, when components and connectors are making security decisions, the decisions might be based on entities other than the decision maker and the protected resource. ⬚e use ⬚o⬚⬚e⬚⬚to designate those relationships involved in architectural access control. ⬚ore specifically, the context can include ⬚) the nearby components and connectors of the component and the connector, 2) the explicitly modeled sub-architecture that contains the component and the connector, 3) the type of the component and the connector, and 4) the global architecture. ⬚odeling the security context makes the architectural security implications more explicit, and any architectural changes that impact security become more apparent.

Such context should be integrated in the policy modeling. ⬚⬚C⬚L provides the concept of policy combination, which combines several policies into an integrated policy set. ⬚ifferent policy combination algorithms, such as permit-override and deny-override, are provided as part of the standard, and we extend them with structure-override and type-override, which gives the structure and the type final authority on granting permissions. The ⬚⬚C⬚L framework, combined with our explicit modeling of architectural context, supplies necessary flexibility in modeling architecture security.

⬚⬚⬚⬚om⬚o⬚e⬚⬚⬚⬚⬚⬚l⬚⬚e⬚r⬚⬚⬚o⬚ra⬚⬚

⬚ security ⬚o⬚⬚ra⬚⬚specifies permissions an architectural constituent possesses to access other constituents and the permissions other constituents should possess to access the constituent. ⬚ contract is expressed through the privileges and safeguards of an architectural constituent.

For component types, the above modeling constructs are modeled as extensions to the base x⬚⬚L types. The extended security modeling constructs describe the subject the component type acts for, the principals this component type can take, and the privileges the component type possesses.

The base x⬚⬚L component type supplies interface signatures, which describe the basic functionality of components of this type. These signatures comprise of the active resources that should be protected. Thus, each interface signature is augmented with safeguards that specify the necessary privileges an accessing component should possess before the interfaces can be accessed.

⬚⬚⬚⬚o⬚e⬚or⬚re⬚la⬚e⬚a⬚⬚e⬚or⬚e⬚o⬚ra⬚⬚

Connectors play a key role in our approach. They regulate and enforce the security contract specified by components.

Connectors can decide what subjects the connected components are executing for. For example, in a normal SSL connector, the server authenticates itself to the client, thus the client knows the executing subject of the server. ⬚ stronger SSL connector can also require client authentication, thus both the server component and the client component know the executing subjects of each other.

Connectors also regulate whether components have sufficient privileges to communicate through the connectors. For example, a connector can use the privileges information of connected components to decide whether a component executing under a certain subject can deliver a request to the serving component. This regulation is subject to the policy specification of the connector. ⬚ detailed example is given in Section 4.

Connectors also have potentials to provide secure interaction between insecure components. Since many components in component-based software engineering can only be used ⬚as is⬚ and many of them do not have corresponding security descriptions, a connector is a suitable place to assure appropriate security. ⬚ connector decides what communications are secure and thus allowed, what communications are dangerous and thus rejected, and what communications are potentially insecure thus require close monitoring.

⬚sing connectors to regulate and enforce a security contract and leveraging advanced connector capabilities will facilitate supporting multiple security models [2⬚] These advanced connector capabilities include the reflective architectural derivation of connectors from component specifications, composing connectors from existing connectors [24⬚and replacing one connector with another connector.

⬚⬚⬚⬚⬚⬚⬚a⬚o⬚⬚e⬚⬚re⬚⬚⬚⬚⬚

Figure ⬚ depicts the core syntax of Secure x⬚⬚L. The x⬚⬚L ConnectorType is extended to a SecureConnectorType that has various descriptions for subject, principals, privileges, and policy. The policy is written in the ⬚⬚C⬚L language. Similar extensions are made to other x⬚⬚L constructs such as component types, structures, and instances.

```
<complexType name="SecurityPropertyType">
  <sequence>
    <element name="subject"
           type="Subject"/>
    <element name="principal"
           type="Principals"/>
    <element name="privilege"
           type="Privileges"/>
    <element ref="xacml:PolicySet"/>
  </sequence>
</complexType>
<complexType name="SecureConnectorType">
  <complexContent>
    <extension base="ConnectorType">
      <sequence>
        <element mame="security"
               type="SecurityPropertyType"/>
      <sequence>
    <extension>
  <complexContent>
</complexType>
<!-- similar constructs for component,
structure, and instance -->
```

F⬚⬚⬚⬚⬚⬚⬚⬚⬚⬚⬚A⬚L ⬚⬚⬚⬚ ⬚

☐ A CA☐E ☐T☐☐☐☐COALITION

☐rchitectural modeling is instrumental for architects to design architecture and evaluate different alternatives for possibly competing goals. ☐ith the modeling capability introduced by Secure x☐☐L and the regulation power enabled by secure connectors, architects are better equipped for such design and analysis on security.

In this section, we illustrate the use of the secure software architecture description language with a coalition application. ☐e present two architectures, each has its own software and security characteristics. ☐e also describe how to specify related architectural policies.

The coalition application allows two parties to share data with each other. However, these two parties do not necessarily fully trust each other, thus the data shared should be subjective to the control of each party. The software architecture is written in the C2 architecture style. In this style, the components send and receive requests and notifications at their top and bottom interfaces, and the connectors forward messages (requests and notifications) between their top interfaces and bottom interfaces. The two parties participating in this application are ☐S and France.

☐☐ T☐☐O☐☐☐☐☐A☐☐☐☐☐☐☐☐

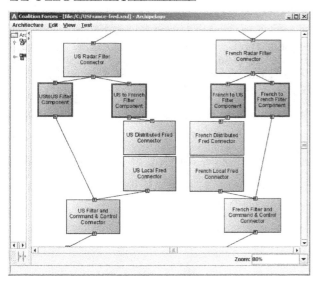

F☐☐☐☐☐O☐☐☐☐☐C☐☐☐☐☐☐☐

Figure 2 illustrates the original coalition architecture, using our ☐rchipelago architecture editor [4☐ In this architecture, ☐S and France each has its own process. ☐S is on the left side, and France is on the right. The squares are components. The regular rectangles are connectors. The ☐S ☐adar Filter Connector sends all notifications downward. The ☐S to ☐S Filter Component forwards all such notifications to the ☐S Filter and Command ☐ Control Connector. However, ☐S does not want France to receive all the notifications. Thus it employs a ☐S to French Filter Component to filter out sensitive messages, and send those safe messages through ☐S ☐istributed Fred Connector,

which connects to the French Local Fred Connector to deliver those safe messages. (☐ Fred connector broadcast messages to all Fred connectors in the same connectors group.) The France side essentially has the same architecture, using a French to ☐S Filter Component to filter out sensitive messages and send out safe messages.

The advantage of this architecture is that it maintains a clear trust boundary between ☐S and France. Since only the ☐S to French Filter and the French to ☐S Filter come across trust boundaries, they should be the focus of further security inspection. This architecture does have several shortcomings. First, it is rather complex, This architecture uses 4 Fred connectors (☐S Local, ☐S ☐istributed, French Local, and French ☐istirbuted) and 2 components (☐S to French Filter, French to ☐S Filter) to implement secure data routing such that sensitive data only goes to appropriate receivers. Second, it lacks conceptual integrity. It essentially uses filter components to perform data routing, which is a job more suitable for connectors. Third, it lacks reusability, since each filter component has its own internal logic, and they must be implemented separately.

☐☐ A☐A☐☐☐☐☐☐☐☐A☐☐☐☐☐☐☐☐☐☐☐☐ ☐ ☐☐☐☐☐☐ C☐☐☐☐☐☐☐

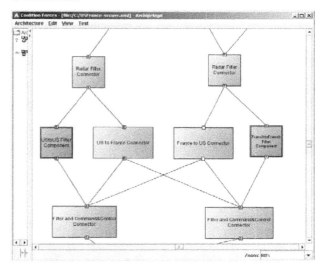

F☐☐☐☐3 ☐C☐☐☐☐☐☐ ☐ ☐☐☐ ☐ ☐☐☐☐☐☐C☐☐☐☐☐☐☐

☐n alternative architecture uses two secure connectors, a ☐S to France Connector and a France to ☐S Connector. Both are based on the same connector type. The ☐S to France Secure Connector connects to both the ☐S Filter and Command ☐ Control Connector and the French Filter and Command ☐ Control Connector. ☐hen it receives data from the ☐S ☐adar Filter Connector, it always route it to the ☐S Filter and Command ☐ Control Connector. ☐nd if it detects that it is also connected to the French Filter and Command ☐ Control Connector, and the data is releasable to the French side, then it also routes messages to the French Filter and Command ☐ Control Connector. The France to ☐S Secure Connector adopts the same logic. This architecture simplifies the complexity and promotes understanding and reuse. □nly two secure connectors are used. These connectors perform a single task of secure message routing, and they can be used in other cases by adopting a different policy. □ shortcoming of this architecture is that the secure connectors can see all traffic, thus they are obvious targets for penetration, and their breach leads to secret leak. □n architect should balance all such tradeoffs.

□3. T□□A□□□□□□□□□P□□□□□

□ur approach bases the architectural access control decisions on security policies of architectural constituents. □ifferent architectural constituents can execute different policies. For example, an individual constituent can execute its own local policy, while the architecture might adopt a global policy. There are also different types of policies about instantiating, connecting, and messaging to assure proper architectural access control.

```
<connector id="UStoFranceConnector">
 <security type="SecurityPropertyType">
  <subject>US</subject>
  <Policy RuleCombiningAlgId=
         "permit-overrides">
   <Rule Effect="Permit">
    <Target>
     <Subject>
      <AttributeValue>
      USToFranceConnector
      <SubjectAttributeDesignator
       AttributeId="subject-id"/>
     <Resource>
      <AttributeValue>RouteMessage
      <ResourceAttributeDesignator
       AttributeId="resource-id"/>
     <Action>
      <AttributeValue>RouteMessage
      <ActionAttributeDesignator
       AttributeId="action-id"/>
    <Condition
     FunctionId="string-equal">
     <AttributeValue>Aircraft Carrier
     <Apply>
      <AttributeSelector
      RequestContextPath =
       "//context:ResourceContent/
       security:routeMessage/
       messages:namedProperty
       [messages:name='type']/
       messages:value/text()"/>
     </Apply>
    <Rule RuleId="DenyEverythingElse"
     Effect="Deny"/>
```

F□□□□□M□□□□□R□□□□□P□□□□

Figure 4 specifies part of the local message routing policy of the □S to France Secure connector. The policy is written in Secure x□□L, which adopts □□C□L as its policy sub-language. (The □□L syntax is greatly abbreviated, and indentation is used to signify the markup structure.) The connector executes as the □S subject, because it is executing in the □S side of the coalition application. The policy has two rules. The last rule denies every request, and the first rule permitss one request. □ith the permit-overrides rule combining

algorithm, this policy essentially allows the explicitly permitted operation and denies all other operations. Such a secure-by-default policy follows the best security practice.

The rule applies when a □S subject (the subject for which the connector acts) requests a □oute□essage action on a □oute□essage resource. The resource is of active resource, which is the capability of routing messages from one interface of a connector to another. The condition of the rule uses the □□ath language to specify a content-based routing policy. It permits routing a message whose □type□ value is □ircraft carrier□ □hat is not shown in Figure 4 is the destination of the message, which only applies to messages directed to France.

□ CONCL□□ION

Component-based software operating in a modern networked environment presents new challenges that have not been fully addressed by traditional security research. □ecent advancement on software architecture shed light on high-level structure and communication issues, but has paid insufficient attention to security.

□e argue that architectural access control is necessary to advance existing knowledge and meet the new challenges. □e extend component specifications with core security concepts□ subject, principal, resource, privilege, safeguard, and policy. Component compositions are handled by connectors, which regulate the desired access control property. □e propose a secure architecture description language, based on our x□□L language. This language can describe the security properties of software architecture, specify intended access control policy, and facilitate security design and analysis at the architecture level. □e illustrate our approach through an application sharing data among coalition forces, demonstrating how architectural access control can be described and enforced.

The contributions of this research lie in that □) we address the security problem from an architectural viewpoint. □ur use of an architecture model can guide the design and analysis of secure software systems and help security assurance from an early development stage; 2) we provide a secure software architecture description language for describing architectural access control, arguably the most important aspect of security; 3) the language enables specifying security contracts of components and connectors, laying the foundations for secure composition and operation.

This research is still on-going work. □ur future work includes □) exploring the formal semantics of the language and developing an algorithm that can check whether an architecture meets the access control policies specified in various architectural constituents; 2) developing a set of tools (visual editing and implementation generation) to support developing with the architectural security modeling; 3) implementing the necessary run-time support for executing and monitoring the security policies. These development activities will extend our existing development environment, □rchStudio □4□.

□ AC□NO□ LE□□EMENT□

This work was supported in part by the □ational Science Foundation award 020□24.

□ REFERENCE□

[□] □llen, □. and □arlan, □., □□□ormal □a□i□□or□ □r□□e□□ural□□o□e□□o□□□C□ Transactions on Software □ngineering and □ethodology., □□□□ □(3)□p. 2□3-24□

[2□] Berghel, H., □□e□□o□□e□□□orm□Communications of the □C□, 200□ □□(2)□p. □□-□□

[3□] Bidan, C. and Issarny, □. □e□□r□□□□e□□e□□□□□rom□ □o□□ware□□r□□□e□□□re. in □roceedings of 2nd International Conference on Coordination Languages and □odels, p.□4-□0, □□□□□

[4□] □ashofy, □.□., □ndr, Hoek, v.d., and Taylor, □.□., □ □om□re□e□□□□e□□□roa□□□or□□□e□□e□elo□me□□□o□□□o□□ar□ □o□□ware□□r□□□e□□□re□□e□□r□□□□□a□□a□e□□□C□ Transactions on Software □ngineering and □ethodology, 200□ □□(2)□p. □□□-24□

[□□] □eLine, □., □□o□□□□□a□□a□□□□□□□□□ma□□□□□□□□□□□ □le□□le□□a□□a□□□□□□I□□□□ Transactions on Software □ngineering, 200□ □□(2)□p. □24-□43.

[□□] □eng, □., □ang, □, Tsai, □□□., and Beznosov, □., □□□ □□□roa□□□□or□□o□el□□□a□□□□al□□□□□o□□e□□□r□□□□□□em□ □r□□□e□□□re□I□□□□ Transactions on □nowledge and □ata □ngineering, 2003. □□(□)□p. □□0□-□□□□

[□□] □ucasse, S. and □ichner, T. □□e□□a□le□□o□□e□□or□□ □o□□ar□□□e□□a□le□□e□□□□□leme□□□ in □roceedings of □th □uropean conference held jointly with the □th □C□□ SI□S□FT international symposium on Foundations of software engineering, p.4□3-4□□□ □□□□

[□□] Halpern, □□. and □eissman, □. □□□□□□□□r□□□□r□er□ □o□□□□□e□a□□o□□□□□□□□ol□□e□□ in □roceedings of □□th I□□□□□ Computer Security Foundations □orkshop, p.□□□-20□□ 2003.

[□□] Humenn, □., □□e□□ormal□□ema□□□□□o□□a□□ml. 2003, Syracuse □niversity.

[□0□] □oshi, □B.□., Bertino, □., and □hafoor, □., □□□ □□□al□□□□□□□re□□□□e□□a□□□□e□□□□□□□□e□□or□□□e□ □e□□eral□□e□□□□em□oral□□ole□□a□e□□□□□e□□□o□□rol□□o□el□□ □ependable and Secure Computing, I□□□□ Transactions on, 200□ □(2)□p. □□□□-□□□□

[□□□] □rjens, □□□ml□□e□□□□e□□□□□□□□ml□□or□□e□□□re□□□□em□□ □e□elo□me□□.in □roceedings of □□L□□02□□roceedings of the □th International Conference on The □nified □odeling Language, p.4□2--42□□ 2002.

[□2□] □atara, □. and □atz, S. □r□□□e□□□ural□□□e□□□□o□□ □□□□e□□□□ in □roceedings of □roceedings of the 2nd international conference on □spect-oriented software development, p.□□-□0, 2003.

[□3□] Lampson, B.□□., □□o□□e□□□□e□□o□□□□eme□□□r□o□lem□□ Communications of the □C□, □□□3. □□(□0)□p. □□3-□□□

[□4□] Li, □. and □itchell, □C. □□□□□□ole□□a□e□□r□□□□ □a□□a□ema□□□□rame□□or□□ in □roceedings of □□□□□□□ Information Survivability Conference □ □xposition III, p.20□-2□2, 2003.

[□□□] Lodderstedt, T., Basin, □.□., □, and □oser, r. □e□□re□ml□□□□□□ml□□a□e□□□o□el□□□a□□a□e□□□or□□o□el□□r□□e□□ □e□□r□□□□ in □roceedings of □□L□□02□□roceedings of the □th International Conference on The □nified □odeling Language, p.42□-44□□ 2002.

[□□□] Lopes, □., □ermelinger, □., and Fiadeiro, □L., □□□□er□□r□□er□□r□□□e□□□ural□□o□□e□□or□□□C□ Transactions on Software □ngineering and □ethodology, 2003. □□(□)□p. □4-□04.

[□□□] □agee, □. and □ramer, □. □□□am□□□□□□re□□□□□ □o□□□ware□□r□□□e□□□re□ in □roceedings of □roceedings of the 4th □C□□ SI□S□FT symposium on Foundations of software engineering, p.3-□4, □□□□□

[□□□] □edvidovic, □. and Taylor, □.□., □□□la□□□□□a□□o□ a□□□om□ar□□o□□□rame□□or□□□or□□o□□□ware□□r□□□e□□□re□ □e□□r□□□□o□□a□□a□e□□Software □ngineering, I□□□□ Transactions on, 2000. □□(□)□p. □0-□3.

[□□□] □ehta, □.□., □edvidovic, □., and □hadke, S. □o□□ar□□□ a□□□a□□□o□□□om□□o□□□o□□ware□□o□□□e□□or□□ in □roceedings of 22nd International Conference on Software □ngineering, p.□□□-□□□□ 2000.

[20□] □insky, □.H. and □ngureanu, □. □□□□□e□□□or□□or□ □e□□ro□□e□o□□□□e□□r□□o□□□□e□□□r□□□□□e□□□□□em□. in □roceedings of □th □S□□I□ Security Symposium, p.□3□-42, □□□□□

[2□□] □oriconi, □., □ian, □., □iemenschneider, □.□., and □ong, L. □e□□re□□o□□□ware□□r□□□e□□□re□ in □roceedings of □□□□ I□□□□ Symposium on Security and □rivacy, p.□4-□3, □□□□

[22□] □□SIS, □xtensible □ccess Control □arkup Language (□acml), http□□docs.oasis-open.org□xacml□2.0□access□control-xacml-2.0-core-spec-os.pdf

[23□] □ay, I., France, □., Li, □., and □eorg, □., □□□□□□e□□ □a□e□□□□roa□□□o□□o□el□□□□□re□□□□o□□rol□□o□□er□□ Information and Software Technology, 2004. □□(□)□p. □□□-□□□

[24□] □en, □, Taylor, □., □ourish, □, and □edmiles, □. □o□□ar□□a□□□r□□□e□□□ural□□rea□e□□o□□o□□ware□□e□□r□□□□□□ □o□□e□□or□□□e□□r□□□o□roa□□ in □roceedings of □ orkshop on Software □ngineering for Secure Systems, 200□

[2□□] Sandhu, □. and □unawer, □. □□o□□□□o□□□o□□ □□□re□□□□ar□□□□e□□□o□□rol□□□□□□ole□ in □roceedings of 3rd □C□□ □orkshop on □ole-based □ccess Control, p.4□-□4, □□□□□

[2□□] Sandhu, □.S., Coyne, □.□., Feinstein, H.L., and □ouman, C.□., □ole□□a□e□□□□□e□□□□o□□rol□□o□el□□Computer, □□□□□ □□(2)□p. 3□-4□

[2□□] Spitznagel, B. and □arlan, □. □□om□o□□□□o□al□ □□roa□□□or□□o□□r□□□□□o□□e□□or□□ in □roceedings of 2nd □orking I□□□□IFI□ Conference on Software □rchitecture, p.□4□-□□□□ 200□

[2□□] Tisato, F., Savigni, □., Cazzola, □., and Sosio, □. □r□□□e□□□ural□□e□le□□□o□□□eal□□□□□o□□□ware□□r□□□e□□□re□□a□□ □e□le□□□e□□□□□□□e□ in □roceedings of 2nd International □orkshop on □ngineering □istributed □bjects, p.□02-□□□ 2000.

[2□□] Tripunitara, □.□. and Li, □. □om□ar□□□□□e□ □□re□□□□o□□er□□o□□□e□□□o□□rol□□o□el□□ in □roceedings of □roceedings of the □□th □C□□ conference on Computer and communications security, p.□2-□□□ 2004.

[30□] □ijesekera, □. and □ajodia, S., □□□ro□□□□□o□al□□ol□□□ □□e□ra□□o□□□□e□□□o□□rol□□□C□ Transactions on Information and System Security, 2003. □□(2)□p. 2□□-32□

[3□□] □in, B.□., □□□□eer□□□□□□□la□□□o□□e□e□□□□e□□r□□ □ro□□□□□□□e□□r□□e□□□□o□□ware□□e□elo□me□□.□2004.

[32□] □ing, □□□., □□□all□o□□□o□□□□oo□□e□□o□□□□e□ □or□□o□□Security □ □rivacy □agazine, I□□□□, 2003. □(□)□p. □2-□□

[33□] □inslett, □. □□□□□ro□□□o□□□o□□r□□□□e□□o□a□□o□□. in □roceedings of □□st International Conference on Trust □anagement, p.2□□-2□3, 2003.

Prioritization of Threats Using the k/m Algebra

Supreeth Venkataraman
Portland State University
1900 SW 4th Ave
Portland, OR-97201
(503) 705-9127
supreetv@cs.pdx.edu

Warren Harrison
Portland State University
1900 SW 4th Ave
Portland, OR-97201
(503) 725-3108
warren@cs.pdx.edu

ABSTRACT

We present in this paper a new methodology for prioritizing threats rated with ordinal scale values while preserving the meaning of ordinal values and respecting the rules that govern ordinal scales. Our approach is quite novel because we present a formal algebraic system called the k/m algebra to derive the equivalence classes into which threats will be placed and define an operation called k/m dominance which orders the equivalence classes. The operations of our algebra always respect the rules that govern ordinal scales and preserve the meaning of ordinal values. We also describe and present the results from a preliminary case study where we applied our k/m algebra to prioritize threats ranked using data from an existing threat modeling system.

Categories and Subject Descriptors

D.2.8 [**Software Engineering**] Metrics – for threat modeling in computer security D.4.6 [**Security and Protection**]

General Terms

Security, Measurement

Keywords

Information assurance, Security metrics, threat modeling, threat prioritization.

1. INTRODUCTION

In today's information age, the need for information assurance has never been greater. With every passing day in the twenty first century, issues of computer security are taking on great importance in all forms of software development.

SSATTM'05, 11/7-11/8/05, Long Beach, CA, USA.
(c) 2005 ACM 1-59593-307-7/05/11

In the past, issues of development and meeting deadlines often were given priority over security issues, and computer security itself was viewed as a "bolt-on", something that could be added to a software system outside of development if security issues became visible.

Whenever such issues arose, the usual solution was to add fixes or patches to existing systems. The problem with such fixes is that they result in an expensive patchwork that does not seamlessly integrate with the existing system. Present day perspectives on software development have gradually begun to view security as an integral component of software, and many experts have stressed the importance of integrating security features into software applications from the very beginning of the software development lifecycle [1, 2, 7, 12].

Unlike traditional software bugs, security vulnerabilities are exploited by thinking adversaries. In order to thwart such adversaries, many organizations have begun to model threats from an attacker's point of view during the design phase and prioritize them using various risk analysis techniques [7, 9, 11]. This process is generally called *threat modeling* and includes methodologies like CERT's OCTAVE[1] and Microsoft's STRIDE/DREAD methodology [7, 11]. Threat modeling is now viewed as an integral part of information assurance design in software.

Threat modeling involves categorizing threats using a scheme such as Microsoft's STRIDE [7], and assessing each threat's relative risk using a technique such as Microsoft's DREAD. This allows mitigation efforts to be prioritized using a given threat's overall risk in relation to the overall risk of other threats the system may face.

A threat's level of overall risk is based on multiple attributes such as the threat's severity, its likelihood of occurring, etc. Each of these attributes is rated on a relative scale such as "High", Medium" or "Low", or more often, a relative numeric scale such as "1", "2" or "3". Customarily, the overall risk is determined by performing some sort of mathematical transformation on the attribute values such as a sum, product or mean. The result of the transformation is used to assign a given threat to an equivalence class representing one or more combination of attribute values. A given threat's relative mitigation priority is based on the relative ordering of the equivalence class to which it is assigned.

The problem with such approaches is that mathematical transformations such as addition and multiplication are impermissible on ordinal values, such as those commonly used to assess individual threat attributes [4, 5, 6]. This raises serious issues involving the propriety of current techniques for assigning threats to equivalence classes.

The motivation behind this paper is to explore a solution to the problem of assigning threats to ordinal equivalence classes in such a way that we preserve the meaning of the individual threat attribute ratings and also obey the rules that govern ordinal values.

We have developed a new algebraic system in order to facilitate the combination of various ordinal threat attribute values. We propose this system as a potential general solution to the threat prioritization problem. This paper presents our algebraic system and the results of a preliminary case study that we undertook to validate our algebra.

All operations in our algebra strictly obey the rules of the ordinal scale. In order to determine the validity of our approach, we applied our algebra to threats ranked with Microsoft's DREAD threat ranking system [7]. We discovered that our prioritization produced a significantly different ordering than the one produced by DREAD. This is a very promising and exciting result and gives us the motivation to conduct further research on validating the k/m algebra by applying it to other prioritization schemes. As of this writing, we are not aware of any other threat prioritization system that works on threats rated using an ordinal scale while *preserving the meaning of the rankings and respecting the rules that govern the ordinal scale*.

The rest of the paper is organized as follows. Section 2 presents a brief description of the ordinal scale from measurement theory. Section 3 describes our k/m algebra and the operations allowed, Section 4 describes a preliminary case study we undertook of applying the k/m algebra to threats ranked with DREAD and the results, and section 5 describes future work.

2. THE ORDINAL SCALE
This section provides a brief description of ordinal scales as defined by Stevens in 1946 and described by Finkelstein in 1984 [5].

There are four basic measurement scales in measurement theory, the nominal scale, the ordinal scale, the interval scale, and the ratio scale. Each of these scales are used for different purposes and each have different permissible mathematical transformations or relations that may be applied to them [4, 5, 6].

The ordinal scale as defined by Stevens is used to rank data with respect to some attribute [4, 5, 6]. Ordinal scales are used for ranking entities based on whether they have "more" or "less" of the attribute in question than another entity. There is no notion of "unit distance" between objects in an ordinal scale [6]. Thus we cannot say that "the distance between 4 and 8 is the same as the distance between 8 and 12" as we can in interval and ratio scales which are necessary for transformations such as sums and products. Consequently, relationships such as "3 units more" or "2 units less" are meaningless without a unit distance, and thus are also confined to interval and ratio scales.

The only permissible relationships on ordinal scales are equality (Vulnerabilities a and b have the same criticality) and the "is more than" and "is less than" relations [5]. For example, "Vulnerability a is more critical than vulnerability b".

Because of the lack of a unit distance, medians are meaningful on an ordinal scale but not means [4]. If vulnerability a has a rating of 8 and vulnerability b has rating of 4 on an ordinal scale, it is meaningful to say that "Vulnerability a is more critical than vulnerability b" but it is not meaningful to say something like "Vulnerability a is twice as critical as vulnerability b" or "The average vulnerability of a and b is 6."

Most threat and risk prioritization schemes that we have seen such as DREAD [7] and Failure Mode and Effects Analysis (FMEA) [10] use ordinal values to rate a threat or failure mode's attributes. In order to derive the overall risk, the attributes of a failure mode or threat are subjected to impermissible mathematical transformations like means and sums (DREAD) or products (FMEA). This breaks the rules that govern ordinal scales, and when looked at strictly from the viewpoint of ordinal scales, renders the result quite meaningless.

Researchers like Kmenta [8], and Bowles [3] have pointed out these mathematical problems with respect to FMEA and have recommended ways to solve this problem by using pareto ranking procedures [3], or probability and expected cost [8]. Fenton [4] notes that some of the most basic rules and observations governing measurement scales have been ignored in many software measurement studies.

We have developed a new formal method for the treatment of this problem. We call our system the k/m algebra and all the operations of our algebra obey the rules of the ordinal scale. This approach is novel because we are not aware of any other methodology that is used to summarize threats with multiple ordinally rated attributes while preserving the meaning of ordinal ranks and also respecting the rules that govern the ordinal scales.

3. THE K/M ALGEBRA

This section introduces our new algebra (from now on called the k/m algebra) and defines the objects and operations allowed by this system. For the purposes of this paper we have viewed this algebra as acting on threats and have defined it accordingly. However, the system is general enough that it can be used for combining any group of entities rated with ordinal attributes without any modifications.

3.1 Overview

The k/m algebraic system facilitates ordering n threats with m attributes each of which are assigned one of k ordinal values. All k/m operations respect the rules that govern ordinal scales as defined by Stevens in 1946. [5].

The k/m algebra defines the equivalence classes into which a specific threat can be placed. In the k/m algebra, the equivalence classes are called k/m objects. The ordering of these equivalence classes is determined by the generic k/m algebra operation called the k/m dominance operation. The following subsections define the equivalence classes in the k/m algebra, constructing the equivalence classes, and the k/m dominance operation.

Assumption: For ease of discussion, it has been assumed that an threat's m attributes associated with one of k ordinal values are represented as a m-tuple $T = (r_1,.. ,r_m)$.

3.2 The k/m object

A k/m object O is an equivalence class denoted as a collection of k numbers $o_1...o_k$,the sum of which equals m. The value of each o_i in a k/m object is the frequency of occurrence of i in every T that is a member of this equivalence class. The following example illustrates a k/m object.

Note: In this example and all the others that follow, it has been assumed that entities have four attributes ($m = 4$) and there are three ordinal ratings $1 - 3$ ($k = 3$).

Example: Let R be a m-tuple representing a mulit-attribute entity (i.e., a threat) as follows : $T = (1, 2, 3, 3)$. The equivalence class into which we place T can be determined as follows.

In this case $k = 3$ and $m = 4$. Hence the k/m object will be comprised of 3 numbers $o_1...o_3$, whose sum equal 4. From T, we observe that there are two 3's, one 2, and one 1. To construct a k/m object for T, we place the frequency of occurrence of 3 into o_1 , the frequency of occurrence of 2 into o_2 and the frequency of occurrence of 1 into o_3. Thus, the k/m object representing T's equivalence class is *211*.

3.3 The k/m dominance operation

Notation: $>_{k/m} (x_a, x_b)$

Definition: The k/m dominance operation is defined by the following rule. x_a and x_b are k/m objects

$$>_{k/m} (x_a, x_b) \Rightarrow \begin{cases} true \ if \ \sum_{i=1}^{k} 10^{i-1} * x_a[i] > \sum_{i=1}^{k} 10^{i-1} * x_b[i] \\ false \ otherwise \end{cases}$$

Example:

a. Let x_a = *211* and x_b = *013*. From the definition of k/m dominance, x_a k/m dominates x_b. Thus, $>_{k/m} (211, 013) \Rightarrow true$.

b. Let x_a = *211* and x_b = *310*. From the definition of k/m dominance, x_b k/m dominates x_a. Thus, $>_{k/m} (211, 310) \Rightarrow false$.

The k/m dominance operation is used for ordering the equivalence classes which are k/m objects.

3.4 Equivalence classes and prioritization

Threats are placed into different equivalence classes based on their attributes' ordinal ratings. Placing threats into equivalence classes avoids the problem of partially ordered sets during prioritization which forces us into ad hoc "equivalent but different" orderings that can result in inconsistent prioritization. By placing threats into equivalence classes such as k/m objects or classes with names like "High", "Medium", and "Low", we ensure that we have a total ordering of the threats via these equivalence classes or categories since the equivalence classes are ordered and not the threats within those equivalence classes. If threats T_1 and T_2 are determined to be equally dangerous, then they are both placed into the same equivalence class.

No two equivalence classes have the same priority, and the k/m dominance operation in section 3.2 is the axiom that defines the strict ordering of equivalence classes. The concept of ordering equivalence classes is certainly not new. Mostly the equivalent classes are implicit. Let us look at some common cases beginning with Microsoft's DREAD ordering system [7]. The initial DREAD system proposed used a 10 point ranking (see section 4.1), and the average of the ranks of each threat's attributes was computed and used as the overall risk value. Many threats can have the same overall risk value. Thus each such value is an equivalence class. Since the minimum ranking is 1 and the maximum ranking 10, the overall risk can range from 1 through 10. Assuming an accuracy of one decimal place, there can be 91 equivalence classes {1, 1.1, 1.2, ..., 9.9, 10}. Determining the ordering of these equivalence classes is trivial. This is an example of a system of implicit equivalent classes. A later version of DREAD [9] using a 3 point scale recommends adding the values of each threat's attributes, and placing threats into categories called "High", "Medium", and "Low" based on their values. In this case, the equivalence classes are quite explicit. Again, ordering the equivalence classes is trivial.

In our system, the equivalence classes are k/m objects and each k/m object is derived based on the frequency of occurrence of ordinal rankings in threat data. If $k = 3$, and $m = 4$ then we can have the following equivalence classes from the rules of k/m object construction, {310, 202, 220, 121, 211, 004, 013, 301, 400, 130, 022, 031, 103, 112}. The ordering of these equivalence classes is determined by the k/m dominance operation.

We have thus presented a system in which we do not have to resort to impermissible mathematical transformations like addition and multiplication to derive the equivalence classes into which threats can then be placed, and have also presented a scheme for ordering these equivalence classes.

4. CASE STUDY – DREAD

This section describes a case study that we undertook in order to explore the ramifications of our k/m algebra by applying it to existing threat prioritization methodologies. We chose Microsoft's DREAD methodology for ranking and prioritizing threats as our target methodology.

We first provide an overview of DREAD and then describe the process of applying the k/m algebra to the threats. We discovered that the ordering of threats obtained by using the k/m algebra was significantly different from the ordering obtained by using DREAD's ordering mechanism which makes us believe that further research is needed into the k/m algebra rankings and an empirical study needs to be undertaken in order to determine if the ordering given by the k/m algebra is better than the ordering given by current methodologies.

4.1 DREAD – an overview

The following brief discussion is derived from "Writing Secure Code" by Howard and LeBlanc [7]. DREAD is a risk calculating mechanism used by Microsoft as part of their threat modeling process. DREAD operates hand in hand with the STRIDE mechanism which categorizes threats. DREAD is an acronym each letter of which stands for a threat attribute. Each of the attributes are ranked using one of 10 criticality ratings with 1 being the lowest rating and 10 being the highest (catastrophic) rating. The attributes are

> **D**amage Potential - How much damage will be done if the threat is exploited by an attacker ?

> **R**eproducibility - How easy is it for an attacker to exploit the threat?

> **E**xploitability - How much skill does an attacker need to have in order to exploit this threat?

> **A**ffected Users - How many users will be affected if this threat is exploited and an attack were mounted?

> **D**iscoverability - How easy is it for an attacker to discover this threat in order to mount an attack?

Once all of the threat's attributes have been ranked, the mean of the five attribute ratings are taken and this value is the perceived overall risk or equivalence class of the threat. Once this process is done for all identified threats, the threats are sorted by the overall risk value in descending order for priority determination. The astute reader will have observed that the DREAD ratings are ordinal in nature, and applying the *mean* operation on ordinal values breaks the rules that govern ordinal values.

Swiderski and Snyder [11] recommend that the DREAD ratings be on a narrower range (1-3) so that each rating can have a simpler definition. Meier and others [9] use a 1-3 rating for DREAD and perform *addition* on the ordinal values instead of taking the *mean*. Each threat in this scheme is handled as follows. The threat's attribute ranks are added up to give each threat an overall value ranging from 5 – 15. Threats are then grouped into three equivalence classes or categories called "High" (12-15), "Medium" (8 – 11), and "Low" (5 – 7). This scheme once again breaks the rules of the ordinal scale since the impermissible addition transformation is used.

We present two examples using our k/m algebra, one using the 10 point DREAD ranking system and the other using the 3 point DREAD ranking system. Table 1 shows 6 threats each of which have been assigned DREAD ratings using the 10 point system. The threats in table 1 are taken from [7]. In order to derive the 1-3 ratings to use in the second study, we assumed the mapping shown in table 2. Table 3 shows the same threats assigned DREAD ratings using the 3 point system by using the mapping in table 2.

Using the 10 point DREAD system, the threats are prioritized as {[T_1], [T_2], [T_4], [T_3], [T_6], [T_5]}, and using the 3 point DREAD system, the threats are prioritized as {[T_1, T_2, T_3, T_4], [T_5, T_6]}.

Table 1: DREAD data ranked using the 10 point scale

Threat ID	D	R	E	A	D	Overall Risk
T_1	8	10	7	10	10	9
T_2	7	7	7	10	10	8.2
T_3	6	6	7	9	10	7.6
T_4	10	5	5	10	10	8
T_5	10	2	2	1	10	5
T_6	10	2	2	8	10	6.4

Table 2: Mapping from a 10 point scale to a 3 point scale

DREAD 10 point scale	DREAD 3 point scale
1 - 3	1
4 - 7	2
8 – 10	3

Table 3: DREAD data ranked using the 3 point scale

Threat ID	D	R	E	A	D	Sum	Overall rating
T_1	3	3	2	3	3	14	High
T_2	2	2	2	3	3	12	High
T_3	2	2	2	3	3	12	High
T_4	3	2	2	3	3	13	High
T_5	3	1	1	1	3	9	Medium
T_6	3	1	1	3	3	11	Medium

4.2 Applying the k/m algebra to threats ranked using DREAD

The first step in applying the k/m algebra to the threats in table 1 and table 3 is to assign an equivalence class or k/m object to each threat. For the data in table 1, m = 5 and k = 10. For the data in table 3, m = 5 and k = 3. We assume that we are given the threat data as 5-tuples. For example the data for threat T1 from table 1 would be represented as $T_1 = (8,10,7,10,10)$. From section 3.2, the corresponding k/m object for T_1 would be *3111000000*. Table 4 shows all the threats from table 1 mapped into k/m objects, and table 5 shows all the threats from table 3 mapped into k/m objects.

We now apply the k/m dominance operation from section 3.3 to the k/m objects in tables 4 and 5 in order to get the two prioritization orders for the equivalence classes.

Table 4: Mapping threats attributes to k/m objects using a 10 point scale

Threat Data	k/m object
T_1=(8, 10, 7, 10, 10)	3 0 1 1 0 0 0 0 0 0
T_2=(7, 7, 7, 10, 10)	2 0 0 3 0 0 0 0 0 0
T_3=(6, 6, 7, 9, 10)	1 1 0 1 2 0 0 0 0 0
T_4=(10, 5, 5, 10, 10)	3 0 0 0 0 2 0 0 0 0
T_5=(10, 2, 2, 1, 10)	2 0 0 0 0 0 0 0 2 1
T_6=(10, 2, 2, 8, 10)	2 0 1 0 0 0 0 0 2 0

Table 5: Mapping threat attributes to k/m objects using a 3 point scale

Threat Data	k/m object
T_1=(3, 3, 2, 3, 3)	4 1 0
T_2=(2, 2, 2, 3, 3)	2 3 0
T_3=(2, 2, 2, 3, 3)	2 3 0
T_4=(3, 2, 2, 3, 3)	3 2 0
T_5=(3, 1, 1, 1, 3)	2 0 3
T_6=(3, 1, 1, 3, 3)	3 0 2

The prioritization order for the threats in table 4 is $\{[T_1], [T_4], [T_2], [T_6], [T_5], [T_3]\}$, and the prioritization order for the threats in table 5 is $\{[T_1], [T_4], [T_6], [T_2, T_3], [T_5]\}$.

Observe that in both examples, the k/m dominance operation produced significantly different prioritization orders when compared to the prioritization orders produced by the corresponding DREAD systems. We feel that this result is significant.

The fact that our k/m algebra, using scale-permissible transformations resulted in a different prioritization order of threats than techniques using scale-impermissible transformations is a very interesting result. One explanation, of course, is that our prioritization is indeed incorrect, and using scale-permissible transformations is counterproductive (of course, this begs the question as to which of the 10-point or 3-point DREAD prioritizations *is* the correct one). However, an alternate explanation is that our prioritization *is* superior to both the 10-point and 3-point DREAD prioritizations, and by using scale-permissible transformations, we have not added to any information that was in the original analysis.

Further research is needed to validate our approach. As a result of this finding, we have decided to undertake further research in order to find out the significance in difference in the orderings produced. Our ultimate goal is to be able to determine with certainty the answer to the question *"Does our k/m algebra produce a better prioritization of threats when compared to existing methodologies?"*

5. FUTURE WORK

In order to further validate our k/m algebra and achieve our goal as stated in the previous section, we intend to apply our algebra to large datasets of DREAD data and also to other security risk analysis techniques and determine empirically whether our ranking scheme is better at prioritizing threats than existing methodologies.

Since our ordering scheme works on any entity with multiple ordinally rated attributes, we are also considering extending our research and experimenting with our algebra on standard techniques like Failure Modes and Effects Analysis (FMEA) which also use ordinally rated attributes for failure modes [10] and comparing the results. In order to prioritize large datasets of threats quickly, we are also developing a software environment that will facilitate threat model analysis and automatically perform the prioritization.

6. CONCLUSION

We described a new methodology, the k/m algebra for prioritizing threats during threat modeling of software applications. We showed that our k/m algebra performed the prioritization of threats while fully respecting the rules that govern ordinal values unlike existing methodologies. We also presented experimental evidence that the prioritization order produced by our algebra was significantly different from the order that was produced by an existing methodology. This result is very promising and exciting since we have arrived at a different threat prioritization ordering by using our k/m algebra without having to resort to impermissible mathematical transformations on ordinal data.

7. REFERENCES

[1] Alberts, C. and Dorofee, A. *Managing Information Security Risks: The OCTAVE Approach*, Addison-Wesley Professional, July 2002

[2] Anderson, R.J. *Security Engineering: A Guide to Building Dependable Distributed Systems* , Wiley, January 2001

[3] Bowles, J.B., The new SAE FMECA standard, *Proceedings of the Annual Reliability and Maintainability Symposium*, 19-22 Jan. 1998 pp. 48 – 53

[4] Fenton, N, "Software Measurement: A Necessary Scientific Basis", *IEEE Transactions on Software Engineering*, Vol. 20, No. 3, March 1994.

[5] Finkelstein, L. and M. Leaning. A review of fundamental concepts of measurement, *Measurement* Vol 2, Issue 1, pp. 25--34.

[6] Harrison, W. Software Measurement: A Decision-Process Approach. *Advances in Computers 39*: 1994, pp. 51-105

[7] Howard, M., and LeBlanc, D. *Writing Secure Code*, Second Edition, Microsoft Press , December 2002

[8] Kmenta, S., Ishii,K. "Scenario-Based FMEA: A Life Cycle Cost Perspective", *Proceedings. ASME Design Engineering Technical Conf.* Baltimore, MD, 2000

[9] Meier, J.D., Mackman, A., Dunner, M., Vasireddy, S., Escamilla, R. and Murukan, A. *Improving Web Application Security: Threats and Countermeasures,* Microsoft Corporation, June 2003

[10] Procedures for Performing Failure Mode Effects and Criticality Analysis, US MIL_STD_1629 Nov. 1974, US MIL_STD_1629A Nov. 1980, US MIL_STD_1629A/Notice 2, Nov. 1984.

[11] Swiderski, S., and Snyder, W. *Threat Modeling,* Microsoft Press, July 2004